Canada Travels
ISSUES AND DESTINATIONS
World Regional Geography

Canada Travels:
ISSUES AND DESTINATIONS

Graham Draper
Senior Author

Authors
Wayne Andrew

Lew French

Ethel Johnston

Todd Pottle (Geo Tech)

Contributing Writer
Patricia Healy

IRWIN
PUBLISHING

Irwin Publishing
Toronto/Vancouver, Canada

World Regional Geography

National Library of Canada Cataloguing in Publication Data

Main entry under title:
  Canada travels : issues and destinations : world regional geography

ISBN 0-7725-2908-6

  1. Geography. 2. Voyages and travels. 3. Tourist trade.
I. Draper, Graham A.

G128.C35 2001   910   C2001-901765-0

Design, layout and artwork by VISU*TronX* Services
Edited by Geraldine Kikuta
Production Coordination by Francine Geraci
Photo Research by Leesa Price, Francine Geraci
Literary Permissions by Lisa Brant
Proofreading and Index by Wendy Thomas

We acknowledge for their financial support of our publishing program the
Canada Council, the Ontario Arts Council, and the Government of Canada
through the Book Publishing Industry Development Program (BPIDP).

1 2 3 4 5   06 05 04 03 02 01
Printed and bound in Canada
Published by Irwin Publishing Ltd.
325 Humber College Blvd.
Toronto, ON M9W 7C3

The authors and publisher would like to thank the following reviewers for
their valuable insights and suggestions:
Mike Ball, Durham District School Board
Peter Healy, Formerly York Region District School Board
Ilze Patrick, York Region District School Board
Linda Sloan, Ottawa Carleton Catholic District School Board
Kim Wallace, Halton District School Board

TABLE OF CONTENTS

Canada Travels
ISSUES AND DESTINATIONS
World Regional Geography

UNIT 1

one

The Geography of Travel and Tourism

NORTH
AMERICA

Chapter 2:
The Niagara Escarpment, Canada. How are regions a useful tool for understanding travel and tourism issues?

This unit provides you with two important tools for analyzing travel and tourism. The first tool is an approach to investigating issues. This issues analysis approach encourages researchers to find solutions considering the variety of viewpoints that surround issues in travel and tourism. The second tool is the geographic application of regions. Using regions, researchers are able to organize ideas and evidence in order to find patterns. These two tools will be invaluable in understanding and using the ideas that are presented in the rest of the book.

Destinations You Will Visit

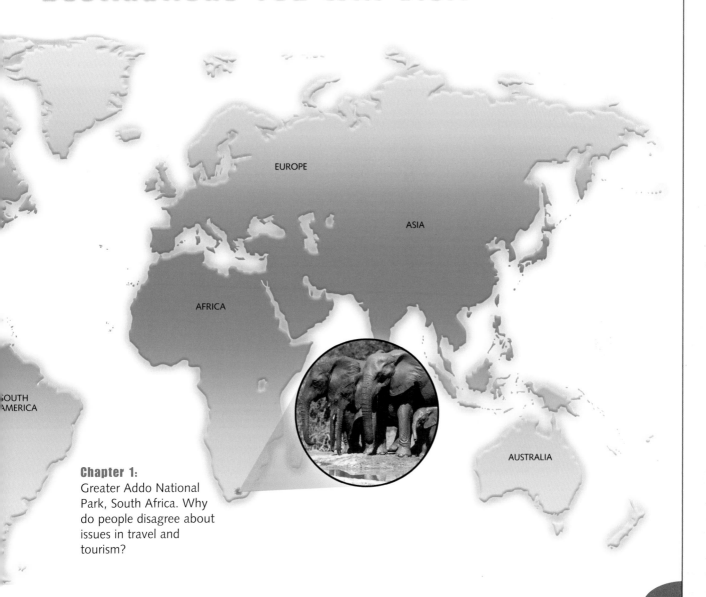

EUROPE

ASIA

AFRICA

SOUTH AMERICA

AUSTRALIA

Chapter 1:
Greater Addo National Park, South Africa. Why do people disagree about issues in travel and tourism?

CHAPTER one 1ᵉ
Analyzing Travel and Tourism Issues

FOCUS ON THESE KEY QUESTIONS AND . . .

1. Why do people engage in travel and tourism?
2. What are some issues that arise from the desire of people for travel experiences?
3. What is the best approach to understanding issues in travel and tourism?
4. What skills are necessary to explore issues in travel and tourism fully?

KEY WORDS & TERMS

cultural motivators
destinations
discretionary money
informed opinion
interpersonal motivators
issue
issues approach
physical motivators
prestige motivators
stakeholders
sustainable
travel motivators
variables

Travel Enriches Us

Most people enjoy travelling. They think that their time spent as tourists is a valuable opportunity to learn more about the world and, perhaps, themselves. Travel brings with it experiences that can be gained in no other way. We will look at different types of tourism and consider issues that are connected with these activities.

Figure 1.1 (Above) Hiking on the trails of Greater Addo National Park, South Africa; (right) exploring the old-world charm of Quebec City. Travel offers many opportunities, whether for rugged physical challenge or for cultural pursuits.

"Travel is fatal to prejudice, bigotry, and narrow-mindedness." – Mark Twain, U.S. humorist

"Travelling is the ruin of all happiness! There's no looking at a building after seeing Italy." – Fanny Burney, English novelist

"The average tourist wants to go places where there are no tourists." – Sam Ewing, tourism analyst

"The time to enjoy a good tour is about three weeks after you unpack." – George Ade, U.S. humorist

"Most travel is best of all in the anticipation or the remembering; the reality has more to do with losing your luggage." – Regina Nadelson, U.S. author

Figure 1.2 These quotations are a sample of people's views on travel and tourism.

We will start in this chapter by looking at the various reasons why people travel and the various factors that influence their travel choices.

EXPECTATIONS

In this chapter, you will have the opportunity to

- identify selected factors that influence travellers' destination choices
- classify the different types of travel and tourism, and explain the reasons why people travel
- compare viewpoints of individuals, businesses, non-governmental organizations, and other groups about sustainable use of the Earth and its resources
- identify the economic, cultural, political, and environmental components of selected issues related to travel and tourism
- demonstrate an understanding of the steps involved in the geographic inquiry process
- describe biases that may inform different viewpoints and perspectives on issues related to regional geography
- evaluate the quality and validity of information found in various sources
- demonstrate an understanding that the travel and tourism industry consists of many interconnected components
- analyze the effects of cultural, economic, and political motivators and barriers on travel and tourism patterns

Why Do People Travel?

Survey your friends and family members to find out why they travel, or want to travel. Perhaps an aunt travels for business reasons. Maybe your uncle enjoys visiting museums in other countries. Possibly your friends are looking for fun and adventure. Most people will tell you they want to experience the excitement of visiting other places. These are popular reasons for travelling, but they are not the only ones. Even though all tourists have their own reasons for booking a trip or planning a vacation, there are four general categories of reasons – these factors are **travel motivators**.

Interpersonal Motivators The desire to meet new people, visit friends and family, or just enlarge the circle of people around them are **interpersonal motivators** for tourists. The travel and tourism industry offers an abundance of opportunities for interpersonal experiences, from "singles" cruises to seniors' bus tours. Activities in this category are designed to get people together, helping them satisfy their interpersonal motivators.

Physical Motivators Many people feel that the world today is extremely stressful. There are too many things to do, too little time in which to do them, too much work, and an incredible amount of information coming at us all the time. These people travel to get away, have a rest, take a break, and renew and refresh themselves. Often people want experiences that are physical – make them use their muscles and limbs in ways that are not routine for them. Activities such as sitting in the sun enjoying its warmth, playing sports, or stretching muscles hiking or mountain climbing appeal to tourists responding to **physical motivators**.

Cultural Motivators Some people seek places that offer them a glimpse of different cultures through dance, music, art, religion, entertainment, and food. The knowledge that they gain through such experiences also helps them to appreciate or understand their own culture better. The travel industry markets to people's **cultural motivators** by offering destinations that include historical landmarks, theme parks, festivals and celebrations, casinos, museums, galleries, and sidewalk cafés.

Prestige Motivators People engage in travel and tourism for personal benefits, such as increasing their knowledge and developing hobbies. They may also travel for the reputation or recognition that comes with travelling to the "newest" popular vacation spot. The tourism industry seeks to satisfy these **prestige motivators** by providing travellers with convention services, student exchanges, study destinations, first-class services, and so on.

Figure 1.3 Spectators enjoy an event during National Aboriginal Week in Corroboree, Australia. Culture may be defined as everything we do in our lives. What part of another culture would interest you enough to motivate you to travel there?

Figure 1.4 Hobbies, such as photography or painting, are a motivating force for many tourists.

66 *The world is a book, and those who do not travel read only one page.* 99

– Augustine of Hippo, fifth century

Important Travel Variables

While the four motivators work in different ways to encourage people to participate in travel experiences, a number of important conditions – **variables** – help to determine how people actually respond to the motivators. These variables include age, education, health, responsibilities, amount of free time, and finances.

Age, Responsibilities, Free Time, and Finances Often, young people – who usually do not have family responsibilities – seek new and exciting experiences. They are interested in new places, different ideas, and meeting people their own age. Many young people do not have a great deal of **discretionary money** – money not needed for living expenses – and are willing to "rough" it, backpacking and staying in hostels. They plan their travel to experience these new situations. As people mature into their middle years, some may look for more comfort and security in their travel. Others want adventurous holidays. In both cases, middle-aged tourists generally have the time, fewer family responsibilities, and discretionary money to obtain the kinds of travel experiences they want. Some seniors may not desire to travel long distances or even at all. They may have declining health or have already travelled to the

Figure 1.5 A family from Japan enjoys the ice sculptures at Ottawa's Winterlude festival. Stage in life affects travel and tourism choices. How might these people's travel choices be different in ten years?

destinations they want to see. They may simply be content with their immediate surroundings. Other seniors continue to seek exciting destinations. Some seniors have the money and time to continue to travel, while others living on fixed incomes cannot afford to travel.

Education Education also affects travel decisions. First, those with more education tend to seek new and different experiences. They may try to go to places that are a little bit "off the beaten track." Second, people with higher education often have higher incomes. It seems that the better educated tourists are, the more money they have to spend on travel. These travellers often choose destinations that are unusual or exotic.

Health Another variable that can affect travel and tourism choices for people of all ages is health. A person who has kidney problems and requires dialysis needs to choose destinations that have dialysis facilities available. A hearing impaired person may not be allowed to travel on some smaller tour boats or overnight cruise boats without a hearing companion who can react to an alarm in case of emergency. As people age, they tend to develop health problems. Those with more serious conditions may choose to travel only to destinations close to home.

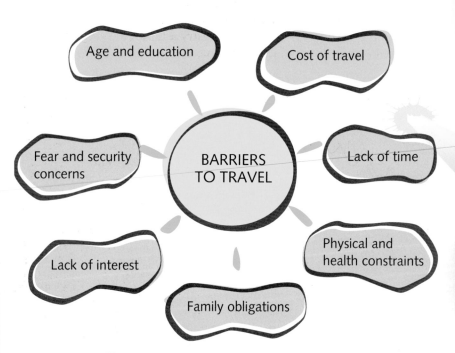

Age and education

Cost of travel

Fear and security concerns

BARRIERS TO TRAVEL

Lack of time

Lack of interest

Physical and health constraints

Family obligations

Figure 1.6 Some barriers to travel that may influence tourists' choices

Interact

Which groups of people in our society are not able to enjoy travel and tourism because of physical limitations? Suggest ways to help these groups enjoy travel and tourism.

www.irwinpublishing.com

Every week new sites are added to the Internet to help you plan and book a trip. To find travel and tourism information for most countries, and online sources for travel agencies, visit the Student Page for *Canada Travels*.

Travel Destinations

The different travel motivators combine with such variables as age, health, education, time, and finances to create diversity in the demand for travel and tourism experiences. People want to be able to choose from a variety of options, according to their needs and desires. The tourist industry responds by offering a wide range of places, or **destinations**. Some destinations offer opportunities to rest and be pampered, some offer excitement and thrills, others offer knowledge and ideas. The options can be a short distance from home or halfway around the world. We can begin to appreciate the range of possible destinations by classifying them. Seven categories of tourism are shown in Figure 1.8 on the next page.

Conflicts and Issues Determining tourist destinations is not always as clear-cut as these categories suggest. Most travellers will engage in a variety of activities while on vacation. They might, for instance, add a bit of "sun, sand, and surf" to a business trip, or visit a museum while on their way to enjoy the quiet of a remote mountain retreat. Nevertheless, travel categories are a useful way to start looking at where tourists go, why they go there, and what they do while they are there. These categories also demonstrate that travel and tourism involves a large number of people and all their activities, from the tourists themselves to the workers in the industry. The size and complexity of the travel and tourism industry and the number of other areas the industry affects mean that there is plenty of room for conflicts and issues to arise around travel and tourism.

Figure 1.7 Visitors to Upper Canada Village see life as it was in nineteenth-century Ontario.

Destination Category	Description	Tourist Activities	Example Destinations
Environmental	Travelling to places that have exotic natural environments	Hiking, mountain climbing, canoeing, photography, camping	Algonquin Park, Canada Grand Canyon, USA Great Barrier Reef, Australia Serengeti Plain, Tanzania Rain forest, Costa Rica
Recreational	Vacationing in relaxing situations	Golfing, tennis, skiing, gambling, shopping, club scene, beaches	Casino Niagara, Canada Nashville, USA Disney World, USA Monte Carlo, Monaco Macau, China
Historical	Glimpsing times past, such as the grandeur of cities and societies or the glory of fallen heroes	Touring museums, cathedrals, mosques, battlefields, archaeological digs	Fort Louisbourg, Canada Quebec City, Canada Smithsonian Institute, USA The Louvre, France Great Wall, China
Domestic Culture	Travelling to experience or participate in parts of your own culture that are changing or vanishing	Visiting rustic inns, historic villages, cultural festivals, battle re-enactments, arts and crafts shows	Upper Canada Village, Morrisburg, Canada Caribana, Toronto McMichael Gallery, Kleinburg, Canada
Urban	Experiencing the excitement of a big city and all the services it has to offer	Going to techno clubs, museums, restaurants, neighbourhoods, galleries	Montreal, Canada Toronto, Canada New York, USA Paris, France Tokyo, Japan London, U.K.
Foreign Culture	Travelling to observe a lifestyle and culture quite different from your own	Viewing dances and ceremonies, religious rituals, marketplaces	Pyramids of the Nile Valley, Egypt Temple of Wat Arun, Thailand Taj Mahal, India Masai villages, Kenya
Business	Engaging in activities for the primary purpose of gaining an advantage in business ventures	Attending conferences, seminars, trade shows, exhibitions	Toronto Convention Centre, Canada Las Vegas, USA World expos

Figure 1.8 Categories of tourist destinations

CHECK IN

1 a) Which travel motivators would you consider to be most important for
      i) you and your friends?
      ii) your family?
      Explain your choices.
   b) Why is the term "motivator" used to describe the reasons that people travel?

2 a) In what ways might gender be an important variable?
   b) Name two other variables that you think influence people in their decisions on tourist destinations. Explain your choices.

3 For each of the categories of tourism shown in Figure 1.8, name a local or provincial destination not listed that fits the category.

Through Different Eyes: Issues and Viewpoints

It is not surprising that people have so many different views on the same subject, such as tourism. Think about the last time you discussed a current movie with your friends. Some probably liked it and wanted to tell everybody about it. Others no doubt were less enthusiastic, making comments such as "It was too long" or "I didn't understand it." Some may have decided not to see it because they disliked the type of movie or the actors starring in it. People have differing views on many other topics, such as books, cars, and clothing styles. Probably nothing shows different views more clearly than a discussion of popular music – most people have very strong likes and dislikes.

We have different views on larger matters as well. It is easy to start discussions about controversial topics such as government spending, how to deal with criminals, immigration policy, and the need to protect the environment. Within any group, there may be a variety of opinions and viewpoints on such topics. In our broader society, the range of viewpoints is huge. These different opinions can be both interesting and frustrating. Some opinions may be interesting when they help us to see topics more clearly and lead us to reshape our own views. Or such discussions can be frustrating if we are convinced that our own view is the only "correct" one.

Figure 1.9 These tourists are on their way to new experiences. People from all walks of life travel and have many perspectives on the experience.

Ways of Investigating Travel and Tourism

There are several approaches that researchers take to explore travel and tourism topics. Figure 1.11 outlines four of them.

All four approaches shown in Figure 1.11 have their strengths. However, their common weakness is that they isolate separate elements of the industry for investigation, such as destinations. In the end, investigators using these approaches have very detailed understandings about specific parts of the industry but not of the industry as a whole.

Using an Issues Approach

Is Cuba a good place for a winter vacation? Should we backpack through Peru? Will whale-watching tours upset the whales' habitat? A wide variety of opinions exist in any discussion of travel and tourism. We need to take this fact into account before we begin to investigate the related issues.

Figure 1.10 A pilot and co-pilot complete their pre-flight safety check. Safety is a key aspect of tourism, no matter how people travel.

Approach	Focus for Studies	Advantages of Approach
Services Approach	Looks at the major agencies and services that comprise the travel and tourism industry. Includes detailed examinations of travel agencies, airlines, hotels, etc.	Leads to an understanding of the components of the industry and how they function on a day-to-day basis.
Destinations Approach	Describes in detail the places where tourists go. Looks at physical and human attractions, facilities, services provided, etc.	Leads to an understanding of the tourist industry in popular destinations.
Product Approach	Examines the different ways that travel and tourism experiences are packaged. Looks at cruises, resorts, ecotours, sports travel, etc.	Leads to a greater understanding of how tourists consume services and what they want for their time and money.
Economic Approach	Organizes investigations around economic ideas, including supply and demand, foreign exchange, etc.	Leads to an understanding of the value of the industry as an economic activity.

Figure 1.11 Different approaches to investigating travel and tourism. Can you think of any disadvantages to investigating travel and tourism using these approaches?

Issue: Should a new ski resort be approved?

Developers: "This is a good use for little-used land. Our studies have shown that there is a strong demand for this type of facility and that such a facility will likely make a profit. To go ahead with the project, we need financial support from local and provincial governments."

Concerns
- profitable use of resources
- market demand for services
- role of governments in resource management

Skiers: "With the new resort, good facilities will be available in the local area and we will not have to go out of province for vacations. The extra traffic and activity is the price we all must pay for good facilities."

Concerns
- access to services
- spending patterns
- stimulation of the local economy

Government officials: "The economic activity and new tax base will benefit the area, but the new resort will require us to invest in local infrastructure, including new sewage treatment facilities and improved roads. We will also have to find a way to regulate activities that will threaten the environment."

Concerns
- economic prosperity
- use of public resources
- role of the government in economic development and environmental protection

Aboriginal peoples: "This resort is planned for a place that is claimed as Aboriginal territory. While it will provide jobs for us, it also threatens our culture, heritage, and lifestyle. Our local band wants conditions built into the approval stage that will protect our culture and that will guarantee benefits."

Concerns
- economic activities for specific groups
- protection of culture and traditions
- role of Aboriginal peoples in use and protection of resources

Townspeople: "The resort will create jobs in our region, which has high unemployment. It will bring new shops and services into the area. It will, however, generate more traffic and change the local lifestyle of our community."

Concerns
- jobs and prosperity
- combating regional inequalities
- protecting social conditions in the community from unwanted change

Environmentalists: "Construction activity will threaten the sensitive mountain ecosystem, and growth will mean greater amounts of sewage, garbage, and air pollution. On the other hand, logging, which also threatens the ecosystem, will likely cease if the resort is developed, since the two uses are often incompatible."

Concerns
- protection of ecosystems
- environmental costs of development
- competing uses for resources

Figure 1.12 Views about a proposed ski resort. This hypothetical situation illustrates the level of complexity of most large issues that involve the travel and tourism industry.

We can better understand different viewpoints by taking an **issues approach** in studying the geography of travel and tourism. All issues deal with problems that affect a number of people – situations that need to be corrected, improved, or at least considered. Losing your luggage while on vacation is a problem. A problem becomes an **issue** when

- people see the problem from a variety of different perspectives
- the problem affects many people

For the airline industry, lost luggage is an issue that the industry is constantly trying to resolve.

So, while you may personally debate whether you should vacation in Cuba this winter, your problem is not an issue because it does not involve many people. Issues are significant concerns that involve many people with differing viewpoints.

The strength of the issues approach in geography is that geographers must explore the complexities of various topics in order to arrive at informed understandings. Figure 1.12 illustrates some of the viewpoints and concerns that might surround a tourist proposal. Any approach that hopes to lead to an understanding of the issues must deal with all the elements and aspects that this example suggests.

Interact

What do you think is the best way to deal with people who do not respect the opinions and viewpoints of others?

CHECK IN

1 Here are ten factors that influence people's viewpoints about travel and tourism issues. Look at the list and identify the two most important and the two least important factors. Explain your choices.

- culture and traditions
- places where people live
- amount of experience with travel and tourism
- amount of education that people have
- political perspectives
- income levels
- gender
- age
- religious beliefs
- racial origins

Explain your top two and bottom two choices.

2 Give two examples of things that you would consider "problems" and two examples of "issues" in travel and tourism.

Investigating Issues in Travel and Tourism

An organized, structured investigation is the best way to gain an understanding of an issue. A good strategy uses these five steps:

1. **Identify the stakeholders** – the people who are involved in or concerned about the issue.
2. **State the issue** as clearly as possible.
3. **Determine the viewpoints** of each group or individual.
4. **Evaluate the viewpoints** of each stakeholder.
5. **Decide for yourself** what would be the best course of action on the issue.

You will note that this five-step issues model follows the same steps as the geographical inquiry process.

Identify the Stakeholders

We need to determine who is involved in the issue. These are the **stakeholders** – all those who are in a position to affect the issue or who will be affected by it. Figure 1.14 shows a helpful way to think about involvement. The more an issue affects people or groups, the more likely it is that they will have strong views and seek direct involvement in any decisions.

Those involved in an issue may be individuals or groups. It is important to find out if individuals speak only for themselves or if they represent larger groups with positions on the issue.

State the Issue

This step is often the hardest. It is very important to identify the issue clearly before you try to improve the situation. If you have not identified the issue, then you will waste time and effort investigating dead ends, unrelated information, and unimportant points.

For any large issue there are usually a number of aspects that can be considered important. As Figure 1.12 on page 13 shows, each stakeholder sees the situation from a different point of view or perspective, emphasizing some concerns above others. It is often helpful at this stage in the investigation to think about categories that can be used to organize the issue, for example:

- economic issues – how money is earned and spent as a part of travel and tourism
- cultural issues – the relationships among groups of people, including tourists and their hosts
- social issues – how a society functions, who makes decisions, who has influence, and how these factors affect travel and tourism
- environmental issues – the relationship between humans and nature in travel destinations
- political issues – how decisions are made in tourist areas

Figure 1.13 Guests can enjoy both downhill and cross-country skiing, as well as snowshoeing, at this resort in Ontario's Caledon Hills.

Figure 1.14 Levels of involvement in issues. Think about where your viewpoint would fit on an issue such as developing a golf course on prime agricultural land.

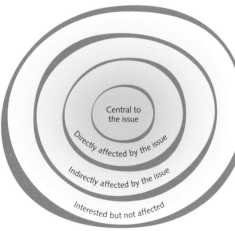

Central to the issue

Directly affected by the issue

Indirectly affected by the issue

Interested but not affected

Issues do not fit neatly into one category. For example, issues that deal with protecting the natural environment have economic aspects to them and probably have political aspects also. Using categories is a starting point, but good investigators must deal with the more hidden parts of an issue, as well.

The next step is to decide the most important aspects of the issue. In any important issue there is normally a range of aspects, from some that are central and crucial to the situation to those that are minor and likely important for only a handful of people. Since it is too challenging to look at all aspects of a situation, it is best to isolate the larger, more important aspects. This means choosing only those that you see as central to understanding the issue. What you hope, of course, is that by considering these critical aspects, you gain understanding of the lesser aspects at the same time.

It is a good strategy to record the issue as a clear statement. The act of stating the issue in words can clarify it further.

Determine the Viewpoints

Once you know who has a voice in an issue, you must determine what the stakeholders' views are. Listen carefully to what they have to say about the problem. Sometimes it is difficult to follow their arguments. In many cases, people are angry or frustrated and have difficulty expressing their views clearly. At other times, individuals and groups may have other issues – other agendas – in mind and may try to hide some information that does not support their view. To understand the issue, you must carefully analyze the views, looking at the facts and opinions being offered.

Figure 1.16 These people are protesting offshore fishing by Americans in Canadian waters. What are the economic, cultural, social, environmental, and political aspects of this issue? How might this issue affect travel and tourism?

Interact

Which aspects of the issue represented in Figure 1.16 do you think are crucial to the situation?

Facts Are Facts? Facts are details that are known to be true and that can be shown to be true. We use facts when we try to convince others of the correctness of our views. We suggest that since our facts are correct, then our viewpoint must be correct. However, as investigators, we must not fall into the trap of thinking that people always use facts in a way that is reliable, neutral, and free of value judgement. We need always to be critical of how facts are used, carefully examining them to ensure they have been used correctly and fairly. Here are some questions to consider when looking at facts used to support a viewpoint.

- How was the data collected?
- Who collected it?
- Would someone else gathering data produce the same "facts"?
- What facts were not given as evidence?

So, a simple fact such as "a million visitors toured the site" should be looked at carefully. Such a fact might be used in two entirely different ways. For example, a person favouring a project may use this fact to support his view that the project is a success. On the other hand, a person critical of the project may use the same fact to emphasize her point that the project has failed because it only attracted a million visitors instead of the projected 5 million. Correctness can be a very flexible thing when people use facts to support their views.

Figure 1.17 Facts and figures help us to understand issues related to tourism, at least to some degree. In what circumstances do you think statistics may not be enough to give a good understanding of issues?

Opinions Count Besides facts, opinions are used to support viewpoints. Opinions are expressions of what people think about a topic. Everyone has opinions, but not all opinions are useful as evidence to support a position or viewpoint on an issue. Opinions from people who do not know much about the issue are not very important and should not be considered as evidence. People expressing their views are not impartial. They are trying to sway the listener. In fact, since every opinion states a point of view, all opinions are biased. In issues where people are deeply involved, it can be hard to find unbiased voices. The challenge is to distinguish the facts from the opinions of the stakeholders.

The opinions of experts can be considered evidence in the right circumstances. Experts are people who know a good deal about the topic. Their opinions are helpful when they are given fairly and impartially. However, experts sometimes have a strong bias. A biologist hired by a developer to survey a situation may present a very different report than a biologist hired by an environmental group to look at the same issue. In investigating issues in travel and tourism, we must always question the authority of the expert witness so that we can determine if the opinions being expressed are legitimate support for a viewpoint.

Detecting Bias Bias is a one-sided or slanted view of an issue. It is often an unbalanced view. People may have incomplete information or they may distort the facts about an issue. Bias can be subtle and difficult to detect. Often, people try to disguise their biases by using misleading, or fallacious, arguments. Here are some things you should look for in the arguments of stakeholders:

Figure 1.18 Bias can be found everywhere – in election pamphlets, speeches, radio and television commercials, newspaper advertising, and conversations about an issue. This composite photograph was digitally produced by Adbusters, a citizens' group that promotes awareness of ethical issues related to advertising.

- The use of emotionally charged words or phrases can indicate that a view is biased. "The new golf course will be magnificent!"
- The omission of important details to oversimplify the issue is another indicator. "Developing a golf course is the only good use for that land."
- The use of an important or high profile person to influence others about an issue can indicate bias. "The mayor thinks that this is a good project, so the golf course should be built."
- The use of sweeping generalizations is a good indication that the view is biased. "Everyone knows that a golf course is the best way to go."

Evaluate the Viewpoints

Once you have an understanding of the different views of those involved in an issue, you can begin to judge those viewpoints. To evaluate an issue you must critically examine the evidence that has been offered and consider the potential outcome of each viewpoint on the issue.

Here are some of the questions that you should ask.

- Has this viewpoint been presented honestly?
- Have holders of this view been fair in their use of evidence?
- Who will benefit if this viewpoint succeeds?
- Who will be harmed if this viewpoint succeeds?

It is important that you be fair and objective at this stage, so that you judge the viewpoints on their own merits. You may personally dislike some of the people involved or their views on an issue, but you must separate your own feelings from what is valid and correct about their position.

Decide for Yourself

As you work at investigating an issue, you are combining and synthesizing – bringing ideas together – the information that you uncover. By the time you have finished your investigation and understand the different viewpoints, you will probably have an **informed opinion** about the issue. You may regard some views as stronger or more legitimate than others, or consider some courses of action to be better than the rest. Remember, though, that opinions need to be supported by evidence, so organize the facts and expert opinions that support your own viewpoint. Occasionally, in spite of all your investigation, you may feel that you still do not have all the facts. In that event, additional research may be required before a complete understanding of an issue is possible.

Figure 1.19 Construction begins on a new dam. While you may have personal views about such a development, as a researcher you must remain fair and impartial until all the evidence is examined.

Once you have an informed opinion, you may feel compelled to do something about the issue, such as write letters, attend meetings, or speak to others about your ideas for solving the issue. These are appropriate actions. Make sure that you use your new knowledge of the situation as you plan your course of action and that your action is designed to improve the situation.

Interact

Is it necessary for a person to take some action once he or she has arrived at an informed opinion about an issue?

 **CHECK IN**

1 Create an illustration or graphic organizer such as this example of a concept web that will help you to remember the five steps in the issues investigation strategy.

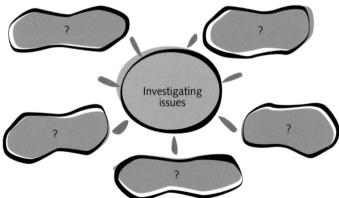

2 The following six quotations show something about how people think issues should be investigated. Which quotations show an issues approach? In your notebook, explain why you think they do.

a) "I try to find out everything I can about the place I will be visiting. That way I can be prepared for anything that might happen to me."

b) "This industry will be most successful if we figure out what people want and then give it to them. Helicopter skiing and white-water rafting are two good examples of meeting the needs of tourists."

c) "When I run into trouble and do not know what to do, I try to talk to as many people as I can. By listening to all their opinions, I usually can figure out a good way to resolve the situation."

d) "Most problems can be solved if we just determine what will earn the most money. Like all industries, travel and tourism is about making a profit."

e) "Everyone has an opinion about issues, but that does not mean that everyone is right. Some people just do not have all the facts or are not thinking clearly."

f) "When I run into a problem I just go to my travel agent. She usually knows who I should contact to make things better."

3 a) Facts can provide support for a viewpoint. Create an example of how facts can prove a viewpoint.

b) Give an example of how opinions would not be acceptable support for a viewpoint. Share your example with others in the class. Do your classmates agree your example would not be accepted?

4 Using the four techniques for detecting bias described on page 19, write a biased speech about an issue of your choice from a single viewpoint.

5 In your own words, explain how you might determine whether a given viewpoint on an issue is legitimate and fair.

LOOKING AT ISSUES

Greater Addo National Park

Issue: Should a national preserve be expanded to protect the habitat of the animals in this tourist area?

This is the study of a real situation related to travel and tourism. To analyze whether a national preserve should be expanded to protect the animal habitat, the stakeholders involved used the five-step approach to investigating an issue. Here are the viewpoints they considered.

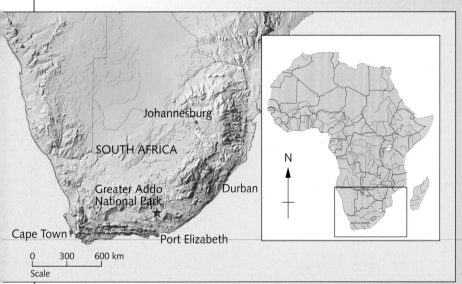

Figure 1.20 Location of the Greater Addo National Park.

In 1997, a report by researchers Graham Kerley and Andre Boshoff of the Terrestrial Ecology Research Unit at the University of Port Elizabeth in South Africa proposed the expansion of the existing Addo Elephant National Park into the Greater Addo National Park, creating a continuous conservation area over 200 km in length. The park would be located about 1000 km south of Johannesburg, South Africa, in the province of Eastern Cape. Here are excerpts from reports, comments, and other information on the expansion of the park. Much of this information comes from the Greater Addo National Park, Southern Africa Environmental Page, which can be

TRAVELLERS' ALERT!

Malaria is a serious disease spread by mosquitoes in tropical countries. If you are travelling to an area where it occurs, you need to obtain antimalarial medication. Begin taking the drug for a full week before departure, for the duration of your trip, and for four weeks after leaving the area. As well, you should try to reduce the risk of mosquito bites.

Figure 1.21 An excerpt from the original report, *A Proposal for a Greater Addo National Park*, suggesting the park's expansion.

Figure 1.22 Part of a newspaper report on public reaction to the proposal for a Greater Addo National Park.

Figure 1.23 Elephants at the Addo Elephant National Park. Why might it be necessary to have such a large national park in order to protect the elephants?

found on the Internet by visiting the Student Page for *Canada Travels* at <www.irwinpublishing.com>. Additional information can also be found there in a report of the Stakeholders' Workshop.

Figure 1.21 shows an excerpt from the report, *A Proposal for a Greater Addo National Park*, prepared by Graham Kerley and Andre Boshoff.

In the 30 November 1997 issue of the *Sunday Times*, Brett Adkins reported the reaction to the proposal for a Greater Addo National Park shown in Figure 1.22

There is growing acceptance that ecotourism/conservation, as a recognised form of land use, can play a major role in promoting development and community upliftment, through the **sustainable** use of natural resources. The issues of land ownership and land use, and the need to accelerate socio-economic development, especially amongst the rural and poorer sections of the population, feature prominently in the government's strategies and plans.

FARMERS VS THE JUMBOS

A group of farmers in the Eastern Cape are furious over proposals to expand the Addo National Park into a huge game reserve. Ecologists believe the enlarged reserve could be a showcase, provide thousands of jobs, and attract tourists. But about 100 farmers whose lands border or overlap the proposed boundaries say that livelihoods will have to be sacrificed and that hundreds of families could be affected by job losses.

The proposed Greater Addo National Park would cover an area of 368 000 ha, compared with the current 12 000 ha, encompass the existing Addo National Park, the Tootabie and Woody Cape nature reserves, and resuscitate large tracts of degraded farmland.

But the farmers believe the National Parks Board should first use the large area of undeveloped property it already owns in the area which, they say, is a haven for jackals and lynxes which prey on their mohair [goat], sheep, and dairy herds.

The board says it has no intention of imposing its will on any of the affected parties and will seek to please all concerned through negotiations.

One group of farmers has asked for a full economic evaluation of the potential earnings of the Addo scheme against the lost revenue from dairy, sheep and mohair farming. The Port Elizabeth Dairy Farmers' Union says the reserve would incorporate prime land which cannot be replaced.

"We naturally could not have expected everyone to agree to the proposal," the board's communications head, Fanyana Shiburi, told the *Sunday Times*. "But through negotiation we're confident that we'll eventually find agreement on it."

"We were totally taken aback when we first heard of this," said Donald Watson, chairman of the Zuurberg Wool and Mohair Growers' Association. "We feel the parks board has to go into this a lot more carefully. We accept that it is a long-term task but the land it already owns must be properly developed. It has remained fallow for 10 to 15 years while we have had to put up with the vermin that breed there."

He said up to 200 families in the area could be affected if the expansion plans in their present form go ahead.

Another reaction, shown in Figure 1.24, was reported by Ed Richardson in the 21 November 1997 issue of the *Eastern Province Herald*, Port Elizabeth, South Africa.

Figure 1.24 An excerpt from the *Eastern Province Herald*.

FARMERS QUESTION MERIT OF ADDO PARK EXTENSION

Farmers bordering on the proposed greater Addo elephant park have called for a full economic evaluation of the project before it goes ahead. "The problem is we feel we are being bulldozed into something on which we have not been consulted," says chairman of the Zuurberg Wool and Mohair Growers' Association, Donald Watson.

"The proposers of the park are forgetting about the people on the surrounding farms. We feel the future of the farmers and the workers is not being taken into account," he says. "We're talking about ground that has been in family hands from the mid-1800s." The farmers have asked for a full economic evaluation of the potential earnings of the Addo Park versus the lost revenue from sheep and mohair farming in the area.

There is concern that plans for mohair and wool beneficiation and processing plants for the Eastern Cape will have to be shelved if too much land is lost to non-farming activities. The area currently produces 60% of the world's quality mohair.

Figure 1.25 Comments by Dr. Graham Kerley, researcher at the University of Port Elizabeth, South Africa.

According to Graham Kerley,
"With 368 000 ha covering six of South Africa's seven ecological niches, the park would represent a massive commitment to the country's conservation cause. It would ensure that the Eastern Cape would become a prime international eco-tourism destination attracting substantial, sustainable foreign capital. Degraded farmland would be restored and the famous Addo elephants would become the new milk cows of the Eastern Cape."

Figure 1.26 A statement by Geoff Barr, a South African environmentalist.

Conservationists have welcomed the plans to bolster the black rhino and elephant populations. Also, they plan to introduce two prides of lion, which would put the reserve on the international wildlife map. Perhaps even more exciting is that the proposed national park would include a 57 000 ha marine reserve – incorporating Bird and St. Croix islands – which would also mean protection for the southern right whale, humpback dolphin and jackass penguin.

The press release shown in Figure 1.27 was issued by South Africa Environment Project (SAEP), an environmental group in the country.

Figure 1.27

SAEP believes that this project has an enormous potential for benefitting local communities through the multitude of job opportunities that will ensue. Why not, we ask the Government of South Africa, focus on this project, instead of putting scarce resources into the very dubious and unquestionably unsustainable Coega project? Both projects have the potential to create jobs and stimulate secondary economic activities, yet one entails the construction of a highly polluting zinc smelter whose lifespan is a mere 25 years, while the other offers environmentally friendly, community-based development opportunities that are sustainable. Which would you choose? We think the choice is obvious.

The article in Figure 1.28, concerning a neighbouring industrial project, appeared in the *Eastern Province Herald*, Port Elizabeth, South Africa, on 22 October 1997.

Figure 1.28

PROJECT SPELLS GLOOM FOR ADDO PARK

The Coega industrial project will have serious negative consequences for the Greater Addo National Park, according to the park proposal document produced by the University of Port Elizabeth's Terrestrial Ecology Research Unit (TERU). The proposed Coega harbour and 10 000 ha industrial development zone (IDZ) would be visible from a large part of the park, especially the Zuurberg Mountain range, it said. "This inevitably will detract from the natural experience for tourists, who will have to drive though a heavily industrialised area to reach the park." The risk of pollution from toxic waste generated by the resident industries also posed a problem. "The prevailing winds blowing from a south/south-west direction will inevitably blow this pollution over the park."

The level of fluoride emissions from the proposed Gencor and Kynoch plants would definitely have a negative impact on vegetation in the Coega area as well as several kilometres downwind of Coega, said the document. It was likely that the bird populations on the St. Croix Islands would be severely affected by the Coega harbour development.

"Unfortunately, it is not possible to evaluate the impact of the proposed Coega development as there is currently insufficient information on their environmental impact." The park's management should in the first instance be identified as an interested and affected party in terms of the Coega project assessment process, it said.

Coega project director Doug Reed was approached for comment on Monday and again yesterday but was not available. Messages were not returned.

Interact

Discuss whether saving the elephant herd was an important issue.

Figure 1.29 on the next page shows some interesting facts about the existing Addo Elephant National Park from the *Eastern Province Herald*, Port Elizabeth, South Africa, 22 October, 1997.

Figure 1.29 Some facts about the existing Addo Elephant National Park.

- The Addo Elephant National Park is already attracting 100 000 visitors a year – more even than Tanzania's Serengeti.

- Last year tourists spent R360 million [rand] getting to the park, excluding what they spent inside the park on accommodation, meals, supplies, game drives, and tips.

- It has been estimated that each ten foreign tourists will create one local job.

- With 8000 direct and indirect jobs, the elephant park was already generating four times the income of agricultural uses of the land.

Find out the value of one rand in Canadian dollars. Calculate the value of R360 million.

Figure 1.30 Tourists in the Greater Addo National Park. In your opinion, were the benefits of expanding the park worth the costs? Why or why not?

On 10 February 2000, the Environment News Services, an online news provider, posted the announcement shown in Figure 1.31 on the opening of the expanded park.

By carefully following the five steps of investigating an issue, the people involved concluded that a national preserve should be established to protect the habitat of the animals in the area. Now the elephants have more space, the region has more employment, and tourism is growing.

Dollars & Sense

The greatest gamblers on health care are Canadians aged 18 to 25, with 22% of this group travelling without health insurance coverage. By comparison, only 5% of those over age 65 report travelling without insurance.

One week of hospitalization in another country can cost more than $10 000. You can protect yourself by investing in a health insurance package, which can start as low as $1 a day. This insurance would cover all or most of your bills for health care while outside Canada. It makes sense to get adequate coverage when travelling outside Canada – even for one day.

In an effort to expand tourism revenues, South Africa launched an international advertising campaign at the beginning of 2000. Using electronic and media sources, the campaign targeted at least 60 million people in the top six markets – the United Kingdom, the United States, Germany, Italy, the Netherlands, and France.

Figure 1.31 An excerpt from an online news report of the opening of the expanded park (Environment News Service, http://ens.lycos.com).

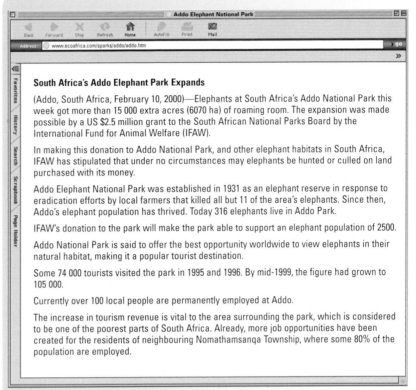

Addo Elephant National Park

Address: www.ecoafrica.com/sparks/addo/addo.htm

South Africa's Addo Elephant Park Expands

(Addo, South Africa, February 10, 2000)—Elephants at South Africa's Addo National Park this week got more than 15 000 extra acres (6070 ha) of roaming room. The expansion was made possible by a US $2.5 million grant to the South African National Parks Board by the International Fund for Animal Welfare (IFAW).

In making this donation to Addo National Park, and other elephant habitats in South Africa, IFAW has stipulated that under no circumstances may elephants be hunted or culled on land purchased with its money.

Addo Elephant National Park was established in 1931 as an elephant reserve in response to eradication efforts by local farmers that killed all but 11 of the area's elephants. Since then, Addo's elephant population has thrived. Today 316 elephants live in Addo Park.

IFAW's donation to the park will make the park able to support an elephant population of 2500.

Addo National Park is said to offer the best opportunity worldwide to view elephants in their natural habitat, making it a popular tourist destination.

Some 74 000 tourists visited the park in 1995 and 1996. By mid-1999, the figure had grown to 105 000.

Currently over 100 local people are permanently employed at Addo.

The increase in tourism revenue is vital to the area surrounding the park, which is considered to be one of the poorest parts of South Africa. Already, more job opportunities have been created for the residents of neighbouring Nomathamsanqa Township, where some 80% of the population are employed.

CHECK IN

1 Use the five steps in the issues investigation analysis model to analyze the issue of the expansion of the Addo Elephant National Park. For each step in the model, record your ideas in point form.

2 Identify biases in the materials presented about Addo Elephant National Park. Describe the biases that you find and what these suggest about the people or groups who hold them.

3 Which of the sources of information given in the Addo study would you consider most legitimate and valid? Give reasons for your choice(s).

4 Who, in your opinion, should be most responsible for resolving issues that involve travel and tourism? Share your opinions with the class.

- apply geotechnologies to a study of regional geography
- produce and interpret different types of maps, graphic organizers, and diagrams
- communicate effectively in written, oral, and visual forms
- explain how tourism-related development can have important impacts on human systems
- analyze specific examples of how tourist activities can threaten fragile environments
- identify the economic, cultural, political, and environmental components of selected issues related to travel and tourism

Tourism Issues Around the World

Purpose: To use ArcView to create a world map that highlights the tourism issues addressed in *Canada Travels*.

Files: country.shp

Functions: View Properties, Legend Editor (Symbol Edit), Zoom, Convert to Shapefile, Find, Table Edit, Add Event Theme, New Theme, Feature Drawing, Legend Editor (Unique Value), Text Labels, Hot Link.

1. Your first step will be to create a blank View and name it "Tourism Issues of the World."

2. Next, add the theme c:\esri\esridata\world\country.shp and use the Colour Palette in the Legend Editor to change the colour to white.

3. Now, scan through your textbook and identify the issues that are discussed and the village/town/city, country, or region in which each occurs. Use this information and the following steps to complete the table on page 29.
   - Determine if the issue is being discussed in relation to a village/town/city, country, or region. Record the name of the village/

town/city, country, or region in the appropriate column of the table.
   Note: If it is a village, town, or city, use an appropriate source, such as the gazetteer of an atlas, to find its latitude and longitude coordinates. Record the coordinates in the table. If it is a region, record a description of the location of the region and/or the countries that it includes.
   - For each village/town/city, country, or region recorded in the table, write a *brief* description of the issue that is examined in the text. An example is provided in the table.

4. Next, create a table in ArcView called "Villages/Towns/Cities" that contains three fields: Villages/Towns/Cities, Latitude, and Longitude. Add records for each of the Villages/Towns/Cities you have recorded in your table in Step 3, then enter the appropriate data. Save the edits to the table, then add it as an Event Theme to the world map in the "Tourism Issues Around the World" View.

5. Now, open the country.shp theme table and highlight each of the countries listed in the Country column of your table. (Hint: You may toggle through the list to locate these, or you may use the Find tool.) Close the table and convert these to a shapefile called Countries.

6. Next, create a new polygon theme called "Regions." Use the polygon drawing tool to

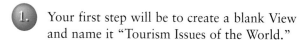

Village/ Town/ City	Latitude and Longitude	Issue	Country	Issue	Region	Location (e.g., countries included)	Issue
			e.g., Madagascar	e.g., deforesta- tion for fuel and farm- land; destruction of the rainforest for sapphire mining			

draw on the world map each of the regions listed in the Region column of your table. (It may be helpful to zoom in on the general area of the region before drawing it.) Then, open the theme table, add one field called "Region," then enter the names of the respective regions. (Hint: If you are unsure which record in the theme table corresponds with which region on the map, then highlight the record and return to the View. The record will be highlighted there as well!) When you have finished, return to the View, save your edits, and stop editing.

 7. Now, use the Legend Editor to apply a Unique Value legend type to each of the three themes you have created: villages/towns/cities, countries, or regions. (For the values field, use the value that denotes the name.)

 8. Last, use the Callout Text tool to create labels for each of the villages/towns/cities, countries, and regions. Each label should contain a brief and general description of the tourism issue experienced in that place.

Extension:

Create ASCI DOS.txt files containing more detailed descriptions of the tourism issues. Then, hot link these text files to the three themes you have created by entering their directory paths in the respective theme tables.

Extension:

Scan or download photos of the issues or places studied in this activity. Then, hot link these to the three themes you have created by creating new Views and adding the .jpeg photos as image data.

(Hint: Do not forget to turn on the JPEG Support extension and name the Views appropriately!)

REVISIT THE chapter 1
Looking Back

Understanding the Concepts

1. Identify three factors that influence travellers' destination choices. For each, explain how it influences decisions.

2. Why do people travel? Answer this question from the view of different sections of society (e.g., students, families, young people, newlyweds), and then from a personal perspective. Explain why your reasons for travelling may not be the same as those for other groups of society.

3. a) Explain why it is important that issues be examined carefully and critically.
   b) Why is it important that investigations recognize that people have a variety of perspectives on issues?

Practising Your Skills

4. Create an ideas web (also called an ideas map) to show the different viewpoints in the issue about the Greater Addo National Park. Your web should include some details about the various positions held.

5. From the viewpoint of either a farmer whose lands were being expropriated by the newly enlarged Greater Addo National Park or a game warden employed by the Addo Elephant National Park, write a diary entry stating your feelings about the creation of the new park and your view of the future.

Figure 1.32 The entrance to the former Addo Elephant National Park. What languages are used on the sign?

Applying Your Skills

6. Think about an issue that involved you personally either at school, in the community, or even in your home.
   a) State the issue.
   b) Give your viewpoint or position on the issue.
   c) Give three facts or opinions that you used to support your viewpoint.
   d) Give other important viewpoints or positions on the issue.
   e) If the issue was resolved, explain how it came to be resolved. If it is unresolved, identify the things that are preventing a resolution.
   f) Describe ways that the issues analysis approach described in this chapter might have helped lead to a resolution of the issue.

7. You are writing a play about an issue such as the expansion of the Addo Elephant National Park. Think about the plot that you would develop in the play to help people understand the various issues in this situation. Outline the plot of your play.

Thinking Like a Tourist

8. You are a tourist planning a visit to the Addo Elephant National Park just as the expansion plan is announced.
   a) What concerns do you have?
   b) What better tourist opportunities might the expansion provide?

9. Make a poster for promoting the new Greater Addo National Park. Carefully consider the images that you will use to attract tourists to the destination. On the back of your poster, point out the images that you used and give reasons for your choices.

JOB SKILLS

Write a one-page analysis in which you explain how using the issues analysis strategy to look at travel and tourism issues will help to develop employability skills. Think about such skills as locating and managing information, evaluating information, and coping with uncertainty.

Figure 1.33 Employers look for workers with skills that include the ability to see different points of view and evaluate them based on facts, to identify the root cause of problems, and to work as part of a team.

CHAPTER two 2
Regions and Tourism

FOCUS ON THESE KEY QUESTIONS AND . . .

1. How do geographers use the similarities and differences among places to help them understand the Earth's geography?
2. What are regions and why are they useful?
3. How can an understanding of what a region is help tourists and tour operators?

KEY WORDS & TERMS

boundaries
functional region
homogeneous
multifactor region
region
single-factor region
transition zone

Geographic Foundations: Regions in Travel and Tourism

Great! After months of working at it, you have just landed your dream summer job. You have been hired by the local municipality to work in the planning office. Only a few students were chosen to conduct studies on tourism in the area. This is a great opportunity to work with interesting people, to apply the research skills you have been developing in school, and to spend the summer doing interesting things. Then, you get your first task – and the real work begins!

Figure 2.1 Ethnic neighbourhoods have qualities that many people find appealing. These neighbourhoods can generate a tourism industry.

Figure 2.2 Shops and services include stores that sell Indian-language newspapers, silk, and tandoori-style barbecued foods.

The municipal council has decided to make some improvements to the streets of a neighbourhood well known for its distinctive culture. By installing specially designed street signs, widening sidewalks so benches can be added, and planting trees and shrubs, the council hopes to make "Little India" a greater attraction for tourists. These additions would invite more tourists into the area and make their time there more comfortable. The difficult part is deciding just how far the neighbourhood extends. Everyone can pinpoint the core of the neighbourhood, but the edges, or boundaries, are much harder to identify. Before the work can begin, the planning office must clearly define the neighbourhood that is Little India. The job is now on your desk.

EXPECTATIONS

In this chapter, you will have the opportunity to

- demonstrate an understanding of how a variety of factors are used to define regions
- explain how natural and human criteria are used to establish regional boundaries
- demonstrate an understanding of different types of regions
- explain how geographers use the concept of regions to investigate and solve problems and issues
- compare viewpoints of individuals, businesses, non-governmental organizations, and other groups about sustainable use of the Earth and its resources
- evaluate the role of UNESCO in protecting significant natural and cultural sites around the world
- evaluate the impact of government policies on travel and tourism in selected regions

Using Your Research Skills

After visiting the location for a few days and talking to experienced planners, you conclude that Little India is recognizable because of four visible characteristics. These include

- the presence of shops and services, such as restaurants, that cater to Indian tastes and traditions
- the use of Indian languages on signs and banners
- the presence of visible links to India, such as Indian newspapers
- the concentration of people who speak Indian languages

You decide to gather detailed information on these characteristics, using the research techniques shown below.

Figure 2.3 Products from India include spices, packaged specialty foods, and clothing such as saris.

Figure 2.4 Data for travel and tourism studies can be obtained in a variety of ways. The four methods below might be used to study regions at the neighbourhood level. What other characteristics might be used?

Characteristic	Data Gathering Technique
Shops and services with Indian clientele	Prepare and distribute a questionnaire to most businesses in a wide area. One question asks business owners to rate their appeal to different ethnic groups, including people from India.
Signs and banners with Indian words	Conduct a sidewalk survey of a large part of the community, noting the use of different languages on street, store, and home signs and banners.
Visible links to India	Visit shops and services in the area and complete a tally of Canada-India links, such as Indian newspapers for sale in convenience stores, travel agencies specializing in destinations in India, and products made in India on store shelves.
Spoken Indian languages	Obtain census data from Statistics Canada about mother tongues and home languages for the city. Establish that census tracts with more than 10% of the population speaking an Indian language at home are significant for the analysis.

Analyzing Your Data

Working with an experienced planner, you load the data from the questionnaire, the sidewalk survey, and tally of links into a database and combine it with the census tract figures. Then, you work with a computer program to analyze the distribution of the four characteristics. One of the first criteria you establish is that the overlap of any three characteristics is necessary for that area to be included in the neighbourhood of Little India. You print out maps using your data. First print one for each single characteristic. Then print a map showing areas where at least three characteristics are present. Now your maps let you clearly define a region that you can identify as a distinctive Indian neighbourhood.

Interact

What characteristics of neighbourhoods make them attractive and inviting for tourists?

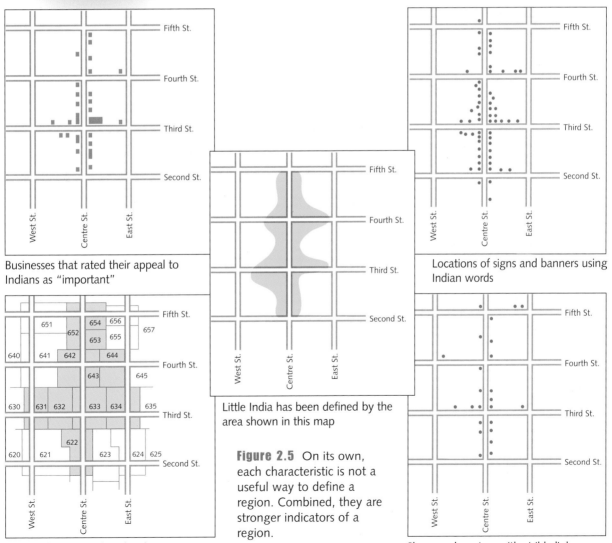

Businesses that rated their appeal to Indians as "important"

Census divisions with Indian home language greater than 10%

Little India has been defined by the area shown in this map

Figure 2.5 On its own, each characteristic is not a useful way to define a region. Combined, they are stronger indicators of a region.

Locations of signs and banners using Indian words

Shops and services with visible links to India

1 In what ways does the Little India example use similarities and differences in analyzing places?

2 Brainstorm two other characteristics that might be used to identify a cultural neighbourhood. Suggest a way to collect data about each.

Regions as Geographic Tools

The geographic idea that was central to the analysis of the neighbourhood, described in the scenario on pages 32–35, was the concept of a region. A **region** is an area of the Earth's surface that has characteristics that make it unique or different from other places. Geographers use evidence about similarities and differences to identify regions.

Geographers use the concept of a region to help understand the way the world works. Within the region, there is one set of characteristics. Outside the region there are many other characteristics. The characteristics that are used to define the region are found everywhere within the region, so the geographic area is **homogeneous** for those characteristics. In the Little India example, that part of the city that had a strong Indian influence – at least three characteristics – made up a region. The **boundaries**, or the edges of the region, were not always clearly defined. City areas around the region's core that had fewer visible Indian characteristics were part of a **transition zone**. Areas of the city that had few, if any, visible Indian characteristics were not part of the region being defined.

Regions Come in Different Sizes

As a geographic tool, regions are very flexible. We can define regions on a small scale, such as our neighbourhood, or a part of the city where most tourist attractions are located. The scale can also be quite large. People often use terms like "the Middle East" or "sub-Saharan Africa" to refer to regions. In these cases the regions contain a number of countries.

The size of the region that you use depends on the purposes of your study. Suppose you need to understand tourist movement

A Region

A region is an area of the Earth's surface that has
- characteristics that are found throughout the region
- characteristics that are different from those in the surrounding areas
- a core where the characteristics are clearly found
- a transition zone where the characteristics decline or are less clear
- boundaries that identify the edges of the region

Figure 2.6 Central Park is clearly visible in this photograph of midtown Manhattan. Central Park can be considered a region within the larger city because its characteristics are very different from the area surrounding it. The boundaries of a region like Central Park are clearly defined.

Figure 2.7 A herd of camels crosses a desert in northern Kenya in search of grazing lands. What would the characteristics of this region be?

patterns within a city, perhaps for the purposes of designing transportation facilities. Then it makes sense to divide the city into regions, each with its own needs. To understand global relationships, working with groups of countries as a region is usually an advantage. An example would be to determine the volume of visitors who travel from Europe to South Asia, perhaps for the purpose of planning future air traffic facilities. The purpose for the study establishes both the size and type of region that is defined.

Three geographic concepts – patterns, movements, and interactions – can be used to help analyze or describe a region.

- *Patterns* are the arrangements of shapes, lines, or items that can be identified on the surface of the Earth, including physical features (for example, the location of mountain ranges) and human-made features (such as the pattern of cities within a country).

- *Movements* are the changes in locations that occur in a place. The movement of tourists to a destination or the migration of animals are two examples.

- *Interactions* refer to connections between humans and natural systems. This can be seen most clearly in the types of agriculture that develop in a region or in the modes of transportation used by people.

When a region is defined, it is done using evidence about patterns, movements, and interactions. Little India could be defined because the data uncovered patterns as a geographic concept. It showed patterns in languages, signs, and services and sales of such items as ethnic products and newspapers.

Patterns, Movements, and Interactions

People identify a region to make it easier to organize vast amounts of complex information for analyzing issues.

When we identify a region, we do so for a purpose. Regions can be identified in a variety of ways.

Single-Factor Regions A region that is identified using only one characteristic is a **single-factor region**. When the Western Cordillera is identified by its mountainous terrain, it is a single-factor region.

Multifactor Regions Other regions are identified using many characteristics, often from both the natural and human worlds. The Little India neighbourhood described earlier used three characteristics. Another example of a **multifactor region** is the area referred to as the Windsor-Quebec Axis. This part of the country contains a high percentage of the nation's manufacturing and economic activity. The region can be identified using such characteristics as high population density, percentage of the

Figure 2.8 Banff National Park is part of the Western Cordillera.

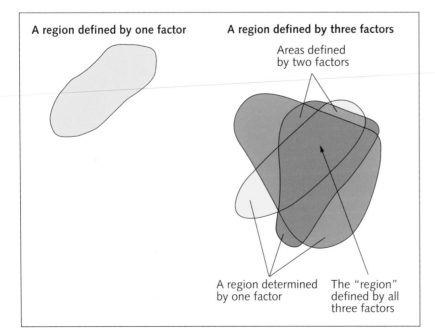

A region defined by one factor

A region defined by three factors

Areas defined by two factors

A region determined by one factor

The "region" defined by all three factors

Figure 2.9 Single-factor regions are simple to identify and use. Multifactor regions are harder to identify because the factors do not always overlap exactly. There may be places that have some but not all of the factors. Should these areas be included in the region or not? The answer to that question depends on the purpose for identifying the region.

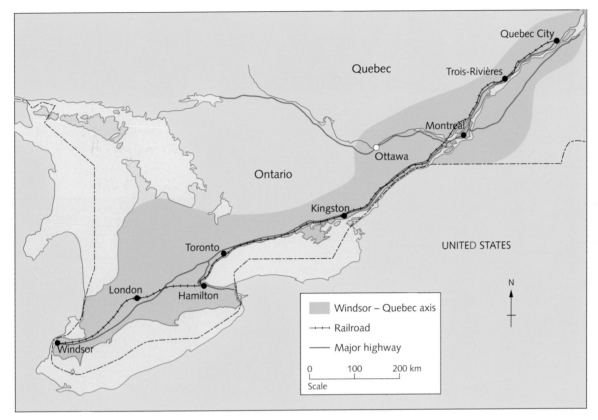

Figure 2.10 The Windsor – Quebec Axis is a region that can be defined by many factors.

population employed in manufacturing, types of landforms, and transportation linkages. This long, narrow region has characteristics that clearly make it different from the rest of the country.

Functional Regions Regions can also be defined by their ongoing activities or functions. A well-known example of a **functional region** is the area served by a pizza outlet. The physical and human characteristics throughout the delivery area may vary a good deal, and so delivery areas are usually not homogeneous regions. Functional regions have a central point around which some activity

Figure 2.11 This table shows some ways that regions are used. You may use regions in your everyday life without realizing their importance.

Single-Factor Characteristics	Multifactor Characteristics	Functional Regions
Landform region	Industrial heartland	Pizza delivery area
Land use region	Ecozones	Newspaper circulation area
Language region	Metropolitan area	River drainage area
Park	Central business district	School bus route
Beach	Tourist business district	Summer festivals

or function takes place. The region extends as far as the functions that are operating. The boundary for the pizza delivery region, for example, is determined by the maximum distance served by a pizza outlet.

Type of Region	Characteristics	Examples
City-centred regions	Large, urban areas	Paris, Cairo, Tokyo
Frontier regions	The edges of development	Antarctica, space
Cultural regions	Places with distinctive cultural characteristics	Islamic Middle Eastern countries, Latin America, Chinatown
Historical regions	Areas with interesting and colourful pasts	Greece, Andean region, India, US South
Political regions	Areas with similar political conditions or regimes	Province of Ontario, European Union
Physical regions	Areas defined by qualities of the physical environment	Great Rift Valley, tropical rain forests, Great Barrier Reef
Economic regions	Areas having distinctive economic activities	Toronto's Bay Street, the Atlantic Provinces, sub-Saharan Africa

Figure 2.12 Regions can be defined using many characteristics. Some examples are given here.

Figure 2.13 The natural region of tropical rain forest on Nevis Island in the Caribbean Sea.

Using Regions in Travel and Tourism

The concept of a region is important in analyzing global patterns of travel and tourism. For example, we can view destinations for tourists as regions. The Caribbean Islands are a region. These island tourist destinations share similar characteristics: they are small, have beautiful beaches and a warm climate, and rely on tourist dollars for economic vitality. The area around Paris, France, can be considered a region because its cultural and historical features attract large numbers of tourists. When analyzing tourist patterns and issues, it is helpful to see the world in terms of geographic regions. Sometimes these regions can be large, like the Middle East, or small, such as the theatre district of a city.

Interact

What is the value of having different types of regions?

Travel FACT

In 1999, tourism in the Middle East was up 17.4% from the previous year.

Figure 2.14 Viewing the many regions of France makes tourism decisions easier.

CHECK IN

1. a) Explain how natural and human characteristics are used to establish regions.
   b) Give two examples of regions defined by natural characteristics alone, two defined only by human characteristics, and two defined by both natural and human characteristics.

2. What are the advantages and disadvantages of defining a region using multiple factors?

3. a) What is the smallest region that you could define? For what purpose might you identify such a small region?
   b) What is the largest region that you know about? For what purpose might you use such a region?

LOOKING AT ISSUES

Protecting the Niagara Escarpment

Issue: Should the protection of the Niagara Escarpment prevail over all other interests in the region?

Tourists often find unique natural environments, like the Niagara Escarpment, attractive. The Niagara Escarpment is a region that can be defined by a number of characteristics, including steep cliffs and the ways humans use the area.

The Niagara Escarpment gets a good deal of use by hikers, campers, and climbers. The escarpment is a 725-km ridge that cuts across the southern part of Ontario, from Queenston on the Niagara River to Manitoulin Island in the north. This landform has much to offer. Housing developers want to take advantage of its scenic beauty; pit and quarry operators hope to use its sand, gravel, and limestone; and farmers prize its growing conditions, especially for tender fruits like peaches and grapes. Cities are expanding all around the escarpment. This is an area under intense development pressure. Tourism is just one of its many possible uses.

Examine the information on pages 42–51 to see how the concept of a region was applied to protect this natural area.

Figure 2.15 The Niagara Escarpment extends through southern Ontario and along the west shore of Lake Michigan.

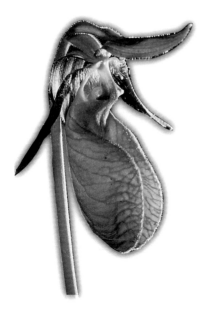

The Physical Environment of the Niagara Escarpment

Figure 2.16 The different environments found along the length of the Niagara Escarpment have produced many species and subspecies that are found in few, if any, other places. The area of the Niagara Escarpment that forms the Bruce Peninsula, separating Lake Huron and Georgian Bay, contains many interesting flowers, including orchids such as this lady's slipper. Admire and photograph the unique flora, but never gather the wildflowers.

Figure 2.17 A cross-section of the Niagara Escarpment. Erosion has removed the softer layers of rock below a more resistant dolomite (a harder form of limestone), creating a steep cliff or escarpment. A feature formed in this way is called a cuesta. Rivers that flow over the edge of the escarpment have spectacular waterfalls. Niagara Falls is the most famous of these natural features.

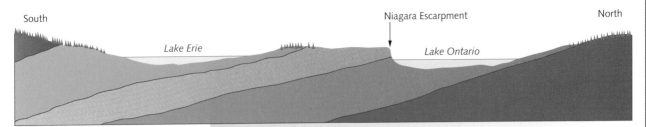

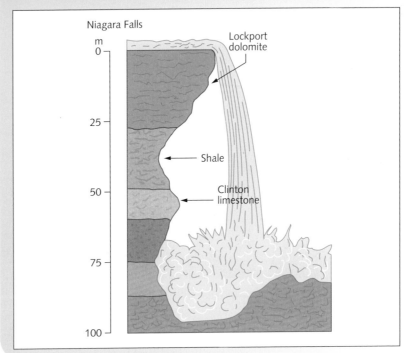

Figure 2.18 A cross-section of the rock layers at Niagara Falls. As the weaker, softer rock is eroded by the water, the upper dolomite collapses. The falls have been retreating upriver since they were formed.

Figure 2.19 A white cedar. Aboriginal peoples taught early French explorers how to cure the disease scurvy by drinking a tea made from the cedar's bark and needles.

Figure 2.20 The Niagara Escarpment in Bruce Peninsula National Park, Ontario. In pioneer times, the escarpment was a barrier to transportation. More recently it has been recognized for its distinctive scenic and ecological character.

Travel FACT

The oldest living tree in Ontario is a white cedar about 950 years old. It stands in the Bruce Peninsula National Park. Another white cedar lived for 1890 years. It grew on Flowerpot Island, off the tip of the Bruce Peninsula.

Figure 2.21 Travel and tourism activities associated with the Niagara Escarpment include this bird sanctuary in Kingsville, hang gliding, historic St. Margaret's Church, and a pow-wow held at Cape Croker by the Chippewas of Nawash First Nation.

Tourism and the Niagara Escarpment

With over 7 million people living within a couple of hours of the escarpment, it is not surprising that its natural beauty attracts tourists. Some tourism developments include

- national parks, including Bruce Peninsula National Park
- provincial parks, such as the Forks of the Credit River Provincial Park
- conservation areas
- ski resorts
- camp grounds and trailer parks
- hiking trails
- caves for exploring
- countless picnic areas and scenic lookouts
- many bed and breakfast locations
- hotels, motels, and country inns
- winery tours
- scenic flights

These developments, services, and facilities attract people to the area, particularly during summer months. The populations of some smaller communities, including Tobermory at the tip of the Bruce Peninsula, more than double during the tourist season.

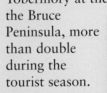

Managing the Niagara Escarpment Area

The pressures to develop the tourism potential of the escarpment, along with the rapid growth of all of southern Ontario, threaten this unique natural area. Many of the potential uses are incompatible. The quarrying of limestone, for example, conflicts with tourism, and industrial development is incompatible with fruit farming. In the past, leaving land use decisions to individual municipalities often proved to be an ineffective way to protect the environment. Towns and townships had different goals and priorities. The result was a patchwork of policies about how the land and resources could be used. The provincial government decided that a comprehensive management plan that covered the entire escarpment would be the best approach. That decision led to the Niagara Escarpment Plan.

Figure 2.22 The eastern massasauga rattlesnake is protected by law.

Figure 2.23 The Dufferin Aggregates limestone quarry

Beware of the eastern massasauga, a native of the Bruce Peninsula. This timid rattlesnake is on Canada's endangered species list. It rattles to warn larger animals of its presence and to avoid being stepped on. It is rarely aggressive and strikes at humans only in self-defence. A rattlesnake bite is poisonous, but if venom antidote is given within a few hours, a healthy person will recover. If you are bitten by a rattlesnake, go to a local hospital as quickly as possible.

Canada Travels

The Bruce Trail Association has set up and maintains an 800-km hiking trail along the length of the Niagara Escarpment in Ontario. The trail is built on publicly owned land and also runs across private property, through the generosity of the landowners. The costs of maintaining the trail are covered largely by membership fees. Volunteers donate hundreds of hours of their time cutting and marking the trail, building bridges, and picking up garbage.

www.irwinpublishing.com

Visit the Bruce Trail Association on the Student Page for *Canada Travels*.

The Niagara Escarpment Plan

In 1985, The Niagara Escarpment Planning and Development Act established a planning process to ensure that development in the area would be managed. From this act emerged the Niagara Escarpment Plan. The plan provides an overall framework of policies that tries to balance economic development of the area with preservation of the natural landscape. The plan ensures that people will be able to enjoy the recreational and aesthetic value of this important resource. Municipalities must make decisions that conform to the criteria set out in the plan. Land use policies identify the uses that are acceptable in the area on or near the escarpment. The plan has received a good deal of criticism from those who want to develop the area in ways that are contrary to the plan's criteria.

Figure 2.24 The Niagara Escarpment Plan area

A World Biosphere Reserve

The United Nations Educational, Scientific, and Cultural Organization (UNESCO) designated the Niagara Escarpment as a World Biosphere Reserve in 1990. This designation was an important event in protecting this sensitive environment and its inhabitants. World reserves are managed in such a way as to find a balance between conservation and development. Core areas are used to protect significant ecological features, such as sensitive lands and threatened species. The national parks and lands owned by the Niagara Parks Commission are the core of the biosphere reserve. Buffer zones around the core provide additional protection.

An important role of world reserves is the opportunity they provide for studying and comparing undisturbed land and developed areas. The world reserves are a standard against which the effects of human impact on the environment can be measured.

Figure 2.26 Wetlands are important places along the Niagara Escarpment.

Figure 2.25 Flowerpot Island, Fathom Five National Marine Park, Georgian Bay, Ontario

Figure 2.27 A winery's proposal to develop a large tourist complex was a recent issue in the Niagara area.

Figure 2.28 The logo of the Coalition on the Niagara Escarpment (CONE)

www.irwinpublishing.com

To learn more about the activities of CONE, visit the Student Page for *Canada Travels*.

DECISION SHOWS ONTARIANS CARE

Last week, the Ontario government released a long-awaited decision on the Niagara Escarpment. It refused an amendment to the Niagara Escarpment Plan (NEP) to permit a winery tourist resort on the escarpment southwest of Vineland.

The escarpment plan played an important role in the emergence of Niagara wineries. The escarpment's unique micro-climate is perfect for growing grapes. Cottage wineries sprang up all over the peninsula.

Wine tours evolved, and the cottage winery industry exploded in Niagara, producing internationally acclaimed wines. Today, wineries host tours all year long, and have a special summer calendar of events.

In 1998, John Howard, owner of Vineland Estates Winery, wanted the NEP changed to permit a specific development. He sought a winery, culinary centre, greenhouse, restaurant and lecture theatre, and 56 guest cottages on 39 hectares in an agricultural area.

A winery requires only a development permit, readily available from the NEP. At issue was a cottage resort right in the "Protection" designation of the NEP. Howard wanted 56 cottages – a subdivision.

An intensive tourist resort is simply not permitted in sensitive areas of the escarpment, so the applicant wanted the escarpment plan changed.

In August 1998, a three-day Niagara Escarpment Plan Amendment hearing took place. Wine industry representatives supported the food and wine components but opposed escarpment cottages.

The Coalition on the Niagara Escarpment (CONE) decided to participate in the hearing, a costly endeavour for volunteers, but they raised funds because they felt strongly that the proposal did not meet the intent of the Niagara Escarpment Plan.

In announcing the decision, a Ministry of Natural Resources spokesperson said that the government found the amendment "too far outside the environmentally protective nature of the escarpment plan."

Source: Joan Little, "Decision Shows Ontarians Care," *The Hamilton Spectator*, 26 June 2000, p. A11.

The Role of Citizen Groups

Citizens concerned about the Niagara Escarpment have formed groups to have a voice in decisions made about the region. One such group is the Coalition on the Niagara Escarpment (CONE). Founded in 1978, it is a nonprofit coalition of conservation organizations and community groups dedicated to the protection of the escarpment. Among its activities, CONE monitors the implementation of the Niagara Escarpment Plan. It looks at proposals for development along the escarpment and opposes those that it sees as detrimental to the region's ecology. It also works to encourage the public to value this natural region.

Criticism of the Niagara Escarpment Plan

Many landowners in the area resent the controls imposed by the Niagara Escarpment Plan. The plan limits uses of the land to only those that are permitted. Even then, owners must submit a permit application to the Niagara Escarpment Commission for any new development. Processing for simple applications can take six to eight weeks. If the proposals are for permitted uses and they meet the goals of the plan, applications are approved. This is the case for about 90% of all applications. Rejected applications can be appealed at a hearing, where the landowner has an opportunity to argue against the commission's decision and in favour of the proposal. A final decision is made by the provincial Minister of Natural Resources based on the report of the hearing.

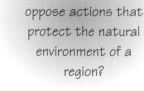

Interact

Why would anyone oppose actions that protect the natural environment of a region?

Figure 2.29 View from Mt. Nemo, Burlington, Ontario

Figure 2.30 Conservation of the Niagara Escarpment must be balanced by considering other land uses, such as tourism and agriculture.

CHECK IN

1   a)   In what ways can the Niagara Escarpment be considered a
         region?
    b)   Explain how the commission responsible for implementing
         the Niagara Escarpment Plan uses the concept of a region to
         investigate and solve problems and issues related to
         development of the area.

2   Sketch a poster to promote the tourist potential of the Niagara
    Escarpment. Explain in a paragraph why you chose the symbols
    or images you used in your poster.

3   The Niagara Escarpment Plan has been criticized because it
    controls the ways that people who live near the escarpment can
    use their land.
    a)   Summarize arguments that these critics might make to the
         provincial government if they were trying to get the plan
         changed.
    b)   Summarize arguments that a supporter of the plan might
         make to keep the plan intact.
    c)   Which side of the issue do you support? Give reasons for
         your opinion.

- apply geotechnologies to a study of regional geography
- produce and interpret different types of maps, graphic organizers, and diagrams
- communicate effectively in written, oral, and visual forms
- analyze the major characteristics of selected tourist regions in terms of natural, cultural, economic, and political criteria

Popular Tourist Regions of the World

Purpose: To use ArcView to create a map that highlights the popular regions of the world and contains hot links to each of these regions.

Files: country.shp

Functions: View Properties, Legend Editor (Symbol Edit), Zoom, Convert to Shapefile, Geo-processing (Dissolve Boundaries), Geo-processing (Merge Polygons), Table Edit, Legend Editor (Unique Value), Auto-label, Hot Link, Layout.

1. Your first step will be to create a blank View and name it "Popular Regions of the World."

2. Next, add the theme c:\esri\esridata\world\country.shp and use the Colour Palette in the Legend Editor to change the colour to white.

3. Now, using an atlas or another appropriate source, identify the countries that make up each of the following regions. Then, using ArcView's zoom, select and convert to shapefile tools to make each region its own theme.

- Caribbean
- Mediterranean
- Middle East
- Oceania
- Scandinavia
- The Orient

4. Next, use ArcView's Geo-processing Wizard extension to "dissolve" the boundaries that separate the countries within each region. (Hint: Each of the countries, or "records," must share a common characteristic, or "attribute." The most obvious common characteristic is the region to which the countries belong. So, your task will be to create this "attribute" in the theme table, then use it as a basis for "dissolving" the boundaries.)

5. Now, use Geo-processing Wizard again to merge all of the region themes together to form just one theme. Then, apply a unique symbol (i.e., a colour) to each of the regions that make up this theme.

6. Next, create a new View for each of the region themes that you created in Step 3. Within each View, label the countries that make up that region. Then, create hot links from the world map (i.e., Popular Regions of the World) to the regional Views you have just created.

7. Last, create a layout complete with all of the essential map requirements.

Figure 2.31 China has become a popular destination for the adventurous tourist. The Great Wall of China, shown here, is the world's longest wall, extending over 2400 km. Construction began in the second century BCE to defend China against invaders, and continued for more than 1000 years. The Great Wall has an average height of 7.5 m; it is wide enough to accommodate riders on horseback.

REVISIT THE chapter 2
Looking Back

Understanding the Concepts

1. Offer one example (other than those used in this chapter) to show that regions may be defined using a variety of factors.

2. What are three important characteristics for the concept of a region?

3. Describe the skills required to identify regions, such as Little India.

4. Using ideas from the Little India example, explain how geographers use the concept of regions to investigate and solve problems and issues.

5. Write a letter to a friend explaining how the concept of a region has been used to improve the tourism potential of the Niagara Escarpment by protecting its natural systems.

Practising Your Skills

6. What factors will affect the characteristics of regions?

7. Use the issues approach described in Chapter 1 (pages 15–21) to analyze the issue of development of the Niagara Escarpment. Answer these questions:
   a) What is the issue?
   b) Who are the stakeholders when it comes to development of the Niagara Escarpment?
   c) What are the viewpoints of the stakeholders?
   d) Write a one-page summary of your position on the issue.

Applying Your Skills

8. Does your community have a tourist region? To answer this question, brainstorm a list of the sites in and around your community that people would likely describe as tourist destinations. Locate these places on a map of your community. Is there a pattern to the locations? What does this pattern indicate about a tourist region?

Figure 2.32 Niagara Falls. In what ways have both Canada and the United States benefited from this natural wonder?

9. Research a region in your local area, such as a land use region or a distinctive neighbourhood. Try to answer these questions about the region:
   a) What characteristics or criteria were used to define the region?
   b) What is the function or purpose of this region?

10. Think of a purpose for using regions, such as what makes a tourist region in the world. Once you have a purpose, determine which characteristics or criteria would help you to define the regions. Conduct research to find information about the topic, then divide the world into regions on an outline map.

Thinking Like a Tourist

11. Identify one way that people might use the concept of a region to plan tourist activities. Share your ideas with others and list the "best" way from everyone's ideas.

12. Suppose you are a world traveller and have numerous videotapes about places you have visited. You need to categorize these videos. Brainstorm three ways that you might use the concept of regions to organize your collection.

J O B SKILLS

Figure 2.33 Problem-solving skills are essential for meteorologists, who map and interpret weather phenomena.

Problem-solving skills are important to employers. The ability to identify the root cause of a problem is one skill.

Suppose you are being interviewed for a position in the travel and tourism industry. During the interview, you are asked to explain how concepts and ideas you learned in school will make you a better problem solver. Write a paragraph on how understanding the concept of regions makes you a more useful employee.

UNIT 2
two

Tourism and the Natural Environment

OVERALL EXPECTATIONS

In this unit, you will have the opportunity to

- analyze the influence of human systems on patterns of travel and tourism and, conversely, the influence of travel and tourism on human systems
- explain the effects of natural systems on travel and tourism patterns
- analyze the impacts of different types of travel and tourism on the natural environment
- evaluate programs and initiatives designed to manage and protect the resources on which tourism is based

Chapter 5:
Toronto, Canada. How are the natural environments of cities important for tourism?

NORTH AMERICA

Chapter 3:
Costa Rica. What is the relationship between travel and tourism and the natural environment?

Overview

This unit investigates issues that arise in the vital connection between travel and tourism and both the natural and urban environments. This connection has both good and bad aspects. On the one hand, people learn about natural systems through tourist experiences, and this understanding often leads to a desire to protect nature. Tourist dollars can also help to pay for protection of the natural environment. On the other hand, use of natural urban environments by tourists can lead to their deterioration.

Destinations You Will Visit

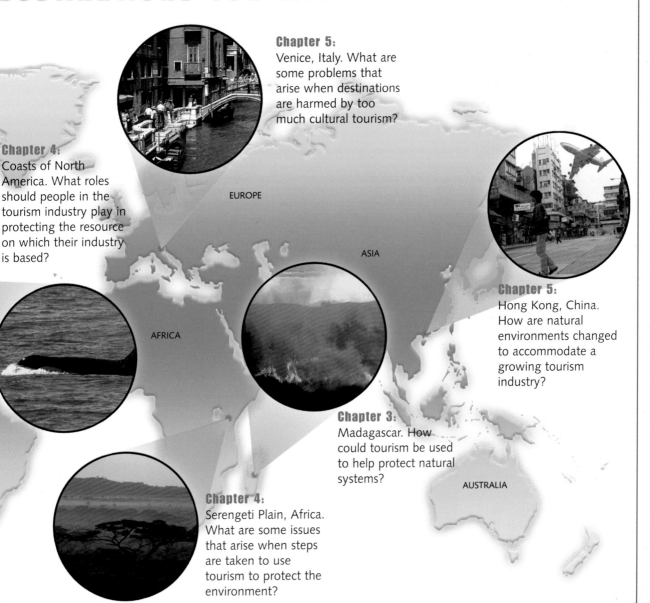

Chapter 5:
Venice, Italy. What are some problems that arise when destinations are harmed by too much cultural tourism?

Chapter 4:
Coasts of North America. What roles should people in the tourism industry play in protecting the resource on which their industry is based?

EUROPE

ASIA

AFRICA

Chapter 5:
Hong Kong, China. How are natural environments changed to accommodate a growing tourism industry?

SOUTH AMERICA

Chapter 3:
Madagascar. How could tourism be used to help protect natural systems?

AUSTRALIA

Chapter 4:
Serengeti Plain, Africa. What are some issues that arise when steps are taken to use tourism to protect the environment?

CHAPTER three 3

Natural Spaces and Tourism

FOCUS ON THESE KEY QUESTIONS AND . . .

1. What factors influence the number of tourists who will visit a destination?
2. How do tourists create problems for natural spaces?
3. Can ecotourism help save threatened environments?

KEY WORDS & TERMS

adventure travel
ecotourism
endangered space
fertility rate
hard adventure
infant mortality rate
life expectancy
literacy rate
site factors
soft adventure
wildlife corridors

Nature Attracts

In 2000, the Canadian Tourism Commission asked U.S. travellers why they had chosen Canada. Here are the reasons they gave:

1. spectacular outdoor vacation
2. lakes, rivers, and mountains
3. camping and hiking
4. to experience nature
5. for an adventurous and exciting vacation
6. a chance to relax
7. cultural attractions
8. good value for money
9. a safe vacation

Figure 3.1 Two attractions that draw tourists to Canada are Quebec City's winter carnival and fishing in Ontario's Kawartha region.

Figure 3.2 Adventure tourism and ecotourism are the most rapidly growing sectors of tourism. Can you define each of them?

> "I'm not a city person. Cities are like anthills. I find urban life nasty and I don't think cities tell me much about the country I'm in. I would rather have crocodiles chase me than stand in New York waiting for a bus. I much prefer ... places that are emptier, wild. I'm trying to find them before they disappear altogether."
>
> – Paul Theroux, travel writer (*Toronto Sun*, May 26, 2000)

Clearly, most of these Americans chose Canada because of the natural beauty of this country. They are typical of many visitors to Canada who seek sparkling waters, majestic mountains, imposing forests, and other natural wonders. Of course, not all visitors journey to wilderness or remote locations. Many people prefer to vacation in or near cities.

Nonetheless, natural spaces attract tourists. National parks, World Heritage Sites, special water features, migratory routes, and trails are all natural spaces that influence tourist destination choices. In fact, nature-based travel is the fastest growth sector in the travel and tourism industry.

Just how people enjoy the natural environment depends on variables such as their age and health, the natural characteristics of the site, and the season. This chapter will focus on how the natural environment, in combination with the other variables, supports the travel and tourism industry.

EXPECTATIONS

In this chapter you will have the opportunity to
- identify the natural resources on which tourism is based
- identify selected factors that influence destination choices
- classify different types of travel and tourism, and explain why people travel
- analyze the positive and negative impacts of ecotourism on people and the natural environment in selected regions
- analyze specific examples of how tourist activities can threaten fragile environments
- demonstrate an understanding of the need for sustainable development and protection of the resources on which tourism is based
- research and report on the potential of natural and human factors to attract tourists to a local region
- evaluate criteria used to determine the selection of park locations for a selected country
- evaluate the impact of government policies on travel and tourism in a selected region
- identify recent trends in travel and tourism

Age Makes a Difference

People of various ages have different ideas about how to enjoy nature. These ideas are often connected to such variables as their interests, income levels, personal experiences, health, and physical endurance levels. Consequently, people in different situations tend to select different types of tourist activities. When polled, tour operators gave the breakdown of general destination selections shown below. Remember, though, these are general patterns and certainly do not reflect individual choices. Some seniors who retire early are fit and ready for adventurous vacations. Some younger people wanting to escape the stress of the business world look for places to relax that offer music, sightseeing, beaches, and a chance to meet other people their own age.

Travel FACT

Nearly 60% of adventure travellers are women.

Category	Activity Type	Examples
Young adults	Hard adventure	Extreme sports, mountain biking, heli-skiing
Families	Packaged trips	Skiing holidays, theme parks, camping
Seniors	Soft adventure	Cruises, bird watching

Figure 3.3 Activities reported by tour operators

Figure 3.4 Rock climbing is usually for younger people who are fit and adventurous. There is also plenty of adventure in a camping trip or a cruise to exotic locations.

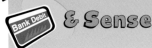
Travel FACT

Snowboarding is growing in North America at an annual rate of 15%. The average snowboarder is a 27-year-old single male.

Many people enjoy **adventure travel**, which is a rapidly growing part of tourism. Adventure vacations usually take place in an outdoor setting and offer experiences that are both mentally and physically challenging. Travellers who select this type of vacation enjoy a challenge that may involve an element of risk. There are two types of adventure travel – hard adventure and soft adventure.

Hard adventure offers exciting activities that require a person to be physically and mentally fit. Examples of hard adventure are hang gliding, rock climbing, kayaking, and mountain biking.

Less physical risk is involved in **soft adventure**. While many of the activities are similar to those in the hard adventure category, soft adventure is less physically demanding. Examples of soft adventure activities are camping, snorkelling, snowshoeing, and wind surfing.

Site Factors

Tourists of all ages want to experience and enjoy what the natural world offers. Geographers refer to the natural or physical attributes of a place as its **site factors**. Since places have different site factors, a wide variety of activities are found in tourist destinations. Seasides provide different opportunities than do mountainsides. The choice of destination depends upon the tourist's needs and wants. Figure 3.5 shows examples of some activities different age groups enjoy. Of course, some members of all age groups enjoy very different activities from those listed.

Natural Location	Young Adults	Families	Seniors
Mountains	Climbing rock faces Wilderness hiking Snowboarding	Visiting look-out sites Horse trails	Tram lifts Gentle walking trails
Beaches	Surfing Beach volleyball	Picnic areas Supervised swimming	Beach walks Swimming
Rivers	Running rapids Canoeing	Rafting Cruising	Tour boats Fishing
Forests	Mountain biking Wilderness camping	Trail hikes Photography	Bird watching Nature walks

Figure 3.5 Typical activities in natural destinations

Seasonal Characteristics

The fact that weather and seasons influence travel plans is familiar to Canadians. Canada has four distinct seasons, and each one brings a variety of travel responses. Often tourists have a preferred season for their vacations. In many cases, Canadians travel outside the country, seeking an escape from winter.

Figure 3.6 shows that the seasons influence the travel choices of young people.

Month	To countries other than the United States	To the United States	Within Canada
WINTER			
December	11%	14%	14%
January	6%	4%	6%
February	9%	13%	13%
SPRING			
March	9%	7%	11%
April	7%	8%	8%
May	11%	7%	8%
SUMMER			
June	16%	9%	9%
July	15%	14%	9%
August	8%	14%	10%
FALL			
September	5%	3%	4%
October	2%	4%	5%
November	1%	3%	3%

Source: TravelCUTS/Voyages Campus; Survey of College-Age Travellers.

Figure 3.6 Canadian youth travel by seasons

Canada Travels

Half of all Canadian pleasure trips to "sun" destinations are to Florida. The fact that Canadians can drive to the state is an important advantage that Caribbean destinations cannot match.

Interact

In what ways might the seasonal nature of tourism be an asset for the tourist industry? How might it be a problem?

TRAVELLERS' ALERT!

In the Northern Hemisphere, June to October is hurricane season. During this period, the climate conditions in the Atlantic Ocean are just right to spawn these ocean storms that feed off warm water and humid air. Hurricanes follow general tracks or routes, but they are very unpredictable as to the exact places they will hit each season. They strike islands and coastal regions with fury, but begin to lose force if they move inland. To gain more information about hurricanes and the damage they can do, visit the Student Page for *Canada Travels* at <www.irwinpublishing.com>.

Dollars & Sense

Bermuda Guarantee

If you travel to the island of Bermuda in the off-season (December to March), some hotels offer a guarantee that the temperature will be above 22°C. If the temperature fails to reach that figure, you receive discounts on your hotel rate and the price of other activities on the island.

TECHNOLOGY and Tourism

The Kawartha Tourist region offers an abundance of activities related to the natural environment. To promote the area as a destination choice, Kawartha Lakes Tourism now uses the Internet to attract tourists. Previously, the annual number of inquiries ranged from 9000 to 17 000. Once the organization went online, inquiries jumped to 22 000. In 1999, their Web site was fully operational, and it had close to 47 000 hits! More significantly, inquiries now came from locations worldwide. To find out more about this site, visit the Student Page for *Canada Travels* at <www.irwinpublishing.com>.

Winter

Summer

Fall

Figure 3.7 Identify four activities that attract people to the Kawartha region in each season.

Spring

CHECK IN

1 Natural characteristics of a location and the season are two variables related to the natural environment that influence tourist destination choices. Select three different natural characteristics, and explain how each characteristic might attract tourists in both the summer and the winter.

2 What natural characteristic(s) of your own community might attract tourists?

3 With other members of your group or class, brainstorm a list of ways to enhance and preserve natural attractions of your community.

Protecting Nature

Tourism to natural spaces has several benefits. By visiting these areas, people learn more about the conservation and preservation of ecosystems and their biodiversity. Tourism to natural spaces also leads to the construction of new accommodations and to increased employment opportunities.

Unfortunately, tourism can have a negative impact on natural spaces. Tourists do not always treat the natural environment with respect, and some tourist activities can threaten ecosystems. Adventure tours that offer big game safaris may endanger certain species; campers may cause forest fires by failing to extinguish campfires properly; mountain bikers may damage the terrain and disturb flora and fauna; tourists engaged in snorkelling or scuba diving may break off souvenir pieces of coral and damage the reef. A natural space becomes an **endangered space** when human activity becomes destructive.

Increased numbers of tourists also put a strain on the facilities of the area, making it difficult to manage garbage and sewage disposal and for available staff to enforce rules to maintain protection of the ecosystem. As a result wildlife is sometimes disturbed and habitats destroyed, endangering the flora and fauna. Figure 3.8 shows how some tourist activities are endangering spaces.

Ecotourism

A segment of special interest travel that focusses on protecting nature is **ecotourism**. Ecotourism is environmentally responsible travel to natural areas that conserves the environment and sustains the well-being of local people. Conservation is the main focus. Essentially, ecotourism

- provides for conservation measures
- includes meaningful community participation
- is profitable and can sustain itself

Whereas adventure travel involves a challenge to the individual, ecotourism stresses the total environment. Examples of ecotourism include photographic safaris and bird and wildlife viewing.

Portrait of an Ecotourist Have you ever had an ant farm? Do you like to watch the birds at a feeder and try to identify them by name? Are you curious about where different living things find their food, water, and shelter? Are you interested in conservation? Do you care about protecting the natural environment? If you answered yes to these questions, you may be a candidate for ecotourism.

Interact

With a partner, brainstorm other examples of how tourist activities can threaten fragile environments.

Travel FACT

Recognizing the global importance of ecotourism, the United Nations designated the year 2002 as the International Year of Ecotourism.

Endangered Spaces	Reasons
Banff National Park — Alberta	Impact of tourist development threatens irreversible harm to the park and its wildlife.
Denali National Park and Preserve —Alaska	Snowmobiles and all-terrain vehicles (ATVs) disturb breeding territories of bear, moose, and wolves.
Everglades National Park/ Big Cypress Preserve — Florida	Disrupted water supplies, influx of non-native species, reduced habitat as a result of development, and invasion by off-road vehicles (ORVs).
Haleakala National Park — Maui, Hawaii	Proposed international airport will generate many new flights over the sensitive and threatened ecosystem.
Joshua Tree National Park — California	Los Angeles has plans to build a massive garbage dump and landfill site beside the park. This will degrade the desert ecosystem, spoil the view, and introduce high noise levels.
Petrified Forest National Park — Arizona	Twelve tons [10.9 t] of petrified forest disappear annually as visitors pocket samples.
Point Pelee National Park — Ontario	Under severe pressure from sheer numbers of visitors.
St. Lawrence Islands National Park — Ontario	Air, water, and noise pollution from recreational boats, as well as soil compaction and shoreline damage from visitors.
Stones River National Battlefield — Tennessee	A proposed expansion of a two-lane highway on property that was part of the Civil War battle site, but not yet part of the park system.
Yellowstone National Park — Wyoming	Winter snowmobile use, over 1000 per day, plus volume of motorized traffic in the summer season.

Source: Adapted from *National Parks Magazine*, May/June 2000; "The Canadian Outdoor Page," http://outdoors.fazeshift.com/campingtips_0003.html (January 2001).

Figure 3.8 Some endangered spaces in North America

Travel FACT

Film used by travellers per week
none = 10%
1–2 rolls = 40%
3–4 rolls = 33%
5+ rolls = 17%

An ecotourist is someone who has a curiosity about nature and wants to learn more about living things by observing them. An ecotourist is also interested in protecting natural areas, minimizing negative impacts upon those areas and the local people, and raising awareness of conservation measures. An ecotourist may prefer to stay in a tree house than in a five-star hotel and use a camera to shoot an elephant rather than a gun.

In areas that have fragile ecosystems, it is especially important that natural resources be protected. The case study that follows shows how Costa Rica has benefited from tourism and, at the same time, protected its ecosystems.

1 Which of the benefits of tourism do you consider most important? Why?

2 Which of the negative impacts identified do you consider to be the most harmful? Why?

3 Identify a natural space in Canada that is an endangered space, and explain how it is being threatened.

Interact

Do you think that you have a moral responsibility to consider when you decide on a tourist destination? Explain your answer.

Figure 3.9 (Top) Copper Canyon, Mexico (Above) A Tarahumara man, one of the indigenous peoples of Copper Canyon, carrying his child on his back

Travel FACT

FONATUR, the Mexican Federal Tourist Agency, wants to capitalize on adventure travel and ecotourism in the remote and spectacular Copper Canyon region (Las Barrancas del Cobre) by raising visitor numbers to this site by six-fold, to over 400 000 per year!

CASE STUDY
Costa Rica: Saving the Perfect Natural Destination

Figure 3.10 Location of Costa Rica

Costa Rica is considered a perfect natural destination for tourists because

- it touches two oceans, both with beautiful beaches and great surf
- it has a tropical climate, creating lush, warm conditions
- it offers topography from coastal plain beaches to volcanic peaks
- it is home to 130 species of freshwater fish, 160 species of amphibians, 208 species of mammals, 220 species of reptiles, 850 species of birds, 1000 species of butterflies, 1200 varieties of orchids, 9000 species of plants, and 34 000 species of insects
- it boasts over 112 volcanoes

Costa Rica's diverse conditions result in 20 "life zones" or ecozones, ranging from mangrove swamps and dune areas on the coast through tropical rain forest to subalpine grasslands. Within this nation's small area of 50 900 km2, comparable in size to Denmark, you find an astonishing 5% of the world's biodiversity. The rugged terrain, active volcanoes, challenging mountain hikes, and beautiful surf and sand appeal to nearly all travellers.

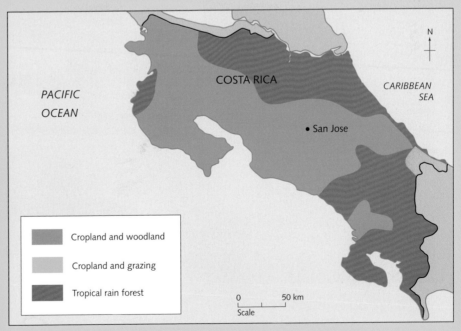

Figure 3.11 Land use in Costa Rica

Tourism Grows

Through the 1960s, tourist arrivals in Costa Rica grew quickly, matching world travel trends. Most of the tourists were from Canada and the United States. While welcoming the tourists and their tourist dollars, the Costa Rican government recognized the need to protect the natural resources that were the base of this new and growing industry. They took three major steps to preserve and enhance the natural characteristics that made their island unique. These major steps focussed on national parks and reserves, new infrastructure, and sustainable funding.

Figure 3.12 These images reflect the beauty of Costa Rica's natural environment. Identify the flora and fauna in these photographs.

Figure 3.13 Tourists to Costa Rica, 1984–1995

National Parks and Reserves As a first step, ten national parks and reserves (see Figure 3.14) were established. Today, over 25% of the land is under some form of protection, with over 12% designated as national parks. Over 500 000 tourists visit these parks every year.

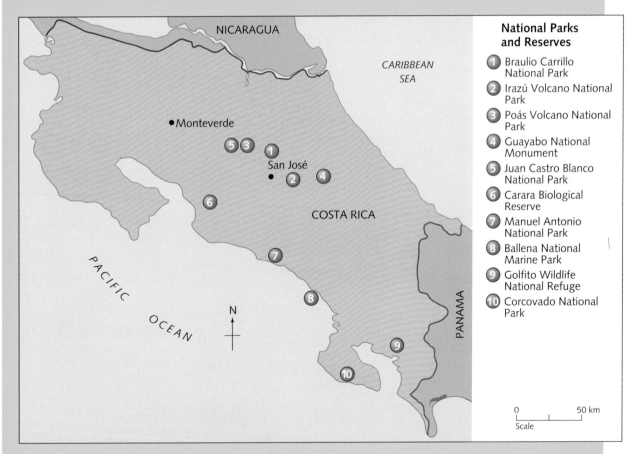

National Parks and Reserves

1. Braulio Carrillo National Park
2. Irazú Volcano National Park
3. Poás Volcano National Park
4. Guayabo National Monument
5. Juan Castro Blanco National Park
6. Carara Biological Reserve
7. Manuel Antonio National Park
8. Ballena National Marine Park
9. Golfito Wildlife National Refuge
10. Corcovado National Park

Figure 3.14 In addition to these national parks and reserves, a further 16% of Costa Rica is protected as biological reserves, Indian reserves, and wildlife refuges and corridors.

Wildlife corridors are important to the protection of Costa Rica's natural environments. These corridors are strands of protected areas that link the national parks and reserves, through which animals can migrate. The corridors are important because they allow animal populations to meet and breed. They also provide access to larger habitats that offer a wider range of food sources and shelter to the wildlife.

In the wildlife corridor that links the Braulio Carrillo National Park to the rain forest surrounding La Selva Biological Station, the land drops from nearly 3000 m to sea level. This creates a diverse habitat for more than 400 species of birds, jaguars, howler monkeys, vipers, sloths, and thousands of species of insects.

Groups like the World Land Trust have helped to create these corridors by buying parcels of land to protect the wildlife and sustain the strong base of ecotourism.

New Infrastructure The Costa Rican government also understood that many tourists would want close, first-hand experiences with the rain forest. But the government felt that too many people wandering on their own were a threat to this fragile ecosystem. Consequently, marked trails and paths were planned and laid out to provide safe, exciting, and educational rain forest walks and tours. As well, a new aerial tram was built to lift tourists up through the branches of the giant trees to the leafy canopy. Tourists can interact with this unique ecosystem without interfering with its delicate systems.

VIRTUAL TRAVEL

www.irwinpublishing.com

The World Land Trust (WLT) is a fundraising charity that seeks to conserve the world's tropical forests, their wildlife, and other important habitats that are threatened by destruction. To find out more about WLT and other areas of the world that the organization has assisted, visit WLT on the Student Page for *Canada Travels*.

Interact

What responsibilities do tourists have to the natural environment of a destination that they are visiting?

Canada Travels

World Wildlife Fund Canada, with support from the government of Costa Rica and the Canadian International Development Agency (CIDA), has sponsored the development of three community-run eco-lodges in Costa Rica. Local farming families do all the cooking, cleaning, and guiding in addition to working on their farms.

Sustainable Funding   Currently, tourists spend over US$650 million in Costa Rica each year. Portions of this revenue go to preserve, maintain, and expand natural attractions to sustain the tourist industry. As well, tourism based on natural environments is providing many jobs throughout the country. These jobs include tour operators, game wardens, conservationists, hotel management and service workers, and other service-related jobs. Tourist income and its economic spinoffs are major incentives for Costa Ricans to preserve and enhance their wonderful and varied ecosystems.

A Success Story

The government of Costa Rica has implemented long-term plans that preserve the natural environment in the best interests of all. By being proactive, Costa Rica has taken advantage of the tourist boom to protect and enhance its wonderful natural characteristics.

VIRTUAL TRAVEL

www.irwinpublishing.com

To discover more about national parks and tourism in Costa Rica, visit the Student Page for *Canada Travels*.

CHECK IN

1   What natural characteristics of Costa Rica would you find most attractive?

2   As a tourist visiting the country, list three things you can do to help Costa Rica preserve and enhance its ecosystems.

3   Describe the role the Costa Rican government has played in sustaining tourism.

4   Find out for yourself whether tourism has benefited the people of Costa Rica. In a chart, compare Costa Rica with the other countries in Central America. Use such statistics as life expectancy, infant mortality, literacy rate, and annual Gross Domestic Product (GDP) per capita. What do your findings indicate?

LOOKING AT ISSUES

Madagascar

Issue: Should governments be responsible for protecting fragile environments and their species when they promote tourism?

Naturalists call this land "the Garden of Eden." Like Costa Rica, Madagascar has unique flora and fauna, such as

- tropical forests that are the source of known, and possibly undiscovered, medicinal plants
- over 30 species of lemurs (relatives to the monkey) found only on this island
- over 800 types of butterflies
- more chameleons than anywhere else on Earth
- breeding grounds for rare sea turtles on coastal beaches
- offshore reefs that match the Great Barrier Reef of Australia

Madagascar's diversity is a product of its large, isolated landmass. It is the fourth largest island in the world and is located 400 km off the eastern coast of Africa in the Indian Ocean. The interior is a massive highland, which in the east descends abruptly to a narrow coastal plain. At one time, rain forest totally covered the east and the north. Most of it has now been cut for fuel. The south and west are progressively drier, and forests give way to savannah (grasslands) and semi-desert conditions.

Figure 3.15 Location of Madagascar

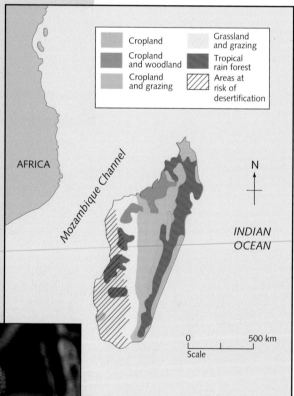

	Cropland		Grassland and grazing
	Cropland and woodland		Tropical rain forest
	Cropland and grazing		Areas at risk of desertification

AFRICA

Mozambique Channel

INDIAN OCEAN

N

0   500 km
Scale

Figure 3.17 Land use in Madagascar

Figure 3.16 The bamboo lemur is one of the most endangered species living in Madagascar's rain forest.

Figure 3.18 Lush rain forest covers much of Madagascar's Masoala Peninsula, but slash-and-burn methods of forest clearance have allowed grasslands and desert to begin to encroach on deforested areas.

Figure 3.19 A busy market at Nosy Be, Madagascar

Human Conditions

Madagascar is a very poor nation. Over the last 25 years, the country's economic growth has been slower than its population growth. As a result, quality of life has declined sharply. Madagascar's annual GDP per capita is less than US$800. The mainstay of the country's economy is agriculture, fishing, and forestry, which account for 34% of the GDP.

The country faces chronic malnutrition and underfunded health and education facilities. The average **life expectancy** at birth is 52.71 and 57.26 years for males and females, respectively. The **fertility rate** averages 5.84 children per woman, and the **infant mortality rate** is 85.26 deaths per 1000. The **literacy rate** – those over age 15 who can read and write – is 88% for males and 73% for females.

Environmental Issues

Unlike Costa Rica, the government of Madagascar has not focussed on environmental issues, such as preserving rain forests and saving the habitats of many of the species found on the island. A weak economy, a growing population, and an ineffective government have resulted in massive destruction to the ecosystems.

More than 85% of the forested land has been cut for fuel or farmland (rice paddies in the north and rangeland in the southwest). Mining for sapphires created a rush of prospectors invading the rain forest in the mid-1990s. Uncontrolled, these miners cleared the forests searching for the precious stones. The tropical rain forest ecosystem, with its unique characteristics, is disappearing at a rate of 2000 km² per year. The government has no plans for sustaining these ecosystems. Current issues include soil erosion from deforestation and overgrazing, desertification, surface water contamination with sewage, and endangered flora and fauna unique to the island.

Figure 3.20 This aerial view of a river bed in Madagascar shows how a badly deforested area has had its soil eroded.

	Number of Known Species	Number of Threatened Species
Mammals	105	46
Birds	202	28
Plants	9000	189
Reptiles	252	17
Amphibians	144	2

Figure 3.21 Threatened species in Madagascar

Travel FACT

Madagascar is home to the rosy periwinkle. This plant contains chemicals that are extremely effective in the treatment of childhood leukemia and Hodgkin's disease. Massive deforestation is rapidly depleting the supply of this unique plant.

www.irwinpublishing.com

To learn more, visit Madagascar on the Student Page for *Canada Travels*.

The rainy season in Madagascar extends from December to April. Cyclones occur during February and March, especially on the east coast.

Is Tourism the Answer?

Although Madagascar's tourism has increased since the early 1990s, compared with the number of tourists to places like Costa Rica, the number is quite small. Eventually, the number of tourists who are attracted to the natural features of Madagascar will dwindle as those features are destroyed. Should the government promote ecotourism and implement programs like those initiated by the Costa Rican government to protect the ecosystems? Or should the rain forests be cut to provide fuel for heat and agricultural land to feed the people? The future of this island may depend on which choice the government makes.

CHECK IN

1 The stakeholders involved in this issue are the people of Madagascar, government officials, environmentalists, and tourists. Explain the economic, cultural, social, environmental, and/or political aspects of this issue from the viewpoint of each of the stakeholders.

2 Using Figure 3.21 and the Travel Fact on page 74, describe some of the problems associated with losing fragile environments in Madagascar.

- apply geotechnologies to a study of regional geography
- produce and interpret different types of maps, graphic organizers, and diagrams
- communicate effectively in written, oral, and visual forms
- identify the natural resources on which tourism is based

Canada's Natural Landscape and Tourism

Purpose: To use ArcView to create a series of maps illustrating the distribution of various geographic phenomena in Canada (i.e., landforms, land covers, and water bodies).

Files: ecoreg.shp, rg_cover.dbf, rg_form.dbf, country.shp, lakes.shp, rivers.shp

Functions: View Properties, Legend Editor (Symbol Edit), Zoom, Convert to Shapefile, Geo-processing (Dissolve Boundaries), Geo-processing (Merge Polygons), Table Edit, Legend Editor (Unique Value), Auto-label, Hot Link, Layout.

1. Your first step is to create a blank View and name it "Canada's Natural Landscape."

2. Next, add the theme x:\canada\ecoreg.shp (from ArcCanada 2.0 Disk #1).

3. Now, add the tables x:\tables\ecoreg\ rg_cover.dbf and x:\tables\ecoreg\ rg_form.dbf (from ArcCanada 2.0 Disk #1) and join each to the ecoreg.shp theme table.

4. Next, return to the Canada's Natural Landscape View and create a map illustrating the distribution of dominant landforms across Canada. To do so, use the Legend Editor to apply a "Unique Value" legend type to the Ecoreg.shp theme using

"Dom_form" as the classification field. Then, change the labels as illustrated in the following table. Finally, change each of the symbols to a colour that is appropriate for the landform it represents. (Hint: Examine several thematic maps in an atlas to determine the conventional colours that cartographers use to represent different landforms and elevations.)

Code	Landform
B:	Plateau
H:	Hill Land
M:	Mountainous
O:	Organic Wetland
P:	Plain
S:	Scarp
V:	Valley

5. Now, make a copy of the Ecoreg.shp theme and paste it into the same View. Then, change the name of the original Ecoreg.shp theme to "Dominant Landform" in the Theme Properties window. Finally, turn the Dominant Landform.shp theme off.

6. Next, create a map illustrating the distribution of dominant land covers across Canada. To do so, use the Legend Editor to apply a "Unique Value" legend type to the Ecoreg.shp theme using "Dom_cov" as the classification field. Then, change the labels as illustrated in the following table. Finally, change each of the symbols to an appropriate colour for the land cover it represents. (Hint: Examine several thematic maps in an atlas to determine the conventional colours that cartographers use to represent different types of land cover.)

Code	Land Cover
1	Mixed Forest: canopy 26–75% coniferous/broadleaf trees.
2	Broadleaf Forest: canopy > 75% broadleaf trees.
3	N/A
4	Transitional Forest: forest land < 50% of area.
5	Coniferous Forest: canopy > 75% coniferous trees.
6	Tundra: Treeless arctic and alpine vegetation.
7	Sparsely Vegetated/Barren Land: plant cover generally < 25%.
8	Perennial Snow or Ice: Perennial snow fields and glaciers.
9	Cropland: Cultivated land.
10	Rangeland and Pasture: Native vegetation with < 10% tree cover.
11	Built-up area: Cities and towns.
36165	(Both 1 and 5 as shown above)
36256	(Both 4 and 6 as shown above)

7. Now, change the name of the Ecoreg.shp theme to "Dominant Land Cover" in the Theme Properties window. Then, turn the Dominant Land Cover.shp theme off.

8. Finally, create a map that shows only the Canadian border (not the provincial borders) and all of Canada's major rivers and lakes. To do so, add the theme c:\esri\esridata\ world\country.shp. Select Canada, convert it to a shapefile, then delete the Country.shp theme. Change the colour of the Canada.shp theme to white, using the Legend Editor. Then, add the themes c:\esri\esridata\canada\ lakes.shp and c:\esri\esridata\canada\ rivers.shp and change the colour of both to blue using the Legend Editor.

Congratulations – you have created a digital atlas of Canada's natural geography! By turning themes on and off you can examine the distribution of Canada's landforms, land covers, and water bodies.

Map Interpretation and Analysis

1. Carefully examine the maps you have created.
   a) Describe the distribution of the different types of landforms, land covers, and water bodies found in Canada.
   b) List at least five relationships that you can observe between the various features (e.g., "Mountainous areas tend to be dominated by coniferous forests").

2. Choose at least five of the different features illustrated on the maps you have created. Identify how tourists visiting Canada might enjoy each feature. Where possible, give at least three examples: one for youth, one for adults, and one for seniors. (Cite specific examples when you can.)

REVISIT THE chapter 3
Looking Back

Understanding the Concepts

1. For each of the four natural locations shown in Figure 3.5 on page 61, give two new examples in each category of activities that you and your friends might do on vacation.

2. Suppose you were being interviewed for an interesting job in the travel and tourism industry. The interviewer has asked you to reply to the question "What would you consider to be the most appealing type of tourist attractions, and why?" Outline three points that you would make to answer the interviewer's question.

3. In your own words, explain the difference between adventure travel and ecotourism. Which type of travel appeals to you, and why?

4. List ten natural resources that attract adventure tourists and ecotourists. Indicate the type of activities associated with each resource.

Practising Your Skills

5. Study the percentages shown in Figure 3.6: Canadian youth travel by seasons on page 62.
   a) Construct a comparative bar graph to show the travel by month. Use a different colour for each column (International, United States, and Canada).
   b) What are the two seasons of greatest travel? Suggest two reasons to account for each season.
   c) Is the pattern the same for all three destinations? Explain.

6. a) Examine the data in Figure 3.22: Top 15 states visited by Canadians, 1999. On an outline map of the United States, label the states and shade them according to the legend below. Complete your map by adding a legend and a title.
   Over 2 000 000 stays .... Dark red
   1 000 000 – 1 999 999 stays . . Orange
   500 000 – 999 999 stays . . . . . Dark yellow
   300 000 – 499 999 stays . . . . . Light yellow
   b) Describe the pattern shown on your map.
   c) Suggest some natural attractions that might explain the pattern shown on your map.

State Visited	Overnight Stays
New York	2 283 000
Florida	1 690 000
Washington	1 644 000
Michigan	1 232 000
California	1 044 000
Nevada	682 000
Maine	661 000
Pennsylvania	644 000
Vermont	557 000
Minnesota	487 000
Ohio	486 000
Massachusetts	462 000
Montana	444 000
Virginia	439 000
North Carolina	367 000

Figure 3.22 Top 15 states visited by Canadians, 1999

d) How do you think this pattern might change if stays for only the summer season were shown? Only the winter season?

e) Suggest two ways that people in the tourist industry might use a map such as this to make decisions about their activities and operations.

Applying Your Skills

7. Select a country or region in Europe, Asia, Australasia, or South America. Use Internet and classroom resources to complete the following parts of this question.

   a) Research the types of seasons your region has, and list the months for each season.

   b) Describe the natural attractions and the types of activities that would draw young single adults, families, and seniors to that region to enjoy the seasonal activities found there.

8. Work in a group of five, with each person taking two of the parks shown on the map in Figure 3.14 on page 69. Using an atlas, the Internet, and other sources, find out why your two parks were established in their locations. Share your findings with your group.

9. Your task is to design a presentation – either a pamphlet, PowerPoint presentation, or Web page – to promote the natural attractions of the region where you live. Your presentation should include a map, photographs, diagrams, and descriptive text.

10. You are an ecotour guide for a fragile environment of your choosing. Prepare a list of "Do's and Don'ts" for ecotourists visiting your fragile environment. Indicate why they should or should not do each activity on the list.

Thinking Like a Tourist

11. Some Hollywood films, such as *The Beach*, tend to glamorize travel. Describe three dangers that young travellers might encounter while seeking travel adventures.

12. Write a case study (one-half to one page in length) that features a type of adventure tourism in which you might participate. Include how the tourist activity has an impact on the local environment and the economy of the region.

JOB SKILLS

ECOTOURISM AND YOU

Governments and companies involved in the ecotourism industry hire staff for a wide variety of jobs. These positions include ecotourism planners, tour guides, interpreters, writers, staff for the visitor information centre, park rangers, curators, destination representatives, game wardens, and educational programmers, to name a few. Formal training in ecotourism is available at many post-secondary schools under geography, hospitality, applied sciences, or recreation departments.

Choose one of the above positions that appeals to you and find out what types of courses you would need to prepare you for this career. Present your findings in a brief report.

Figure 3.23 A local guide escorts travellers in Everest Park, Nepal.

CHAPTER four 4

Tourism and Preserving and Protecting Natural Spaces

1. In what ways do World Heritage Sites help to protect natural environments?
2. How can tourism help protect and also threaten natural areas?
3. In what ways did tourism help solve problems facing the Serengeti Plain in Africa?
4. What impact does whale watching have on the natural environment?

KEY WORDS & TERMS

biodiversity
direct tourist spending
indirect tourist spending
intrinsic value
non-governmental organizations
poaching
safari
savanna

Tourism and Nature

The splendour and grandeur of Earth's natural spaces range from national parks to biosphere reserves, to trails, to marine environments, and to heritage sites. These treasures, and the beautiful creatures that inhabit them, draw tourists. Ironically, this attraction begins a process that could soon endanger those places and threaten the flora and fauna that so attract us. Too many people visiting too often! This chapter looks at protecting some of the natural spaces that tourists visit.

Figure 4.1 Mananara Nord Biosphere Reserve, Madagascar, is a UNESCO World Heritage Site.

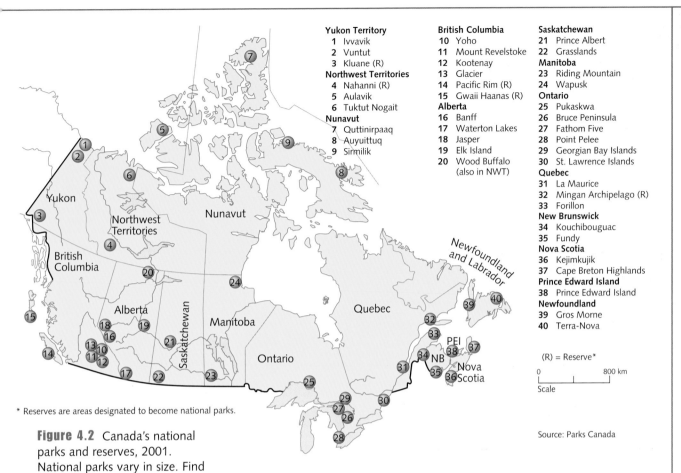

Yukon Territory
1 Ivvavik
2 Vuntut
3 Kluane (R)
Northwest Territories
4 Nahanni (R)
5 Aulavik
6 Tuktut Nogait
Nunavut
7 Quttinirpaaq
8 Auyuittuq
9 Sirmilik

British Columbia
10 Yoho
11 Mount Revelstoke
12 Kootenay
13 Glacier
14 Pacific Rim (R)
15 Gwaii Haanas (R)
Alberta
16 Banff
17 Waterton Lakes
18 Jasper
19 Elk Island
20 Wood Buffalo
    (also in NWT)

Saskatchewan
21 Prince Albert
22 Grasslands
Manitoba
23 Riding Mountain
24 Wapusk
Ontario
25 Pukaskwa
26 Bruce Peninsula
27 Fathom Five
28 Point Pelee
29 Georgian Bay Islands
30 St. Lawrence Islands
Quebec
31 La Maurice
32 Mingan Archipelago (R)
33 Forillon
New Brunswick
34 Kouchibouguac
35 Fundy
Nova Scotia
36 Kejimkujik
37 Cape Breton Highlands
Prince Edward Island
38 Prince Edward Island
Newfoundland
39 Gros Morne
40 Terra-Nova

(R) = Reserve*

0 |_____|_____| 800 km
Scale

Source: Parks Canada

* Reserves are areas designated to become national parks.

Figure 4.2 Canada's national parks and reserves, 2001. National parks vary in size. Find out how much area the national parks in your province cover. What percentage of your province's land mass has been set aside for national parks?

EXPECTATIONS

In this chapter, you will have the opportunity to

- identify the natural resources on which tourism is based
- evaluate the role of UNESCO in protecting significant natural and cultural sites around the world
- identify selected natural and cultural World Heritage Sites and the factors responsible for their selection
- identify criteria used to determine the selection of park locations for a selected country
- analyze specific examples of how tourist activities can threaten fragile environments
- compare viewpoints of individuals, businesses, non-governmental organizations, and other groups about sustainable use of the Earth and its resources
- analyze the distribution of Canada's tourism regions and national parks, and explain the observed patterns

National Parks

The hundreds of national parks we enjoy around the world were created, in part, to protect land. The governments that establish national parks want to preserve places for present and future generations where time seems to stand still – reserves where tourists and visitors can escape everyday life and renew their spirits. In these parks resource extraction is prohibited. However, in many cases there is no buffer zone around the parks. This means that activities such as logging and mining often take place just outside park boundaries. These activities disturb the wildlife in the parks and sometimes pollute water resources that run through the area.

Figure 4.3 Bow Falls, Banff National Park, Alberta (left); Point Pelee National Park, Ontario (right)

Park areas are chosen to promote scenic vistas that have tourism potential, to protect endangered wildlife, and to preserve unique or fragile habitats. Some sites are chosen to preserve their historic or cultural significance. According to the definition of national parks provided by IUCN (the International Union for the Conservation of Natural Resources), national parks are natural areas of land or sea designated to

- protect ecosystems for present and future generations
- exclude uses or activities that harm the ecosystem
- provide spiritual, scientific, educational, and recreational activities for visitors

Parks protect the natural environment by restricting people's activities when they visit (no motorized vehicles, for example), limiting routes through sensitive areas, placing daily and annual quotas on visitor numbers, and restricting camping or canoeing zones.

Travel FACT

The first national parks in North America were Yellowstone, Wyoming, in 1873 and Banff, Alberta, in 1883 in the United States and Canada, respectively. Today, Banff National Park is endangered by constant and heavy pressure from tourist development as resorts within the park increase in popularity for both summer and winter recreation.

Figure 4.4 As people recognize that intense recreation and tourism can harm the environment, support mounts for protective action.

VIRTUAL TRAVEL

www.irwinpublishing.com

To find out more about world parks, visit the Student Page for *Canada Travels*.

Figure 4.5 Elk Island National Park in Alberta is the only national park in Canada surrounded by a fence. The park, located just outside Edmonton, has intense suburban development pressure on its boundaries.

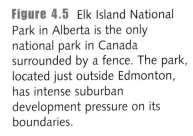

Travel FACT

The United Nations recommends that each nation protect at least 12% of total land area in wilderness preserves.

Biosphere Reserves

Biosphere reserves are parcels of land, marine, or coastal ecosystems identified by the United Nations Environmental, Scientific, and Cultural Organization (UNESCO) as areas for conservation. The goal is to preserve the **biodiversity** (variety of life) in these areas, while allowing local communities to benefit from the resources. For example, the Golden Gate Biosphere Reserve, which extends through the central California coastal region, is unique. It protects about 810 000 ha of marine, coastal, and land resources, including Angel Island and Alcatraz within San Francisco Bay. In addition to protecting wilderness, species, cultures, and traditions, biosphere reserves are used for scientific research, education, and tourism and recreation. By November 2000, UNESCO had designated 391 reserves in 94 countries.

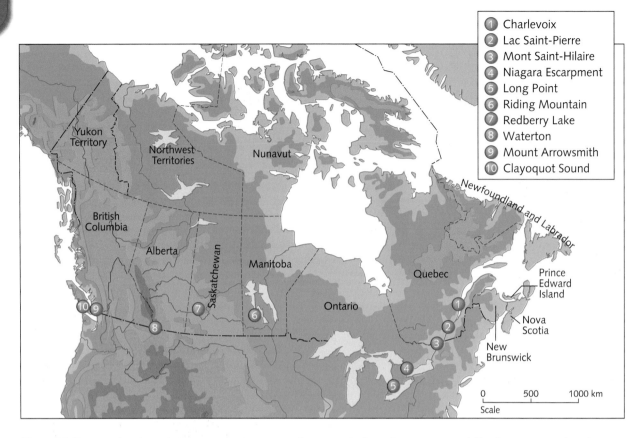

Figure 4.6 Canada's biosphere reserves, 2001. In what way do biosphere reserves differ from national parks?

1. Charlevoix
2. Lac Saint-Pierre
3. Mont Saint-Hilaire
4. Niagara Escarpment
5. Long Point
6. Riding Mountain
7. Redberry Lake
8. Waterton
9. Mount Arrowsmith
10. Clayoquot Sound

Trails

Trails are pathways created over time by frequent use. They help protect endangered spaces by providing passage for visitors through attractive terrain. Walkways, bridges, and signs keep travellers on routes that have minimal impact on the surrounding wilderness. Trails can take many forms.

Hiking Trails At 16 419 km, the Trans Canada Trail is considered the longest hiking trail in the world. It stretches from St. John's, Newfoundland, to Victoria, British Columbia, and travels north to Tuktoyaktuk on the Beaufort Sea in the Northwest Territories, then east to Chesterfield Inlet in Nunavut. Besides hiking, the trail accommodates cycling, riding, in-line skating, cross-country skiing, snowmobiling, and canoeing.

The American Discovery Trail in the United States encompasses 200 trails with 10 000 points of interest. Many European countries, including the United Kingdom and Switzerland, also have many kilometres of hiking trails.

Interact

What are some ways that we might determine which activities are destructive of the natural environment and which should be allowed in a protected area?

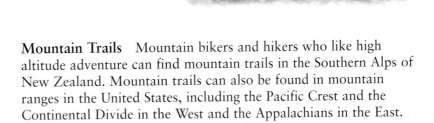

Figure 4.7 Canadian students hiking on the Appalachian Trail in Pennsylvania, USA; climbing in the Monashee Mountains, British Columbia

Mountain Trails Mountain bikers and hikers who like high altitude adventure can find mountain trails in the Southern Alps of New Zealand. Mountain trails can also be found in mountain ranges in the United States, including the Pacific Crest and the Continental Divide in the West and the Appalachians in the East.

Other Trails Water trails, such as the Intracoastal Waterway along the Eastern Seaboard of the United States, are marked trails for boaters. Route 66, a major highway running between Chicago, Illinois, and Los Angeles, California, was the focus of a popular song and a 1960s hit television series. Today, it is a famous historic trail for tourists who want a nostalgic trip across the country. Even air currents provide a trail of sorts, as balloonists and hang gliders follow predominant winds to enjoy their sports.

Marine Environments

While the majority of efforts to protect ecosystems have involved terrestrial environments, aquatic environments have also benefited from actions to protect the natural world from human activities.

Coral Reefs Coral reefs thrive in the clear, shallow waters of tropical seas. These reefs are living colonies of polyps (small water animals) that live inside limestone cups. When a polyp dies, another polyp takes up residence in its limestone cup. The material builds up, with living polyps growing on the skeletons of past generations.

Coral reefs occupy less than 1% of the marine environment, yet they provide a home to more than 25% of all fish species. This spectacular, colourful marine life attracts a huge and lucrative tourist industry – divers, snorkellers, and glass-bottom boat tours. Tour boats or pleasure cruisers will damage reefs if their hulls come in contact with the living coral. Because of their popularity with today's adventure travellers, coral reefs are endangered water spaces.

Places like Australia, Thailand, Florida, and Madagascar have taken steps to preserve and protect these endangered spaces for future generations. Activities that destroy or damage coral reefs, such as fishing, polluting, and collecting and removing coral and shells, are illegal within the marine parks in these areas.

Freshwater Lakes Fresh, clean water is a valuable resource for many reasons. We need it for consumption, agricultural and industrial uses, and recreation. Canada is blessed with thousands of lakes and river systems that contribute to the quality of life. These bodies of water are major attractions for recreational use. Many people buy shoreline properties or plan their annual vacation around a holiday near or on the water.

Figure 4.8 Touching coral kills the polyps. Even though coral is very sharp, many snorkellers damage reefs by breaking off pieces for souvenirs.

Interact

Tourists like souvenirs to remind them of their experiences. What are appropriate souvenirs? Brainstorm souvenirs that you do not think are appropriate. Give reasons for your choices.

Figure 4.9 Describe the types of damage that tourist activities can cause to freshwater areas like this one.

Figure 4.10 A kayaker passes a cave along the Apostle Islands National Lakeshore, Wisconsin, USA, in Lake Superior. Lake Superior, the biggest body of fresh water in the world, is bounded by Ontario to the north and east, Michigan and Wisconsin to the south, and Minnesota to the northwest.

www.irwinpublishing.com

You can join the World Heritage Club, find out about a Canadian WHS, or take a virtual tour of a World Heritage Site by visiting the UNESCO link on the Student Page for *Canada Travels*.

The Kawartha Lakes, which you read about in Chapter 3, form a freshwater geographic region in Ontario. These beautiful blue lakes were created when giant glaciers from the ice age scraped and gouged their way off the Canadian Shield onto the softer limestone plains to the south. As the glaciers melted, these depressions filled with water and remain today as prime recreational spaces. The Trent Canal system allows boaters to travel through the Kawartha Lakes to the Great Lakes.

The Great Lakes themselves are a unique tourist attraction. The shared border with the United States allows tourists to boat between the two nations. Pleasure craft and tour boats use this system of freshwater for travel and tourist sites. Cities like Montreal and Toronto in Canada and Cleveland and Chicago in the United States attract visitors to their waterfronts designed for recreational use.

World Heritage Sites

World Heritage Sites (WHS) are special places recognized by the United Nations. As of December 2000, there were 690 designated sites on the World Heritage list. The location of Canada's 13 World Heritage sites is shown on the map in Figure 4.13.

It is not easy to qualify for WHS designation. In fact, in many recommended areas, conflicting needs (such as those of loggers and environmentalists) and desires (including camping and hunting) present major obstacles to a site ever reaching World Heritage designation.

World Heritage Sites are significant natural and cultural sites protected for all citizens of the world. The idea of setting aside specific areas in different parts of the world to preserve them for all time was developed by UNESCO in 1977. To be designated as a World Heritage Site, a location must have one or more of these features:

- an outstanding example of the Earth's evolution
- a spectacular feature or formation
- an illustration of biological evolution
- rare fauna and flora
- a demonstration of human/environmental interaction

ENVIRONMENTAL		CULTURAL	
Type of Feature	WHS Site	Type of Feature	WHS Site
Nature	Victoria Falls, Zimbabwe/Zambia Galapagos Islands, Ecuador	Monuments/ Ruins	Great Wall of China Pyramid fields of Egypt
Geology	Burgess Shale Marine Fossils, Yoho National Park, British Columbia Puerto-Princesa Subterranean River National Park, Philippines	Architectural Value	Old walled city of Jerusalem Medina of Marrakesh, Morocco Lunenburg, Nova Scotia
Waterway	Canal du Midi, France Danube Delta, Romania Lake Baikal, Russia	Religious Importance	Nikko Temples, Japan Westminster Abbey, England Vatican City, Italy Gardens of Lubina, Nepal

Figure 4.11 Examples of features used to designate World Heritage Sites.

Figure 4.12 Mount Everest (above) and the Grand Canyon (right) were two of the first sites designated as World Heritage Sites.

① Kluane/Wrangell – St. Elias/Glacier Bay/
   Tatshenshini – Alsek (Yukon/B.C., Canada
   and Alaska, USA)
② Gwaii Haanas National Park Reserve
③ Nahanni National Park
④ L'Anse aux Meadows Archeological Site
⑤ Head-Smashed-In Buffalo Jump Provincial
   Historic Site
⑥ Dinosaur Provincial Park
⑦ Wood Buffalo National Park (Alberta and NWT)

⑧ Canadian Rocky Mountain Parks (Alberta
   and B.C.)
⑨ Historic district of Quebec
⑩ Gros Morne National Park
⑪ Old Town, Lunenburg
⑫ Waterton – Glacier International Peace Park
   (Alberta, Canada, and Montana, USA)
⑬ Miguasha Park (Quebec)

Figure 4.13 Canada's World
Heritage Sites. Conduct research
to make a chart similar to the
one in Figure 4.11. In your chart,
list the features that these sites
had in order to qualify for
designation as a WHS.

CHECK IN

1 How might having resource extraction, such as logging, just
   outside a national park affect the natural environment inside the
   park?

2 Why is it important to protect coral reefs?

3 Explain the difference between a biosphere reserve and a World
   Heritage Site.

Protecting Nature

Around the world, natural lands are under pressure by many human activities – forestry, farming, hunting, and residential developments, to name a few. These activities may generate income and create livelihoods for local people.

Many environmentalists believe that natural spaces are important for their **intrinsic value**, in other words, for their own sake. We should appreciate these spaces as important ecosystems, not for the dollars they can generate. People who argue that natural areas should be preserved usually encounter many voices arguing that economic development is more important than natural preservation. These voices may be muted only when nature can generate as much income as other activities. Tourism may have the potential to provide this income.

Tourism Income

Tourists spend money. In part, they spend on necessary items, like food and lodging. Other spending includes things that tourists desire, such as souvenirs, beverages, and entertainment. Combined, this **direct tourist spending** supports businesses and services in tourist destinations. The biggest economic influence is in local employment. For many regions, employment related to tourism has become the dominant sector of the economy. In fact, in some areas it has provided such lucrative employment on a fairly steady basis that some people have abandoned illegal activities, like poaching, for employment in the tourism industry.

www.irwinpublishing.com

The World Wildlife Fund has been involved in protecting the forests and other parts of the natural environment. Visit its Web site on the Student Page for *Canada Travels*. List the major campaigns this organization is waging currently.

Figure 4.14 A day of skiing generates tourist income for the resort.

Tourist dollars end up as **indirect tourist spending** as well. Suppliers and support services benefit from tourists' activities. For example, when restaurants buy food that is produced locally to feed tourists, the food producers earn income. Indirect tourist spending benefits the whole region. Some tourist money flows to local governments in taxes, fees, and licences. These funds support the development of other services such as roads, hospitals, electric power, and other infrastructure components that help the whole population.

Donations to Protect Natural Environments

An appreciation of nature also generates income through donations. Concerned people give money to **non-governmental organizations** (NGOs) like the World Wildlife Fund that fight to preserve fragile environments in a number of locations around the world. Through an international effort to protect tropical rain forests, Canadian donations, for example, have spared thousands of hectares of rain forest in Costa Rica from development. In part, people make these donations to ensure that natural environments will exist for their enjoyment as tourists.

Tourism and Economic Activities

Over time, tourism can dramatically alter the nature of local economic activities. In Canada, for example, as Atlantic coastal fisheries declined, the local people turned their attention to attracting tourists. They promoted the quaintness of picturesque fishing villages in rural settings, offering boat tours, sport fishing, and whale watching. Homes were converted into bed and breakfast establishments, craft, souvenir and antique shops, and restaurants. Income from tourist activities, at least in part, replaced earnings from the fisheries. The Atlantic Canada economy, which was previously based on exploiting the natural environment, is now more focussed on using the natural environment for tourism. Similar economic reorganization has occurred in other parts of the world.

Figure 4.16 Although tourist dollars are helpful to Peggy's Cove, Nova Scotia, tourism is a seasonal activity that must be supplemented with other economic activity in the off season.

Tourism and Protecting the Environment

Tourism is a two-edged sword. On the one hand, it can bring destruction that threatens natural spaces. On the other hand, it can be the instrument for protecting these spaces.

Growth in tourism connected to natural environments can stimulate an interest in keeping the environment as natural as possible. Operators know that any deterioration in the natural setting will discourage tourism. This desire for natural settings has often led to protective measures that have influenced local economic activities. Activities like logging and mining may be prohibited. Even some types of recreational activities, such as snowmobiling or all-terrain vehicles, may be banned to protect ecosystems.

To ensure that tourism continues, tourist industries pressure governments to implement policies to preserve and protect the resources that tourists come to enjoy. For instance, the governments of Zambia and Zimbabwe have established game reserves that prohibit farmers from expanding their cultivation into the reserves, providing a safe haven for the animals. Some funding for these reserves came from tourist activities in the area.

Tourists and their dollars have a great impact on generating public and government support for setting aside areas for protection. The hundreds of national and provincial parks we enjoy were created, in part, to protect land.

Figure 4.17 Trash at the foot of Garhwal (in the Himalayas). Visitors to the Himalayas threaten the beauty of the world's highest mountain chain.

CHECK IN

1 Explain in your own words how tourism can be a villain or a hero.

2 Why do you think people make contributions to NGOs that work to protect the environment?

3 a) Brainstorm a list of tourist activities that can damage a natural environment. Using a scale of one to five (one being the most harmful and five being the least harmful), rank these activities according to their harmful effects on the environment.

   b) Suggest one action that a government might take to reduce the harmful effects from those activities that you identified.

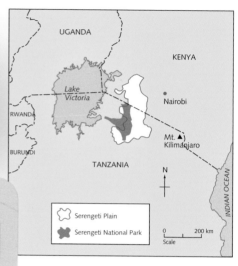

LOOKING AT ISSUES

The Serengeti Plain, Africa

Issue: Should countries with developing economies be allowed to sell ivory taken from elephants that die of natural causes?

If it were not for tourism, every elephant, leopard, and rhino on the Serengeti Plain would now be dead. Illegal hunting threatened many animal species, especially big game. Tourist dollars and tourist pressure are working to overcome the killing on the Serengeti.

The Natural Environment

The Serengeti is in the eastern part of Africa, largely in Tanzania, southeast of Lake Victoria. The area is about 130 000 km², roughly equal to the size of New Brunswick and Nova Scotia combined. The plain is made up mainly of flat, open grassland with some small hills. The western part of the region has areas of woodland and bushy **savanna** with clumps of grass 2 m tall in the rainy season. In the dry periods, the grass withers and dies. Both animals and plants have had to adapt to the marked wet and dry seasons. Most grazing animals, including gnus,

Figure 4.18 Location of the Serengeti Plain, Africa

Travel FACT

There are over 350 recorded bird species on the Serengeti Plain, including 34 species of raptors.

Figure 4.19 The tall grasses, during the wet season in the Serengeti, provide excellent camouflage for many animals. Can you name five animals that may be hidden in the tall grass other than zebras and gazelles?

Figure 4.20 This is the Serengeti during the dry season.

Figure 4.21 In a modern-day "big game hunt," tourists carry cameras, not guns. Why have people's attitudes toward animals changed over the last century?

Travel FACT

In 1991, the last packs of wild dogs on the Serengeti died, apparently victims of a rabies epidemic.

gazelles, elephants, and zebras, have developed patterns of migration. During the rainy season, from November to May, millions of animals graze on the southeastern plains. However, this area has few rivers and becomes bone dry once the rainy season ends. Then, the animals migrate to the western savanna and as far north as the grasslands on the Kenya–Tanzania border.

Hunting and Protection of Wildlife

For many centuries, the animals of the Serengeti were hunted by tribes of central and eastern Africa, including the Masai in present-day Kenya and the Zulus of southern Africa. Never were the animals in danger of extinction during this period. The people hunted to meet their needs for food, clothing, and medicine. They used all that they killed. The arrival of big-game hunters in the 1800s changed that. These European and North American hunters killed for sport, taking only the pelt, head, or tusks as trophies. They showed no regard for the animals or the ecology of the area. Local people contributed to the hunt by acting as guides and labourers. Animal populations began to drop.

Protecting the Serengeti

Action was needed to protect the wildlife of the Serengeti Plain. The first step was the declaration in 1929 of a game reserve over a part of the Serengeti. Controls on hunting in the reserve ended big-game hunting as a form of tourism in the region. The most important action was the establishment of the Serengeti National Park in 1951, which ended other forms of human activity such as agriculture in the park area. The park was to be used exclusively for wildlife conservation and tourism. Even tourism was regulated. **Safaris,** expeditions that took tourists into the Serengeti, had rules to follow, to minimize their impact on the ecosystem. Development around the park was also controlled. International recognition came in 1981 when the Serengeti National Park was included as a UNESCO biosphere reserve.

Hunts Out, Cameras In

As the game reserve and the national park were established, the camera replaced the elephant gun. Now the thrill was to photograph a rhino in the wild, not to kill it. Tourists today can either stay in various resorts for shorter treks into the wild country or go on longer safaris deep into the plain. The modern safari is a different experience from the days of big-game hunting. Gone are treks on foot or on the back of an elephant. Travellers today go into the Serengeti in rugged four-wheel drive vehicles.

Travel FACT

Parts of the Serengeti were never settled to any great extent because of disease-carrying parasites, including the tsetse fly. The tsetse fly transmits the African sleeping sickness to both humans and their cattle.

Interact

Was it fair to local farmers to remove them from the national park?

Dollars & Sense

Would you like to travel to Africa when you graduate? Some NGOs, like World Vision, offer opportunities for service and experience in African countries as well as other nations.

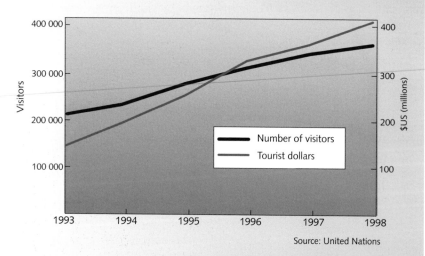

Source: United Nations

Figure 4.22 Tourist visitors and receipts in Tanzania, 1993–1998. People visiting are very important to the economy. Not only has the number of visitors climbed steadily, but the proportion of dollars entering the economy from tourism has increased significantly.

To go on a Serengeti safari, people should be in good health and able to tolerate heat. They should also be immunized against diseases prevalent in tropical areas. These diseases include yellow fever, malaria, cholera, dysentery, and hepatitis.

Estimated Worldwide Trade in One Year
Value: US$7 billion

Traded items:	
50 000	live primates
70 000	elephant tusks
4 000 000	live birds
10 000 000	reptile skins
15 000	pelts
350 000	tropical fish
1 000 000	orchids

What's Available for a Price (US$)	
Rhino horn dagger	— $12 000 each
White Rhino horn	— $6350/kg
A pair of Spix's Macaws	— $80 000
A Vicuna coat	— $100 000+
A Clouded Leopard coat	— $100 000
Rare cacti	— $15 000

Source: Atlas of the Environment

Figure 4.23 Poaching involves big dollars and includes rare plants.

Ongoing Park Problems

While generally considered a success, the Serengeti Park still has problems to solve and issues to face. Locals raising cattle have tried to move into the protected areas to find food and water for their animals. There have also been disputes about the licences needed to operate tours and other tourist-related activities.

Many people think that there are too many visitors to the park to protect the habitat. However, if the number of visitors is restricted, funding for protection of the natural environment will be limited. The future of the Serengeti, and areas like it, depends on political goodwill, education, and tough protection, all of which requires money.

Poachers' Paradise

In spite of all the controls on activities in and near the park, illegal hunting, or **poaching**, continues to be the major park problem. Capturing exotic animals or killing particular species for their parts is very lucrative. A rhino horn when powdered may be worth $28 000–$33 000/kg for medicines. Elephant tusks are also very valuable. Armed park rangers try to catch poachers day or night, sometimes engaging in deadly gunfire.

Figure 4.24 A park warden displays an elephant tusk confiscated from poachers; caretakers lead a herd of baby elephants orphaned after the Kenyan government temporarily lifted a ban on trade in ivory.

Canada Travels

Some Canadians pay high dollars to obtain exotic animals like tropical snakes, birds, cats, and other creatures. They also buy products made from animal parts. Although trade in most of these items has been banned by world agreement, it still continues.

White Gold – Ivory

In the Serengeti, and in many other parts of southern Africa, rhinoceros' horns and the ivory tusks of elephants lure poachers into the park. Most African nations struggle with weak economies and high unemployment rates. With their opportunities limited, some Africans view poaching as a way to survive.

Elephant poaching exploded in the 1970s. This expansion was due largely to the availability of automatic weapons that could kill with greater efficiency. Poaching was encouraged by the high prices that could be earned by selling raw ivory. In the 1960s, ivory sold for $7 to $25/kg. The price had reached $125/kg by 1975 and $480/kg by 1989. Most of the raw ivory was sent to Hong Kong, where it was processed and shipped to consumers around the world.

The worldwide consumption of raw ivory in 1989 amounted to 770 t. This quantity required the killing of 75 000 elephants per year. An estimated 10 000 of these animals were killed in the Serengeti. The extent of the destructiveness of this trade can be seen in nearby Burundi: between 1976 and 1986 the tusks of 200 000 elephants were exported; in 1988, there was only one live elephant left in the country. Clearly, African elephants were in danger of being exterminated. Action was needed.

Fighting Back

The Convention on International Trade in Endangered Species of Wild Fauna and Flora (CITES) was signed in 1989 by 152 countries. This treaty banned the sale of ivory on a global scale. Tourists who bought banned items were subject to fines, and the items were confiscated. Poachers no longer had a market for their illegal trade. The number of elephants killed in Tanzania dropped to about 100 per year. The ivory trade virtually dried

Figure 4.25 Would you buy one of these ivory products, knowing that it cost an elephant its life? Why or why not?

www.irwinpublishing.com

For more information on the Serengeti, visit the Student Page for *Canada Travels*.

up. Similar bans have been placed on other species in attempts to halt trade in those animal parts as well.

The ban on the sale of elephant ivory has its critics. Governments in countries like Tanzania must collect and guard the ivory taken from elephants that die of natural causes. Many African countries now have large stockpiles of ivory. Some of these countries have weak economies. They would like to sell the ivory and use the revenue to build and equip schools and hospitals, or even to develop their tourist potential. Environmentalists, on the other hand, fear that any softening of tough rules will lead to renewed poaching.

CHECK IN

1 What factors might encourage people to hunt illegally?

2 How would you discourage Canadian tourists from purchasing exotic animals and animal parts?

3 Work in a group of five, with each member preparing an argument for one of the following people about a worldwide ban on the sale of ivory.
   • the government of a country with a weak economy
   • a tourist
   • a local resident of a region where elephants live
   • an environmentalist
   • a poacher
   Share your arguments in a role-play with the class.

LOOKING AT ISSUES

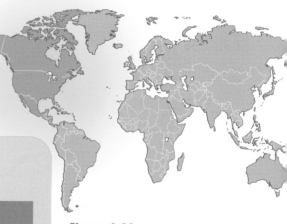

Figure 4.26 Location of North America

Whale Watching off the Coasts of North America

Issue: Should whale watching be regulated?

Off the coasts of North America, whale watching is immensely popular. People take boat tours to spot whales or watch from cliffs along areas where whales are nudged inshore by boaters. This activity is in sharp contrast to how whales have been treated in the past, when they were hunted for their blubber, flesh, and bones.

Figure 4.27 Whale watching has become an important economic activity along Canada's coastline as well as throughout the world. How many people in your class have gone whale watching?

Travel FACT

The popular activity of whale watching has had significant effects. The *Globe and Mail* reported in June 2000 that new regulations on whale watching were under way!

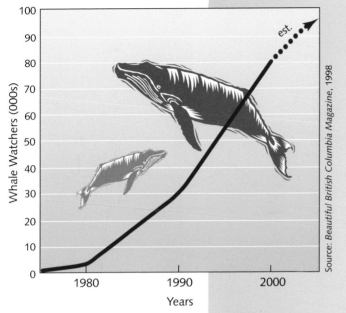

Whale Watchers (000s)

100
90
80
70
60
50
40
30
20
10
0

est.

1980   1990   2000

Years

Source: *Beautiful British Columbia Magazine, 1998*

Figure 4.28 British Columbia reported 80 000 visitors for whale watching in 1997. Ten years earlier there had been only 1400.

A New Wave

Thanks to the Canadian Fisheries Act of 1970 and the United States' Marine Mammals Protection Act of 1972, along with world whaling agreements, the killing of whales has sharply declined. Whale numbers have made quite a comeback.

On a Sea Safari

Finding and watching whales has taken on a kind of "sea safari" atmosphere. West Coast resorts have inflatable craft to speed tourists to the whales. Hundreds of other vessels, like noisy speedboats, sailboats, yachts, and kayaks, transport tourists looking for whales along the coast to Alaska. On the Atlantic side, most whale watching is done from converted fishing boats.

Boaters, keen to be as close as possible, often drive their vessels through the centre of whale pods, breaking up the groups and separating mothers from their young. Short-term studies of beluga whales in the St. Lawrence River indicate that such disruptions, along with the noise of the boats, interfere with whale communication – truly a case of whale harassment!

Figure 4.29 What skills and training should a whale watching tour operator have?

Figure 4.30 How do you think the proximity of these tourists might affect this whale?

VIRTUAL TRAVEL

www.irwinpublishing.com

For more information about the whaling industry, visit the whaling museum on the Student Page for *Canada Travels*.

Figure 4.31 Did you know that the sound made by the blue whale is the loudest sound on Earth, even louder than the engines of a 747 jet?

Action Now!

Whale watching has become so popular that the number of whale guides and tours has more than tripled. Environmentalists have suggested that the industry needs more regulation to protect the wildlife. Proposed regulations recommend that tour operators and guides attend compulsory classes to better understand whale behaviour, that they learn how to operate their vessels at reasonable speeds and in a respectful, caring manner, and that they be licensed.

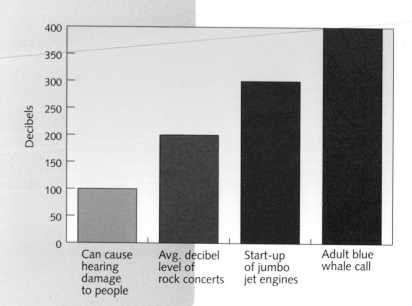

Bringing more and more tourists onto the oceans without care and regulation will upset the animal and sea life. This could have significant effects on the nesting and breeding of creatures like sea birds and whales.

Figure 4.32 Spectators line the bow of the boat *Flyer*, to view an Orca whale during a whale watching excursion to the San Juan Islands during the Orcas' annual migration into the region. How do you think the whale watching business might affect the whales' migration?

CHECK IN

1 How might whale watching as a tourist activity influence public opinion about preservation and conservation concerns in our oceans?

2 How might tour operators and guides view proposed regulations? Explain.

3 As a tourist, do you think the whale watching industry should be regulated? Why or why not?

4 Do you think governments have a responsibility to protect the environment, even if doing so means the tourist industry and the economy may suffer? Explain your view.

LOOKING AT ISSUES

The Queen Charlotte Islands

Issue: To what extent should the views of economic developers be considered in making decisions about the designation of World Heritage Sites and national parks?

An abandoned Haida village on the Queen Charlotte Islands of Canada's West Coast became a World Heritage Site in 1981, thanks to the actions of some people committed to preserving this cultural site. The special attention this designation caused in part led to the establishment of the Gwaii Haanas National Park Reserve in the Queen Charlotte Islands in 2000. Figure 4.34 shows why this site is so exceptional.

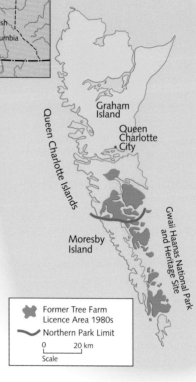

Figure 4.34 The official opening of Gwaii Haanas National Park and Haida Heritage Site capped a 15-year effort by individuals, community groups, NGOs, and some government officials to achieve designation.

Figure 4.33 Location of Queen Charlotte Islands, British Columbia

Figure 4.35 Growth of tourist visitors to the Queen Charlotte Islands. Visitors love what they see and want the area to stay in pristine condition.

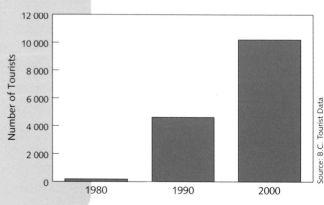

Source: B.C. Tourist Data

Criteria to Qualify as a WHS	Features Found at Gwaii Haanas
The area should be a habitat where populations of rare or endangered species of plants and animals still survive.	• Unexcelled coniferous forest (temperate rain forest) of old-growth status in size and grandeur • Taxa plants, native to the region, found nowhere else on Earth • Peale's Falcon, a subspecies of the peregrine; the only stable peregrine population in Canada, and one of only two in the world • One third of Pacific Canada's nesting seabirds
The region should be an outstanding example representing the major stages of the Earth's evolutionary history.	• Many examples of Earth's geological development • Rugged mountains and fiords
The site should be an outstanding example representing significant ongoing geological processes, biological evolution, and human interaction with the environment.	• Visible stages of mountain-building and weathering • Outstanding natural habitats, particularly salmon, that are dependent on the quality of local rivers for reproduction • Many Haida ancestral village sites and burial grounds
The area should contain unique, rare, or superlative natural phenomena, formations, or features or areas of exceptional natural beauty.	• Extraordinary fiords • Muskeg composed of stunted trees and varicoloured peat moss • Cathedral-like rain forest • Fog-shrouded mountains with snowy peaks • Green islands and blue sea

Figure 4.36 Establishing a World Heritage Site involves applying a set of criteria. These sites become attractions to some tourists.

Figure 4.37 The park scenery is "food for the spirit."

The Haida

Because of the attention the site received, many tourists came to see the rich heritage of the Haida – their totem poles, carvings, lodges, and villages. Visitors also learn that the history of the Haida dates from about 10 000 years ago. The Haida used western red cedar for their carvings and lodgings, and their diet consisted mainly of salmon and other seafood. Over 110 archaeological sites date from 7400 years ago, and there are likely many more to be found. The Haida have unsettled land claims to the islands and the seas around them.

Despite being concerned about too many tourists, most Haida and other Aboriginal peoples on the islands felt that a park or WHS would be better than allowing unsustainable economic development of the region's natural resources.

Viewpoints Opposed to the World Heritage Site

While environmentalists, Haida, and those concerned about heritage preservation have generally been pleased with this establishment of World Heritage Site and national park, not everyone is in agreement. Some groups fought against these developments.

Loggers   Bobby Thompson, a logger in British Columbia, believes that having jobs is more important than protecting the area from tourist development. According to Thompson, "one cubic metre of wood produces $300 for the British Columbia economy from its cutting to processing and related transport industries." Thompson also argues that forest covers only 40% of British Columbia and that much of that is immature or not properly restocked. So, the province needs to use its remaining good forests for logging, not preservation.

The Logging Industry   The logging industry was against the establishment of the WHS. They viewed the stands of spruce, hemlock, cedar, and other valuable timber species on the Queen Charlotte Islands as critical to their long-term forestry needs. The industry argued that they had been granted licences for the use of the forests and their rights had to be protected.

Figure 4.38 Using the figures that Bobby Thompson quotes, how much of British Columbia's land area is covered by forest? Hint: The total land area of British Columbia is 929 730 km².

Interact

To what extent should the views of local Aboriginal peoples be considered in making decisions about the use of natural resources?

> 66 Outstanding biological and cultural features alone should be enough to save Gwaii Haanas, but it is impossible to assign a money value to either, and in this society, where money talks, tourism becomes the logical rationale. 99
>
> — Tom Schneider, spokesman for the Island Protection Society

Victory for the Conservationists

Local tourist operators and Aboriginal peoples supported the WHS designation. They claimed that the new site would generate more tourist-oriented employment. Conservationist groups gradually gained support for their proposals from thousands who had viewed the area and other citizens. Their efforts helped to sway the government to support the WHS designation by the United Nations.

Figure 4.39 This village site, called Nunsting, is the earliest recorded Haida village in the Gwaii Haanas National Park Reserve. Today, the Haida live in the villages through the summer to protect the sites, act as guides, and use the sites for traditional activities.

Canada Travels

David Suzuki taped a *Nature of Things* episode for CBC television in the Queen Charlotte Islands to help the protection cause in 1981. The program had a great impact in supporting the WHS designation.

Support from Tourists

Without tourists from all over North America and beyond who provided money and letters of support for WHS designation, it is unlikely that Gwaii Haanas would now be a national park. Threats from development would still be mounting against this unique environment. It could even have been destroyed by now.

CHECK IN

1   How does the following quote by a conservationist relate to support for a WHS?
    "Before we cut and sell the last of it and pollute it beyond the last hope of recovering an environment worth living in, we must return to treating the Earth with some reverence."

2   Can you think of other stakeholders who would have argued for or against this region's designation? Identify them and their probable arguments.

3   Is protecting a unique place on Earth for all citizens, present and future, more important than local interests? Explain your answer.

- apply geotechnologies to a study of regional geography
- produce and interpret different types of maps, graphic organizers, and diagrams
- communicate effectively in written, oral, and visual forms
- demonstrate an understanding of how a variety of factors are used to define regions
- explain how natural and human criteria are used to establish regional boundaries
- identify the natural resources on which tourism is based

Protected Areas Around the World

Purpose: To use ArcView to create a series of maps illustrating the distribution of protected environments (i.e., terrestrial, forest, marine and coastal areas, and biospheres) throughout the world.

Files: cont_bnd.shp, wri_3m.dbf

Functions: Convert to Shapefile, Join Tables, Geo-processing (Merge Polygons), Legend Editor (Graduated Colour), Hot Link.

Continent	Shapefile	Data File
Africa	x:\af\cont_bnd.shp	x:\af\tables\wri_3m.dbf
Antarctica	x:\an\cont_bnd.shp	x:\an\tables\wri_3m.dbf
Australia	x:\as\cont_bnd.shp	x:\as\tables\wri_3m.dbf
Europe	x:\eu\cont_bnd.shp	x:\eu\tables\wri_3m.dbf
North America	x:\na\cont_bnd.shp	x:\na\tables\wri_3m.dbf
Oceania	x:\oc\cont_bnd.shp	x:\oc\tables\wri_3m.dbf
South America	x:\sa\cont_bnd.shp	x:\sa\tables\wri_3m.dbf

1. Your first step will be to create a blank View and name it "Protected Areas Around the World."

2. Next, you will need to add each of the seven continents to your View. Each time a continent is added, you must convert it to a shapefile, name it using the continent's name, then delete the original theme. Then, you will have to join a series of .dbf files (containing data on protected areas) to the theme tables of their respective continents. The following table provides the names of each of the seven continents and the directory paths required to locate the necessary files.

   Note: All required data can be found on ArcCanada 2.0 Disk #2.

3. Next, you will join all of the continent themes to create a single theme for the entire world. To do so, return to the View and turn on the Geo-processing extension. Then, use the Geo-processing Wizard to merge the seven continent themes and name the new theme "world." Finally, delete the seven continent themes.

4. Finally, copy and paste the World.shp theme until it appears six times in the legend. Then, using the Legend Editor, create six statistical maps as they are defined in the following table. Lastly, rename the World.shp theme in the Theme Properties window as also shown in the table. (Note: Each time you create a map, turn off the theme before proceeding to the next.)

Theme	Legend Type	Classification Field	Details	Rename Theme
World.shp	Graduated Colour	Protclof80	• Natural Breaks • Null Value: –99 • Show no data class (make semi-fill, light grey) • Green Monochromatic	Protected Closed Forest Area
World.shp	Graduated Colour	P_protline90	• Natural Breaks • Null Value: –99 • Show no data class (make semi-fill, light grey) • Brown Monochromatic	% National Land Protected
World.shp	Dot	Prmarine90	1 dot = 1 blue dots, size 4	Number of Marine/Coastal Protected
World.shp	Graduated Colour	Prmarn_a90	• Natural Breaks • Null Value: –99 • Show no data class (make semi-fill, light grey) • Blue Monochromatic	Area of Marine/Coastal Protected
World.shp	Dot	Bioresrv90	1 dot = 1 red dots, size 4	Number of Biosphere Reserves
World.shp	Graduated Colour	Biores_a90	• Natural Breaks • Null Value: –99 • Show no data class (make semi-fill, light grey) • Red Monochromatic	Area of Biosphere Reserves

Congratulations – you have created a digital atlas of the world's protected environments! By turning themes on and off you can examine the variations in the amount of protected forests, land, marine and coastal areas, and biospheres throughout the world.

Map Interpretation and Analysis

1. Carefully examine the maps you have created. Describe the global variations in each of the measures of protected environments covered in this activity. In each case, attempt to account for the noted differences.

2. Explain how protected spaces are enjoyed by tourists. Where possible, give specific examples of ecological reserves, bird/wildlife sanctuaries, conservation areas, national parks, etc., that comprise these protected spaces.

Extension:

Create ASCII DOS .txt files containing detailed descriptions of specific protected spaces. Then, hot link these text files to the appropriate countries on the world map by entering their directory paths in the respective theme tables.

Extension:

Scan or download photos of specific protected spaces. Then, hot link these to the appropriate countries on the world map by creating new Views and adding the .jpeg photos as image data. (Hint: Don't forget to turn on the JPEG Support extension and name the Views appropriately!)

REVISIT THE chapter 4
Looking Back

Understanding the Concepts

1. a) Describe the role of UNESCO in protecting significant natural and cultural sites around the world.
   b) In your opinion, is UNESCO doing enough to protect threatened environments? Explain your answer.

2. Describe how the expansion of world tourism is placing various pressures on the environment. Give two examples to support your answer.

3. In what ways can tourism help protect lands in their natural state?

4. Using the example of the Serengeti Plain, explain how tourism indirectly made poaching a more profitable activity.

Practising Your Skills

5. Compare the Serengeti National Park in Tanzania and Gwaii Haanas National Park Reserve in British Columbia. Some criteria that you might use are date of establishment, important features, stakeholders, and major problems. Organize your information in a comparison chart.

6. From the viewpoint of an environmentalist or a tour operator, express your feelings in a letter to the local newspaper about whether or not the whale watching industry should be regulated to protect the whales.

7. Using the maps in Figures 4.2, 4.6, and 4.13, analyze the distribution of Canada's tourism regions and national parks and explain the observed patterns.

Applying Your Skills

8. a) Name a natural space in your local region that is being protected.
   b) What type of natural space is it, and why is this space being protected?
   c) What types of tourist activities are restricted in this protected space?

9. a) Give an example in Canada where a marine environment is an endangered space.
   b) Why is this marine space threatened?
   c) What has government done to protect this area?

Figure 4.40 Delphi, in Greece, which was once considered by the ancients to be the centre of the world, is now a UNESCO World Heritage Site.

10. Research to find out more about the impact that safari-style tourism has on both the economic and environmental aspects of the Serengeti region.

11. Research one World Heritage Site outside Canada and determine the factors that were responsible for its selection. Prepare a poster to show your findings.

12. Research to find out how close Canada and the various provinces come to meeting the UN suggestion of protecting 12% of land area.

Thinking Like a Tourist

13. Suggest some practices with respect to animals in nature (like deer hunting or fishing for marlin) that are generally acceptable today but may be unacceptable 20 years from now. Explain your answer.

14. Research at least two species of animals or birds that are significant in world animal and product trade. On an outline map of the world, show the major source areas for each species, and if possible, the five leading nations that import them. What actions have been taken by the UN, governments, or NGOs to protect them?

15. a) Plan a vacation to enjoy a natural space. To determine how much money you will need, make an itemized list of the expenses you will have, i.e., your direct tourist spending at your destination.

    b) Explain how some of your tourist spending will end up as indirect tourist dollars.

JOB SKILLS

Brainstorm a list of five to seven characteristics that you would consider important in a Web site for the tourism industry. You might include characteristics like the following:
• up-to-date information
• links that are easy to understand and navigate
• useful Canadian links

Use your list of characteristics to evaluate three Web sites related to travel and tourism. You can choose your own sites, or select from those offered on the Student Page for *Canada Travels* at <www.irwinpublishing.com>.

Figure 4.41 An important job skill is locating, gathering, and managing information. With many new Web sites being created in the travel and tourism industry, this is an important skill to practise.

CHAPTER five 5

Urban Tourism

FOCUS ON THESE KEY QUESTIONS AND . . .

1. Why do so many people travel to cities?
2. What are the problems and issues related to tourism in a city?
3. What is the best way to decide which city to visit?
4. Why is there so much competition for tourists?
5. What is sustainable tourism, and why is it important?

KEY WORDS & TERMS

area of influence
city-centred region
ecological footprint
economic functions
green space
hinterland
infrastructure
subterranean system
sustainable tourism
system

Cityscapes

Cities! People are drawn to them as dwelling places and travel destinations. Over half the world's population lives in cities, and this percentage is increasing. Most of the world's travel takes place to or within cities. Cities have a wide range of services to attract different types of tourists. Consider accommodation, for example. From five-star hotels to inexpensive hostels, cities can satisfy people of all age groups and income levels, whether business travellers, culture seekers, sports fans, or backpackers.

Figure 5.1 (Left) The Colosseum, Rome, Italy (Right); the *souq* (market), Marrakech, Morocco. People visit cities to learn about history and heritage, to appreciate the arts, and to experience cultures different from their own.

Figure 5.2 The Seattle skyline at night. Unlike the peace and nature found in the surrounding countryside, cities attract people to bright lights and excitement.

What do you think of cities? Do you find them exciting places with culture, entertainment, and night life? Or do you find them uncomfortable places that are crowded, noisy, and polluted? Whatever your perspective, cities are certainly diverse and complex places.

This chapter focusses on cities that are significant global tourist attractions and their natural and human features. It also looks at some of the issues that arise from the impact of huge numbers of people in one place and the many changes that are occurring within and around cities.

66 *The city should become a magnet, drawing to it those who wish to enjoy life.* 99

– Daniel Burnham,
1909, Chicago

EXPECTATIONS

In this chapter you will have the opportunity to

- identify significant global tourist attractions
- evaluate the natural and human attributes that contribute to the success of selected globally significant tourist attractions
- explain how tourism-related development can have important impacts on human systems
- analyze the effects of human systems on travel and tourism
- demonstrate an understanding that the travel and tourism industry consists of many interconnected components
- select criteria and compare travel and tourism characteristics for two world-class city-centred regions
- research and report on the economic, environmental, and cultural impacts of travel and tourism associated with international sporting events
- analyze the effects of an increase in tourism on the natural and human systems of a selected region
- evaluate the impact of government policies on travel and tourism in a selected region
- explain the effect of natural systems on travel and tourism

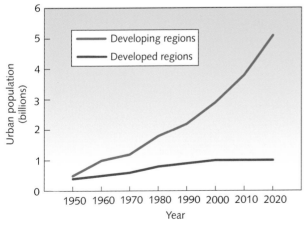

Figure 5.3 Urban growth, 1950–2020, in developed and developing regions

Cities and Their Sites

When geographers investigate why cities are located at particular places, they look at the site and situation of the city. *Site* refers to the physical features of the area. The world is filled with spectacular natural sites, and urban areas have evolved at many of them. Often cities began as small settlements on flat land for building or in sheltered ports or harbours.

The *situation* of a city is its location in relation to economic factors such as access to major transportation routes and availability of natural resources and other trade centres.

> **"**Cities are at one and the same time centres of civilization and centres of social and environmental chaos.**"**
>
> – William Norton, human geographer

a)

b)

c)

Figure 5.4 a) Rio de Janeiro, Brazil; b) Hong Kong, China; c) Vancouver, Canada. What site features do these cities have in common? Why would these features appeal to tourists?

Cities as Regions

Geographers use regions to investigate places and solve problems. Cities are focal points for the area surrounding them. Every city has a complex, interdependent relationship with its surrounding countryside or hinterland. The area that encompasses a city and its **hinterland** is called a **city-centred region**.

Figure 5.5 Toronto is the focal point for the city-centred region known as the Golden Horseshoe. Why do you think it is called this?

A city's influence reaches beyond its political boundaries. Opportunities and services include jobs, technology, capital, entertainment, contact with other people, and so on. The larger a city, the wider its city-centred region or **area of influence**. The size of a region can be measured using criteria such as the distances people will travel for jobs in the city or to attend theatre and sporting events, and the circulation area for the city's newspapers.

While the city influences the hinterland, it also relies on it for food, water, building materials, energy, recreation, a place to dispose of wastes, and space to expand. There is a trend for the largest cities in the world to decline in population as more and more people move to medium-sized and smaller cities. Nonetheless, as the globalization process continues, many large cities are extending their influence over wider areas.

Within cities, smaller regions exist. These unique neighbourhoods, each with a distinct character, contribute to the overall image tourists may have of a city.

Figure 5.6 San Francisco has a unique image partly because of its renowned Chinatown and because of the steep hills at its site.

Cities as Central Places

Cities are central places that perform **economic functions** for the people who live in and around them and for those who visit them. Some cities have predominant functions: New Delhi, India, Ottawa, Canada, and Washington, DC, United States, are centres of government; Las Vegas, Nevada, United States, is an entertainment capital; Mumbai (Bombay), India, is an industrial centre; Milan, Italy, is famous for design and fashion; and Miami, Florida, United States, is a tourist haven.

Cities offer a variety of different kinds of functions, depending on their size. These functions range from low-order services such as pizza outlets and convenience stores, through medium-order functions including banks, movie theatres, art galleries, and hospitals. High-order functions such as national sports team franchises and medical specialists are found in the largest cities, which attract people from the greatest distance.

Figure 5.7 Some businesses, like this dry cleaner, need only a small number of customers, or market, to be successful. Identify businesses in your community that only need a small market.

Figure 5.8 Hotels with casinos seem to multiply in Las Vegas for the millions of visitors eager to try their luck. There is also a large wedding industry to accommodate those who feel lucky in love.

Canada Travels

Casino activity produces significant revenue for the Province of Ontario. Over $2 billion from casinos has flowed into public accounts, and over 15 000 jobs have been provided. Of the visitors to Ontario casinos, 40% come from outside Canada. Conflicting viewpoints have made casinos an issue. Some residents object to the large influx of people; others frown on gambling because it can become addictive.

Figure 5.9 Fans enjoy the action as Leicester City plays against Chelsea in London, England. Sports enthusiasts may travel great distances to see their favourite teams.

Some city functions are directly related to tourism, appealing to visitors seeking entertainment or interesting experiences. Tourist districts within the city have a concentration of hotels, restaurants, theatres, tourist bureaus, currency exchanges, and transportation links. Cities also have recreational districts where seasonal businesses are located. In a city like Calgary, Alberta, for example, the outdoor ice rinks and ski lifts of winter give way to rodeo activities in summer.

1 Harlem (African-American neighbourhood)

2 Hell's Kitchen (Irish neighbourhood)

3 Theatre district

4 Times Square

5 Greenwich Village

6 SoHo (*So*uth of *Ho*uston St.)

7 El Barrio (Hispanic neighbourhoods)

8 Central Park

9 Garment district

10 Little India

11 Little Italy

12 Chinatown

13 Financial District

Figure 5.10 Manhattan tourist districts

Figure 5.11 Some regions within cities, like Times Square in New York City, are well-known tourist attractions.

1 Describe the site and situation of your community.

2 Identify the ways in which the city closest to where you live influences the region around it.

3 What city functions provide services for tourists?

4 Identify a unique region within a city close to where you live. What natural and/or human features make it so distinct from other regions?

Systems

We use the word **system** to describe something that is made up of different parts and joined to form a unified whole. With a system, the whole is more than the sum of its parts. You are a system with interconnected parts. As a human being, you are much more than a collection of your digestive system, circulatory system, nervous system, and so on. A car is another example of a system. All the individual parts go together to make up the whole car. Any one part is not much good without all the others. If the parts do not work well together, the car will not get you far!

Systems thinking is at the heart of geography. It helps us to understand the nature of the planet Earth that is our home. It is useful to think in terms of systems, because we are surrounded by them.

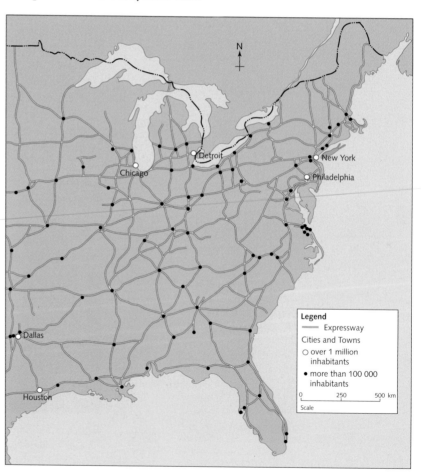

Figure 5.12 If you study a map of a country such as the United States, you will see an interconnected system of urban places.

Legend
— Expressway
Cities and Towns
○ over 1 million inhabitants
• more than 100 000 inhabitants

0   250   500 km
Scale

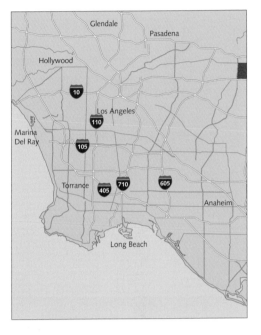

Figure 5.13 The city of Los Angeles is defined as much by its roads and highways as by its coastline.

Cities as Systems

If you were to fly in a space ship over North America, Europe, or coastal parts of Asia and Africa, you would see very different patterns of urban settlement. But everywhere, you would see cities and towns of different sizes strung out along transportation routes, forming a network of interconnected places. Within each of these cities and towns there are both *human* and *natural systems*.

Looking at a map of any large city, you will see a maze of lines representing roads and highways (human systems) and natural features like rivers and coastlines.

Human systems within cities include transportation networks, water and sewage pipelines, and patterns formed by different land uses and distinct districts or neighbourhoods.

Systems that deliver important services, such as supplying clean water, disposing of sewage and other waste, and moving people from place to place, make up what is called a city's **infrastructure**. Roads, expressways, bridges, ferries, canals, airports, pipelines, sewage treatment plants, and power plants are all part of the infrastructure. Think of the complex network of underground pipes, or the underground and overhead wires and towers on which you depend for telephone, television, and computer services.

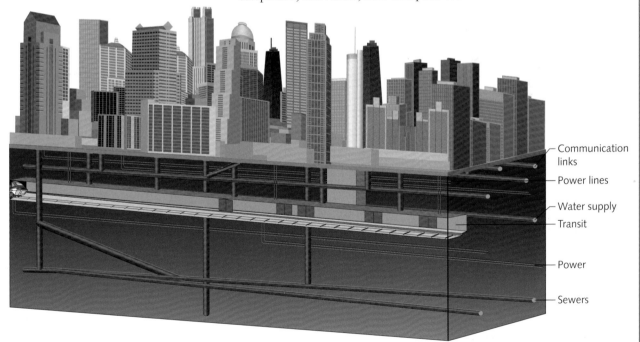

Figure 5.14 Diagrammatic Underground Infrastructure, showing water, sewage, utility corridor (cable, fibre optics, and electricity), and subway. How important is infrastructure to your life? Where does the water come from when you turn on the tap? Where does the waste go when you flush the toilet?

In most cities, infrastructure systems are getting old and are deteriorating. Services are not growing fast enough to meet the demand put on them by growing populations and increased numbers of tourists. Public transportation systems are often inadequate to meet demand or are outdated.

In the latter half of the twentieth century, as the economy shifted to one based on information and services with fewer manufacturing jobs, commercial, residential, and industrial land uses moved to the suburbs and outskirts. In many cities this left large parts of the inner core with slums and decay – not very attractive to tourists! More recently, however, new development has occurred in the downtown core of many North American cities. This redevelopment has enticed residents to purchase and renovate older houses in the downtown area.

Decaying infrastructure along the waterfront is often torn down and the land is redeveloped into attractive waterfront land uses, like parks and hotels, that attract tourists to the city centres. Marinas are adding attractive restaurants to draw both boaters and local residents. Old canals are now used for recreational boating, railroad beds for hiking, biking, skiing, or snowmobile trails, and railway stations as museums or restaurants.

TECHNOLOGY and Tourism

The first modern urban sewers in North America were not built until 1857 in New York City.

Figure 5.15 Toronto's waterfront as it was in 1974 (top) and today. Habourfront Centre, with its theatres, walkways, marina, and skating pond, has rejuvenated this former industrial site. Can you identify one or two features that are the same on each picture?

A Subterranean System

Natural systems can affect patterns within a city and the development of urban travel and tourism. In response to Canada's extremes of cold winters and hot summers, for example, cities like Winnipeg, Manitoba, Toronto, Ontario, and Montreal, Quebec, have built **subterranean systems**.

In Toronto's downtown core beneath 50 skyscrapers, there are 10 km of tunnels containing over 1000 stores and restaurants. These underground passages provide tourists and local residents with comfortable, efficient ways to get from place to place. Links to hotel lobbies, subway entrances, the bus terminal, and the train station create easy access to accommodation and transportation. Theoretically, a tourist could shop, dine, and stay in a Toronto hotel for a week, take a train to Montreal and do the same there for another week, then return to Toronto, without ever having to go outside!

Figure 5.16 The underground walkways use colour-coded signs to guide pedestrians.

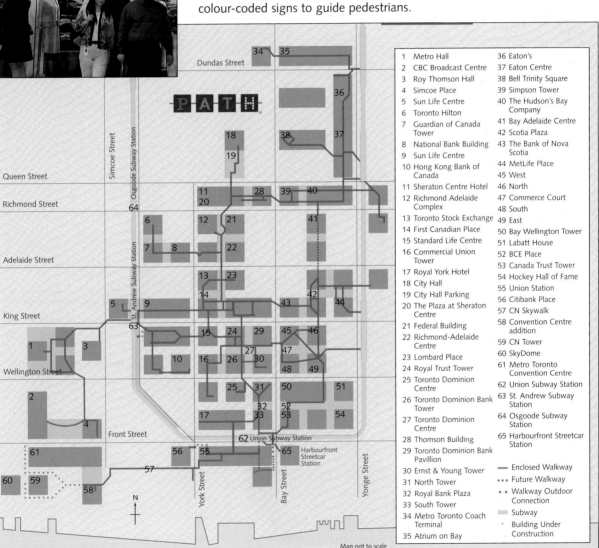

1 Metro Hall	36 Eaton's
2 CBC Broadcast Centre	37 Eaton Centre
3 Roy Thomson Hall	38 Bell Trinity Square
4 Simcoe Place	39 Simpson Tower
5 Sun Life Centre	40 The Hudson's Bay Company
6 Toronto Hilton	41 Bay Adelaide Centre
7 Guardian of Canada Tower	42 Scotia Plaza
8 National Bank Building	43 The Bank of Nova Scotia
9 Sun Life Centre	44 MetLife Place
10 Hong Kong Bank of Canada	45 West
11 Sheraton Centre Hotel	46 North
12 Richmond Adelaide Complex	47 Commerce Court
13 Toronto Stock Exchange	48 South
14 First Canadian Place	49 East
15 Standard Life Centre	50 Bay Wellington Tower
16 Commercial Union Tower	51 Labatt House
17 Royal York Hotel	52 BCE Place
18 City Hall	53 Canada Trust Tower
19 City Hall Parking	54 Hockey Hall of Fame
20 The Plaza at Sheraton Centre	55 Union Station
21 Federal Building	56 Citibank Place
22 Richmond-Adelaide Centre	57 CN Skywalk
23 Lombard Place	58 Convention Centre addition
24 Royal Trust Tower	59 CN Tower
25 Toronto Dominion Centre	60 SkyDome
26 Toronto Dominion Bank Tower	61 Metro Toronto Convention Centre
27 Toronto Dominion Centre	62 Union Subway Station
28 Thomson Building	63 St. Andrew Subway Station
29 Toronto Dominion Bank Pavillion	64 Osgoode Subway Station
30 Ernst & Young Tower	65 Harbourfront Streetcar Station
31 North Tower	
32 Royal Bank Plaza	—— Enclosed Walkway
33 South Tower	••• Future Walkway
34 Metro Toronto Coach Terminal	•• Walkway Outdoor Connection
35 Atrium on Bay	Subway
	• Building Under Construction

Map not to scale

Figure 5.17 Toronto's subterranean system. One survey revealed that 55 million people pass from Union Station into the tunnel system annually.

Impact of Systems

Natural systems are complex. They are driven by a constant flow of solar energy and work together in the air, water, rocks, soil, and life of the planet. Of course, natural and human systems interact with one another as well. Think of pollution, garbage, ozone layer depletion, and climate change, and you will see that humans and their activities have an impact on natural systems. Then think about how dependent you are on nature for the basics of survival. Natural hazards such as floods, ice storms, hurricanes, and earthquakes seriously damage or destroy human systems, such as roads, bridges, power lines, buildings, and other things people need.

People living and travelling in cities significantly change the natural environment. Construction of roads, bridges, and buildings can change ecosystems and destroy the natural habitat of many species. Burning energy for industry, transportation, and heating or cooling homes has serious environmental consequences. As a city sprawls over the surrounding countryside, the size of its **ecological footprint** – its impact on natural systems – increases.

Figure 5.18 An earthquake that struck the Washington State area in March 2001 resulted in millions of dollars in property damage, including this gift shop in Seattle.

Figure 5.19 Ecological footprint. An increase in tourism puts pressure on the capacity of natural systems to satisfy people's needs and wants.

Technology and Tourism

Engineers and scientists work on improving the design of infrastructure so that damage, injury, and death caused by natural disasters is lessened. High-rise hotels that are better able to withstand earthquakes can decrease the risk for travellers as well as local residents.

Travel and Tourism as a System

Even the travel and tourism industry, with its interrelated features, can be considered a system. Some of the components of the industry are included in Figure 5.20. The suppliers that serve travellers include travel agents, tour operators, transportation companies, and hotels and other types of accommodations. Businesses in the travel and tourism system face increasing international competition as consumer demands change and international travel increases.

COMPONENT	FUNCTION
Travel agents	Offer advice; provide retail tourism services; arrange travel insurance, transportation, and accommodations
Tour operators	Buy (usually wholesale) travel and accommodations to put together holiday or business packages
Transportation companies	Offer regular or charter airlines, bus, train, car rental, and taxi services
Hospitality associations	Provide hotels, hostels, resorts, bed and breakfast establishments
Entertainment facilities	Provide cultural activities such as theatres, galleries, and restaurants; include concert companies
Tourism consultants	Conduct research and offer management advice to the hospitality and tourism industry

Figure 5.20 Some components of the travel and tourism industry system

CHECK IN

1 Identify the parts of a city's infrastructure that collect and dispose of waste, move people to work or school, and transport messages between family and friends.

2 List two characteristics that all systems have in common.

3 What parts of a city's infrastructure would be most important to tourists? Why?

World-Class Cities

World-class cities are centres of global economic activity, power, and wealth. They are home to the headquarters of many of the largest transnational corporations and banks. They are entertainment, cultural, economic, and administrative centres. A main focus of business in these world-class cities is on producing and distributing information, including financial, media, education, medical, and tourism services. Of course, low-order functions are also available for local residents. World-class cities are usually identified by their large area and high density of people, cars, and buildings.

New York City, London, and Tokyo have been called true global or world-class cities, but many others with international influence also claim world-class status: Paris, Seoul, Hong Kong, Mexico City, Bangkok, Sydney, Zurich, Buenos Aires, Madrid, and Toronto are just a few cities that have made this claim. Major attractions that help create an international image can include world fairs, major sporting events, huge amusement parks, or unique features such as the Champs Elysée, the Louvre, and the Eiffel Tower, for which Paris is noted.

Figure 5.21 In the late 1990s, 192 cities around the world were ranked by a company based in Geneva, Switzerland, according to how pleasant it was to live in them. Vancouver ranked first, Toronto third, and Montreal fifteenth. Megacities such as Tokyo, Mexico, and New York ranked much farther down the list.

Figure 5.22 Cities with metropolitan areas of over 10 million people, 2000

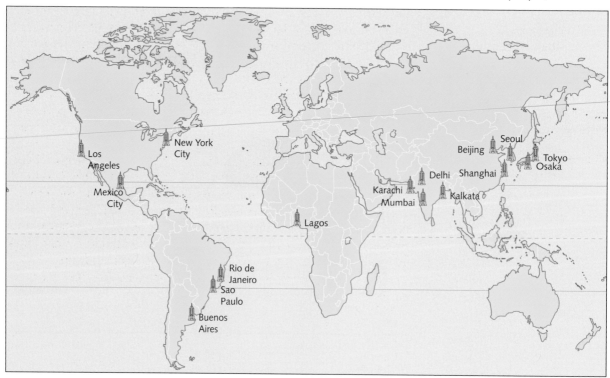

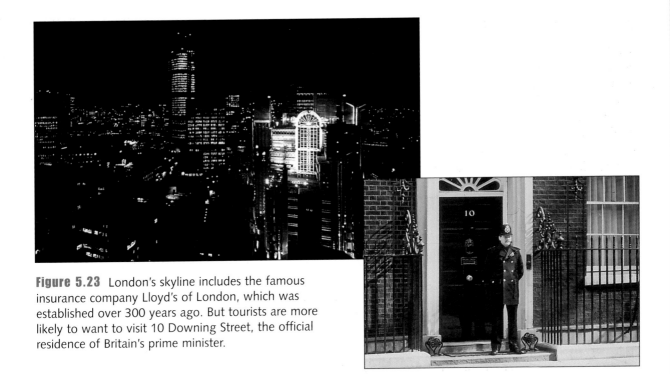

Figure 5.23 London's skyline includes the famous insurance company Lloyd's of London, which was established over 300 years ago. But tourists are more likely to want to visit 10 Downing Street, the official residence of Britain's prime minister.

Comparing Cities as Travel and Tourism Centres

Imagine that you have been offered a trip to any city in the world. How would you decide where to go? A comparison of the natural and cultural features of each city can help you learn more about the "character" of a city and its region, and make an informed choice. Geographers, travel magazines, and travellers all like to compare the natural and human attractions of various cities. As well as helping us make decisions about where to travel, comparison can help us understand the nature of cities and their problems and find solutions to urban issues.

To make an effective comparison, you must first establish criteria on which to base your study. When *Condé Nast Traveler*, a well-known U.S. travel magazine, surveyed its readers asking them to pick their favourite city destinations, the magazine received 26 687 replies! The survey's criteria were: ambiance, people/friendliness, culture/entertainment, and restaurants. People compared many cities by judging these criteria on a five-point scale, ranging from excellent through very good, good, and fair to poor. Figure 5.24 shows the results.

> " Cities are different places for different groups. "
>
> – William Norton, human geographer

World Cities (excluding United States)	Cities in the United States
Sydney, Australia	San Francisco, California
Florence, Italy	New Orleans, Louisiana
Rome, Italy	Charleston, South Carolina
Paris, France	Santa Fe, New Mexico
Venice, Italy	New York City, New York
Salzburg, Austria	Savannah, Georgia
Vienna, Austria	Chicago, Illinois
London, England	Seattle, Washington
Vancouver, Canada	Boston, Massachusetts
San Miguel de Allende, Mexico	San Diego, California

Figure 5.24 Top cities chosen by *Condé Nast Traveler* readers

In January 2001, *Ski* magazine surveyed its readers to determine the best ski cities in North America where enthusiasts could have a career as well as easy access to great skiing. The criteria they selected included

- population
- big ski areas within a reasonable drive
- best on-slope events
- unemployment rate
- average annual income
- median price of a 2000-square-foot [186 m²] home
- tax rates

The five best cities selected were Vancouver, British Columbia; Seattle, Washington; Salt Lake City, Utah; Denver, Colorado; and Boston, Massachusetts.

There are many criteria to choose from when comparing travel and tourism characteristics of different cities. Some important criteria are shown in Figure 5.26.

Figure 5.25 Easy access to a variety of information sources helps today's sports tourists choose destinations that suit their interests and their budget.

CRITERIA FOR COMPARING CITIES AS TRAVEL AND TOURISM CENTRES	
Population	Size, ethnic make-up
Site and situation	Landform features, climate, economic attributes of location
History	Development, traditions, city design
Functions	Special functions and/or those related to travel and tourism
Major attractions	Natural and cultural features
Unique image	Distinct regions within city, landmarks, sounds and smells
Infrastructure	Transportation, accommodations, and other services
Tourist data	Type and number of tourists
Impact of tourism	On natural systems, on local economy, on local inhabitants
Political system	Conflict or authoritarian governments can have implications for travellers
Cost	Of accommodations, food, transportation, currency exchange
Issues	Congestion, pollution, declining infrastructure, health, safety

Figure 5.26 Which of these criteria would be most important to you when choosing a city to visit?

Criteria can be further divided and refined, depending on the purpose of the analysis. Suppose you are trying to choose a hotel to stay in while visiting Spain. A decision-making organizer (see Figure 5.28) can be a useful tool to organize information you might find in a travel guide. For a quick overview, you could use a simple check mark for each hotel that fits each category. Or you may wish to rank the hotels giving three points for the best hotel, two for the next best, and one for the third. Total the points for best overall choice of hotels. If one of the criteria is more important than the others, it could be weighted by assigning it more points – perhaps doubling its value to 6, 4, and 2.

Figure 5.27 No motor vehicles are permitted in Madrid's Plaza Mayor, where the buildings date from the early 1600s.

WHICH IS THE BEST HOTEL?

Criteria	Hotel Madrid	Hotel Sevilla	Hotel Granada
Clean	2	1	3
Safe	Yes	Yes	Yes
Inexpensive	3 (7000 pesetas/single)	1 (9000 pesetas/single)	2 (7500 pesetas/single)
Central location	1 (need taxi to station)	3 (across road from station)	2 (short walk from station)
Toilet/shower in room	Yes (tub)	Yes (shower)	Yes (shower)
Balcony/view	3	1	2
Restaurant/bar	Yes 1	No 3	Restaurant 2
Amenities (telephone/ television/air conditioning)	1	2	3

Figure 5.28 A sample decision-making organizer

Source: Adapted from Margo Classe, *Hello Spain! An Insider's Guide to Spain Hotels*, Los Angeles: Wilson Publishing,1998.

Toronto as a Travel and Tourism Centre

Over 200 years ago, the Huron people called the area on the north shore of Lake Ontario Toronto, which means meeting place. Today, this meeting place is home to more than 2.5 million multiethnic people and attracts more than 21 million tourists annually. Why do so many people want to come to Toronto?

Not only does Toronto abound in investment and employment opportunities, which makes it an attractive place to call home, it is also known as the entertainment and cultural capital of Canada. This makes it an attractive place to visit. Toronto is also a very clean and remarkably safe city. Indeed, it is considered the safest large city in North America. It is not surprising that tourists are attracted to this urban centre. In fact, tourism generates more than $5 billion in revenue for the city annually.

Toronto has a vast array of attractions. For sports fans, the city has three major sports franchise teams in hockey, baseball, and basketball. Racing fans can attend the North American Cup (harness racing) or the Queen's Plate for thoroughbred racing. Toronto is also on the Indy car touring circuit, bringing in the biggest names in CART racing. The Tennis Master Series is held in Toronto every summer. In addition to spectator sports, Toronto hosts a number of sports-related trade shows and is home to the Hockey Hall of Fame.

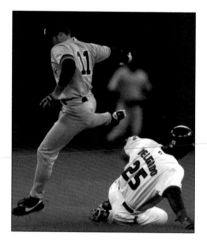

Figure 5.29 During the two seasons that the Blue Jays won the World Series, proud Canadians from across the country flocked to the SkyDome. The stadium, which seats 50 516 for baseball, was packed to capacity for every game.

Figure 5.30 Caribana, Toronto's celebration of Caribbean music and dance, draws one million people annually from all over North America.

Music lovers can visit Roy Thomson Hall and Massey Hall, or any of the numerous clubs in the downtown area, which showcase outstanding performers. During June, July, and August, Toronto offers the Downtown Jazz Festival, the Beaches International Jazz Festival, and Caribana.

Multicultural festivals include the Dragon Boat Race, Krinos, and Caravan. These festivals feature pageantry, shows, and food and drink of the many ethnic groups that make Toronto their home.

Cultural attractions include the Royal Ontario Museum, the National Ballet of Canada, the Canadian Opera Company, the Toronto Symphony Orchestra, and the International Festival of Authors.

Another attraction that Toronto holds for tourists is "stargazing." The city's International Film Festival, which celebrated its twenty-fifth anniversary in September 2000, attracts some of Hollywood's biggest names. The festival is not the only opportunity to see the stars. Many can be spotted year round.

Toronto is often called "Hollywood North." Moviemakers find it less expensive to film on location in Canada than in the United States. Not only is there a difference in value between Canadian and U.S. dollars, there are also tax incentives. Provincial tax credits provide film companies with savings of 20% of the amount of labour costs in a company's total budget.

Interact

Toronto Tourism uses the slogan, "The world within a city." Does Toronto measure up to this claim?

Figure 5.31 Film trucks and equipment lining the curb may be a temporary inconvenience for Toronto residents, but location work boosts the city's economy. At right, a film crew borrows the press room of the *Toronto Star*.

TORONTO PRODUCTIONS					
Year	Features	Movies of the Week	Mini-Series	Specials	TV Series
1994	38	35	2	28	30
1995	40	55	1	25	25
1996	36	45	3	31	31
1997	33	48	4	43	39
1998	41	55	5	45	31

Source: Toronto Film and Television Office

While Montreal and Vancouver are also home to the making of many movies, Toronto is the film and television centre of Canada, with world-class production facilities. Moviemakers claim that Toronto can be used to create the illusion of many cities in the world. It has "played" New York, Boston, Washington, Chicago, Vienna, Warsaw, Tokyo, and Teheran. The quaint villages, small towns, and rolling farmland that surround Toronto, and the natural settings of such parks as Algonquin Park and the Sand Banks, provide additional locations for filming.

Many people are involved in producing a film, which can take weeks to complete. They require accommodation, food, and transportation, and they most likely indulge in some shopping and entertainment, helping to boost the tourism industry and the economy.

Figure 5.32 Toronto productions, 1994–1998. Among the features shot in Toronto were *Three to Tango, Blackheart,* and *Pushing Tin.* Have you seen any of these moves? Did you recognize any Toronto landmarks?

Next time you watch a movie, look for these Toronto features:
- office towers
- industrial landscapes
- university campus
- Casa Loma
- Pioneer Village
- ethnic districts and their populations
- Toronto Islands
- Leslie Street spit
- ravines and river valleys

Figure 5.33 In 2000, celebrities like Burt Reynolds and Sylvester Stallone, shown here with their director and co-stars, could be seen dining and shopping in downtown Toronto.

Green Toronto

Besides entertainment and cultural attractions, Toronto has "**green space**." These natural areas can be seen on air photographs, where the tree cover shows up along city streets, and in river valleys, ravines, and shorelines.

The Green Tourist Association, a non-government organization, works to protect the city's natural setting and encourages tourists to enjoy it. The association produces a "green map," which it calls "The OTHER Map of Toronto." This map provides information shown in Figure 5.35 about natural features and things to see and do in and around them.

Figure 5.34 The Toronto Islands are a green refuge in the city's harbour.

This is not your regular tourist map.... It was designed ... to give you quick access to the greener side of the big city. Tour the parks, shop at the green businesses, stroll from gallery to historic site. Learn about the fascinating and rich heritage of this beautiful city. Eat an organic lunch! ... join in on a Don River tree planting or follow the meandering course of the Humber River and all of its parks.... bike along the Waterfront Trail and picnic by the lake or on one of Toronto's islands.... By being a green tourist, not only are you having fun, you're also fighting smog locally and climate change globally; you're protecting and preserving Toronto's land and water; and you're supporting local businesses and culture at the same time! You are part of a growing community of people around the world who are treading lightly in the city.

Source: Green Tourist Association, "The Other Map of Toronto."

Figure 5.35 Some tourists want to see the "green" side of cities, not the usual "concrete and glass" view.

www.irwinpublishing.com

To discover other green map projects around the world, visit Green Maps on the Student Page for *Canada Travels.*

CHECK IN

1 Choose two world-class cities shown in Figure 5.22 and describe features of their natural site that would attract tourists.

2 Which hotel in Figure 5.28 would you choose to stay in? Explain why.

3 As a tourist, make up an itinerary for a one-week visit to Toronto.

LOOKING AT ISSUES

Figure 5.36 Location of Toronto, Ontario

Toronto, Ontario – Olympic Games

Issue: Should cities use taxpayers' dollars to attract tourism rather than address local concerns?

The economic benefits of tourism associated with hosting the Olympic Games leads to fierce competition among cities. Toronto, Canada, was one of five finalists that bid to host the summer Olympics in 2008. The other finalists were Paris, France, Beijing, China, Osaka, Japan, and Istanbul, Turkey. In July 2001, Beijing was awarded the 2008 summer games.

Media coverage of Olympic events opens the eyes of the world to the host city and its hinterland. For example, millions of people knew nothing about Lillehammer, Norway, before that city hosted the Winter Olympics in 1994. Economic benefits for the host city continue long after the Olympic flame is extinguished as people visit the city to enjoy its attractions.

City, regional, and even national governments, as well as corporations and other businesses, provide funds and spend years creating development plans to encourage the International Olympic Committee to choose their city. To help the Toronto bid for the 2008 games, the federal, provincial, and municipal governments pledged $500 million each to develop Toronto's polluted port lands. This investment was sparked by the Olympic committee's plan to use the port lands for a stadium, athletes' village, and a swimming and diving centre. Local politicians and the Board of Trade felt this investment in Toronto's infrastructure was vital to the economic growth and revitalization of the city, regardless of whether Toronto's bid to host the games was successful.

Not everyone favoured the Olympic courtship, however. Some residents resented the disruption that the events and visitors would bring to the city. The influx of thousands of tourists and athletes would place added stress on public transit and on roads and highways that were already overcrowded.

Bread not Circuses, a coalition of groups concerned about the bid, raised questions about the amount of public money that

Figure 5.37 Canadian athletes parade a giant flag around the Olympic Stadium during the closing ceremonies in Sydney, Australia, October 2000.

Figure 5.38 Sydney, Australia, set a new standard with its Green Games initiatives, which introduced new technologies and environmental practices. Solar energy was utilized, and a car-free site provided facilities for walking and biking.

would be spent at a time when programs for women, housing, and recreation were in need of support. They pointed to the negative impacts of Olympic Games in past host cities. Other critics saw the bid as a massive shift in priorities, in an area that had serious problems such as accessible day care, a housing shortage, and a deteriorating infrastructure.

There was also environmental clean-up to be considered. Over 8000 t of plastic bottles, cups, cans, food wrappers, and food scraps were produced by more than 2 million spectators and participants throughout the 17 days of the Atlanta 1996 Olympics. Who would pay for the clean-up, and where would the trash go? Disposal of Toronto's garbage was an ongoing concern, even without increases.

Then, on January 31, 2001, only months before the Olympic site selection was to be made, the mayor of Toronto announced serious budget problems for the city. Toronto homeowners could face property tax increases totalling 77% over five years. Without provincial aid, the city faced $120 million in possible cuts to services in 2001, affecting such services as dental care for children of low-income families and seniors and breakfast clubs that feed 4500 children. Another $185 million in cuts would follow, possibly closing libraries and community and recreation centres. These fiscal problems cast a shadow on the whole Olympic bid for the city.

CHECK IN

1 If you were a Toronto homeowner, would you have wanted your tax dollars spent to attract tourism or to support local initiatives? Explain.

2 As a taxpayer living in small-town Ontario, would you have approved of the $500 million provincial grant to develop Toronto's waterfront to attract tourism? Why or why not?

3 Complete a chart like the one shown in Figure 5.39 for Toronto's 2008 Olympic bid. Using this information, prepare an argument either supporting or opposing the bid. Present your argument to the class.

Economic Aspects	Political Aspects	Environmental Aspects	Cultural Aspects	Stakeholders Involved

Figure 5.39

Sustaining Urban Tourism

Tourism brings wealth to a city. It generates business for stores, restaurants, taxis, theatres, and many other industries. Tourism provides a larger market that helps to support attractions such as sports, entertainment, museums, and art galleries. Because of the direct and indirect benefits tourism brings to a city's economy, competition for business and leisure tourism is fierce among most cities. The challenge for many large cities is to capture a bigger share of tourist business.

This challenge is twofold. To attract tourists, the city must be able to respond to the needs and expectations of the growing number of tourists. This includes continuously improving facilities and renovating infrastructure to maintain its share of tourism. At the same time, the city must consider the interests of its residents. This means ensuring that tourism is developed and managed in such a way that it

- benefits the city
- enhances the urban environment rather than contributes to its deterioration
- does not become a financial burden.

Many cities, including Madrid, Spain, and Zhuhan, China, have hosted recent international conferences on urban tourism in an effort to discuss and find solutions to urban tourism issues. Many of the issues examined at these conferences are the very issues that are analyzed in this text. **Sustainable tourism** and the impact of tourism on local people and the environment are common topics. Tourism is unsustainable when it destroys the very resources on which it depends, whether natural or human.

The Bad with the Good

Although there are many positive aspects of tourism in cities, tourists can create problems for the residents and have an impact on human systems. In New York City, for example, the influx of tourists combined with one of the largest urban populations in the world creates problems that require solutions. Most of these concerns are common in large cities that invite tourism.

A Worm in the Big Apple!

- traffic congestion that borders on daily gridlock
- traffic congestion compounded by limited routes (bridges and tunnels) for traffic to get in and out of downtown on Manhattan Island

Figure 5.40 Tourists enjoy the old-world atmosphere of Quebec City.

Interact

Discuss the advantages and disadvantages of a car-free downtown city core.

Dollars & Sense

The World Travel and Tourism Council calculated that direct and indirect contribution of tourism to the global economy in 1998 was US$3.6 trillion, providing jobs for 255 million people.

Figure 5.41 Tourists often feel intimidated in the crowded streets of Manhattan.

- high crime opportunities and high policing costs to make the city safe for residents and tourists
- vandalism and graffiti on public surfaces
- terrorism – the United Nations Headquarters, business districts, Parliament Buildings, U.S. stock exchange, and other places are targets for international terrorists
- pollution of air, disposal of sewage, managing litter and garbage disposal overburden city services

Figure 5.42 Is graffiti an urban art form or unsightly vandalism?

CHECK IN

1 In your own words, write a definition of the term "sustainable tourism."

2 Do you think businesses that benefit from a city's tourism should contribute to the improvement of the city's infrastructure over and above their regular taxes?

3 What measures could a city take to ensure that tourism is sustainable?

Figure 5.43 On September 11, 2001, terrorists flew passenger aircraft into the two World Trade Center towers (shown here) in New York City and into the Pentagon in Washington, DC. Both Trade towers were destroyed, with the loss of over 5000 lives.

CASE STUDY
Case Study: Hong Kong, China— Solving an Airport Dilemma

Figure 5.44 Location of Hong Kong's new airport on the island of Chek Lap Kok

Increasingly, people are travelling by air. This is not surprising, as it is usually the fastest and the most efficient way to move people from one city to another. Hundreds of millions of passengers are flown over just the United States every year. As international travel increases, the airline industry will continue to grow and airports will need to keep pace.

Air traffic congestion and decaying airport infrastructure are two travel concerns that need immediate solutions. Other related concerns include noise levels for local residents, access to airports, inefficient design and layout, and airline marketing strategies that leave demand for flights greater than the supply and cause delay, frustration, and sometimes even "air rage."

Hong Kong's tiny Kai Tak Airport was the world's busiest international air cargo and the third busiest passenger airport in the world. The airport could not keep up with demand and turned away hundreds of flights every week.

Figure 5.45 Pilots needed to be especially skilled to land at Kai Tak Airport. Planes sometimes appeared to be flying through laundry hanging on balconies as they descended over local apartment buildings.

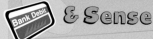

Air travel has a significant impact on the natural environment and on people's wallets! In a ten-minute flight, a Boeing 747 jet consumes 144 000 L of fuel. Faced with high fuel costs, airline companies are raising rates. At the same time, many Canadian companies are freezing their travel budgets, along with other cost-cutting measures.

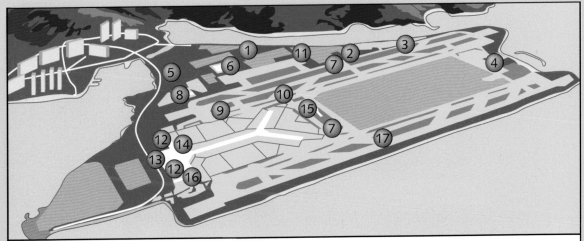

1	Freight Forwarding Centre	7	Fire Station	12	Multistorey Carparks
2	Business Aviation	8	Police Station	13	Ground Transportation Centre
3	Government Flying Service	9	Airmail Centre	14	Passenger Terminal Building
4	Aircraft Maintenance Facilities	10	Southern Runway	15	Backup Air Traffic Control
5	Cathay City Office	11	Air Traffic Control	16	Airport Hotel
6	Super Terminal 1		Complex & Tower	17	Northern Runway

Figure 5.46 More than 60 airlines from 130 cities use the new facilities at Chek Lap Kok.

Interact

To help pay for the new infrastructure, travellers using Hong Kong International Airport must pay an airport tax of HK$50 [US$6.50]. Should travellers be forced to pay user fees?

In order to improve the infrastructure to accommodate the demand from tourists and business travellers, Hong Kong began an ambitious land-reclamation project. To expand the island area, 340 million cubic metres of landfill were blasted from rock to add 938 ha of land to Chek Lap Kok in the South China Sea. The Hong Kong International Airport at Chek Lap Kok, the most expensive airport in the world, cost close to US$30 billion. The area is 6 km long and 3.5 km wide. The new airport symbolizes Hong Kong's role as the gateway to China and transportation hub for Asia, competing with Shanghai and Singapore.

The Y-shaped terminal has two runways, each with a maximum capacity of 50 to 60 take-offs or landings per hour. A taxiway leads planes to the runways. Air traffic is monitored from a control tower, which covers air traffic within eyesight, and a control centre, which covers a much wider area and is four times larger than the one at Kai Tak Airport. To move passengers and cargo to and from the island airport, there are two suspension bridges, a six-lane highway, and a high-speed railway. There is also a ferry service.

Figure 5.47 Although tourists to Hong Kong may find the houseboats in its harbour quaint, the presence of these boats demonstrates a real problem for the city's residents: scarcity of land. With more than 6400 people per square kilometre, Hong Kong has one of the highest population densities in the world. Using landfill to create the land needed for Chek Lap Kok Airport was a costly but innovative strategy.

In 2000, passenger movements rose 9.8% from 1999 to 33.4 million passengers, and cargo was up 13.3% to 2.24 million t. To further increase movements, the Hong Kong Airport Authority offered airlines a 50% rebate on landing charges for the first year and 25% the following year on flights they operate to a new destination effective March 2001.

TECHNOLOGY *and* *Tourism*

Passengers travelling on all Air Canada flights can access the Internet using Bell Mobility phones in place at all seats for laptop-carrying travellers.

Canada Travels

Pearson International Airport in Toronto, about the thirtieth busiest airport in the world, is undertaking a $4.4 billion multi-phase improvement project. Features include a new wing-shaped terminal with 116 gates, 258 check-in counters, 15 km of conveyer belts for moving luggage, the largest parking garage in Canada for 12 600 cars, more and improved runways, and improved highway access. Toronto airport users will pay a tax of $10.

CHECK IN

1 What are the economic, cultural, social, environmental, and political aspects of this case study?

2 Do cities like Hong Kong have a responsibility to world travellers to deal with the problem of increased demand by expanding airports? Explain.

3 How would you deal with the problem of air traffic congestion at major international airports?

LOOKING AT ISSUES

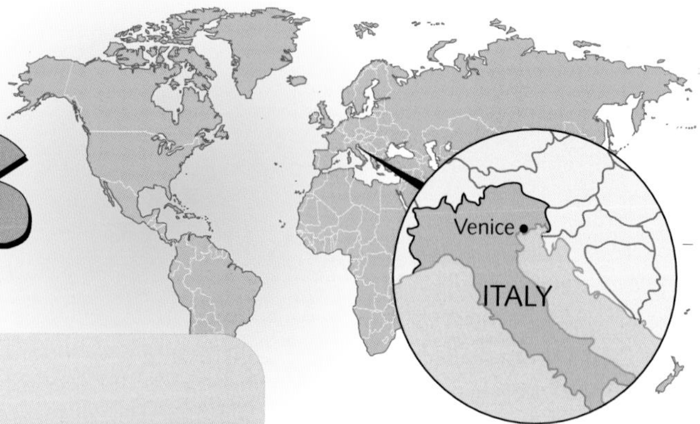

Venice, Italy – Keep Out!

Issue: How should a city deal with the threat of unsustainable tourism caused by large numbers of tourists?

During the peak travel season, tourists outnumber inhabitants in many places, with negative effects. One of these places is Venice, Italy. The words "Venice" and "tourism" are practically synonymous. Whether strolling through the city absorbing the rich architectural history, touring the Basilica of San Marco, or taking a romantic gondola ride, visitors are overwhelmed by the city's beauty and art history. But with a population of 292 000 and approximately 7 million visitors a year, many problems have occurred.

The steady stream of visitors, mostly in July and August, has led to extremely high prices at restaurants, congested narrow streets, and overloaded sanitation equipment. Day-trippers, tourists who arrive just for the day on tour buses, spend little or no money, but they overload the infrastructure. In a city with canals that serve as streets, traffic congestion becomes severe. Overcrowding, litter and pollution, and damage to monuments have been so acute that some residents have moved elsewhere!

It took an extreme example to draw public attention to the unsustainability of tourism in Venice. In 1989, a Pink Floyd concert attracted 200 000 fans to St. Mark's Square. The city was totally unprepared. Some fans climbed ornate sixth-century pillars, chipping off parts of the carvings. Garbage and an overloaded sewage system took days to repair. Preservationists and local residents realized that tourism was too much of a good thing. They now wished the tourists would stay away.

The issue of unsustainable tourism surfaced again when a group of politicians and business people, with

Figure 5.48 Location of Venice, Italy

Travel FACT

Venice is not the only place trying to reduce the number of tourists and their impact. Haines, Alaska, wanted fewer tourists from cruise ships in their coastal town. To reduce the numbers they imposed a 4% tax on all cruise ships. Some no longer include Haines on their itinerary.

Figure 5.49 Algae, silt and untreated sewage from Venetians and millions of tourists each year result in polluted canals.

140 CANADA TRAVELS

Figure 5.50 Venice is sinking due to rising sea level and overuse of artesian wells, causing economic and cultural damage.

Interact

Should people have a say about events in other countries?

the support of large corporations, such as Fiat, Benetton, Olivetti, and Coca-Cola, lobbied to have Expo 2000, the millennium World Fair, held in Venice. The huge event would generate revenue to pay for improvements in telecommunications and the transportation infrastructure. It would also bring an additional 200 000 visitors a day over the four months of the exposition. One group proposed increasing revenue by charging visitors a toll just to enter the city.

Many residents, led by the mayor, were strongly opposed to their city hosting this event. Even people from other countries, who were interested in preserving the heritage of Venice, protested. Huge events like the Olympics and World Expositions can create massive waste and consume vast amounts of energy and resources.

The environment minister for the European Community, of which Italy is a member, called for an environmental impact study. The study indicated that the number of visitors would cause irreparable damage to the natural environment. In the face of this opposition, the Italian government withdrew Venice's application to host Expo 2000. The World Fair was eventually held in Hanover, Germany.

Venice's municipal officials are working on a number of ways to help control the flow of tourists and reduce damage. Government tourism Web sites provide information for tourists to make them aware of how crowded Venice is in peak travel times.

When huge numbers of people assemble in a relatively small area, all cities can experience serious problems, conflicts, and issues. Tourism businesses and the governments that help to support them continually make decisions that affect the natural and human systems on which tourism depends.

CHECK IN

1 How can a government Web site help control the flow of tourists into a country?

2 Explain how holding Expo 2000 in Venice could make tourism unsustainable for that city.

3 In groups of four, assume the roles of a Venetian resident, a tourist, the chief executive officer of one of the four corporations, and a city official. Prepare arguments for the viewpoint of your stakeholder about the issue. Role-play your arguments for the class.

- apply geotechnologies to a study of regional geography
- produce and interpret different types of maps, graphic organizers, and diagrams
- communicate effectively in written, oral, and visual forms
- analyze the major characteristics of selected tourist regions in terms of natural, cultural, economic, and political criteria
- identify the natural resources on which tourism is based

Site Characteristics of the Montreal-Ottawa Corridor

Purpose: To use ArcView to determine the places within the Montreal–Ottawa corridor that meet the following site characteristics: located in an area of flat land adjacent to the St. Lawrence River or Ottawa River.

Files: places.shp, lakes.shp, soil.shp

Functions: View Properties, Legend Editor (Symbol Edit), Zoom, Convert to Shapefile, Geo-processing (Dissolve Boundaries), Geo-processing (Merge Polygons), Table Edit, Legend Editor (Unique Value), Auto-label, Hot Link, Layout.

1. Your first step will be to create a blank View, name it "The Quebec – Montreal Corridor," and change its Distance Units to kilometres.

2. Next, add the following themes: x:\imagery\ccrs\ott-mont\places.shp, lakes.shp, and soil.shp (found on ArcCanada 2.0 Disk #2).

3. Now, place the themes in the following order in the map legend: places.shp, lakes.shp, soil.shp.

4. Next, determine the areas of flat land by using the Query Builder to highlight all of the soil polygons that contain a slope of "<4%," "non-applicable (water)," or "non-applicable (water)."

5. Now, determine the places that are located in areas of flat land. To do so, use the Select by Theme function to highlight all the places that intersect the selected soil polygons. Open the theme table to see how many of the 68 places are located on flat land.

6. Next, determine the number of selected places (i.e., those located in areas of flat land) that are found near the Ottawa or St. Lawrence Rivers. To do so, use the Select by Theme function to find the places that are found within 5 km of the "lakes." Remember that you are actually "selecting from set" here rather than creating a new set! Open the theme table to see how many of the 68 places are located on flat land and are within 5 km of the Ottawa or St. Lawrence Rivers.

7. Now, convert the selected places to a shapefile, naming it "Sites" and adding it to the View.

8. Next, delete the soil.shp theme and the original places.shp theme. Add a provinces theme (c:\esri\esridata\canada\province.shp) and use the Legend Editor to apply a Unique Colour scheme so that you can easily distinguish Quebec and Ontario in your map.

9. Now, show the different sizes of the cities by using the Legend Editor to apply a Graduated Symbol scheme to your "places" theme. Change the symbol type, colour, and sizes as you see fit. Edit the Legend Labels by replacing the population classes with the actual population ranges. (Hint: you will have to go back to the theme table to get this information, then return to the Legend Editor.)

10. Next, auto-label the provinces making sure to select "label only features in view extent." Use the Bullet Leader Label tool to label the two rivers. Use the Callout Label tool to label Ottawa, Hull, Gatineau, and Montreal. (If you are unsure which they are, either select them in the theme table or use the Identify tool.) Re-size and move labels as you see fit and/or experiment with changing the Text and Label Defaults.

11. Now, create a final Layout of your map. Change the scale bar to "kilometres" and change the type of the scale bar and north arrow as you see fit.

12. Now, turn on the Legend Tool extension and use it to create a customized legend that contains only the "places" theme.

13. Using the Pointer tool, select, re-size, and move the various objects in your layout to make room for a text box. Using the Text tool, create a text box and write an explanation for why you think the site characteristics of "flat land" and "near water" were important in the settlement and development of these places. Include as well an explanation of why these factors might be important to the tourism industry in this region today. (Remember that you have to hit Enter at the end of each line when keying in the text!)

Extension:

Scan or download pictures that show the flat land and water in and around the various communities in your map. Then, create hot links from the "places" to the photos.

Extension:

Using other data available on the ArcCanada 2.0 CDs or in the Esridata directory, determine the site factors that have helped determine the location of communities in another region of Canada. For example, you may want to see if productive farmland was an important determinant in the distribution of communities in southern Ontario.

Extension:

Create a map containing your own community and add / manipulate various themes to illustrate the site characteristics that helped to determine its location.

REVISIT THE chapter 5
Urban Tourism

Understanding the Concepts

1. Study the quote by William Norton on page 114.

   a) Suggest three examples of functions that enable cities to be called "centres of civilization."

   b) Suggest three examples of "social and environmental chaos" in cities.

2. Identify two disadvantages (barriers) and two advantages (motivators) for people travelling to cities.

3. Prove, with supporting evidence, that cities are globally significant tourist attractions.

4. Identify the role played by government in the tourism industry in Toronto, Hong Kong, and Venice. What impact has there been on tourism in each case?

Figure 5.51 A ride in a gondola is considered a "must do" by many tourists to Venice.

Practising Your Skills

5. Draw a diagram to represent the relationship between a city and its hinterland. Use arrows to show the movement of goods and services in and out of the city.

6. Refer to the graph in Figure 5.3.

   a) Analyze the growth patterns for developed and developing countries.

   b) Predict how the growth pattern observed will affect future travel and tourism patterns.

7. a) On an outline map of the world, locate and label the cities most preferred by *Condé Nast Traveler* readers as shown in Figure 5.24.

   b) Write an analysis of the patterns that you can see on the map.

Applying Your Skills

8. Contact your local municipal government for information on infrastructure improvements taking place or being planned in your area. How will the improvements likely affect tourism in the region?

9. In a three-column chart, identify low-order, medium-order, and high-order businesses that might benefit in a city hosting an Olympic Games.

10. Design a plan outlining three initiatives to make your city or community a "green city" to attract tourists who appreciate nature.

11. Conduct a geographic inquiry to investigate one of the following issues:

   a) building a new Disneyland in Hong Kong

   b) the Green Games initiatives for the Sydney 2000 Olympics

   c) airspace congestion and how air traffic control works to reduce the risk of mid-air collision

Thinking Like a Tourist

12. What is your image of your city or the city closest to where you live? Compare your ideas with those of other members of your class.

13. You have been offered a trip to any city in the world.

   a) Select six criteria of your choice, including both natural and human features, for comparing two cities.

   b) For any two cities that you would like to visit, construct a comparison organizer listing the criteria you have chosen in the first column.

   c) Conduct research on both cities using a variety of sources such as travel brochures, the Internet, books, and if possible, interviews with people who have visited the cities.

   d) Based upon the information you select and include in your comparison organizer, decide which city you will visit. You may wish to create a decision-making matrix similar to Figure 5.28.

   e) Write a one-page article for a travel magazine, explaining your choice. Be sure to refer to the natural and human attributes your city has to offer.

Director – Economic Development & Tourism Services

The successful candidate will have strong leadership, management, and interpersonal skills. You will supervise, organize, and direct the day-to-day operations of our dynamic and forward-looking division. You will develop strategies to increase our tax and economic base through expanding business and tourism opportunities. As the city spokesperson on economic development matters, you will create networks and be the point of contact for potential investors, commercial interests, brokers, and tourism partners. Your responsibilities will include preparing capital and operating budgets along with business forecasts. You will develop and maintain business, commercial, and tourism information databases in a variety of formats. As team leader, you will develop programs and partnerships with neighbouring communities to expand the economic base of our community.

Only university graduates in Business Administration or in related programs with emphasis on economic development, marketing, and/or tourism will be considered. Applicants must have five successful years of relevant experience in a municipal or public sector environment with experience developing promotional programs and related budgets for the expansion of business and tourism opportunities. Candidates must be proficient in a computerized environment and have highly effective communication and leadership skills.

Salary range:
$70 000 to $87 000 per annum

JOB SKILLS

Study the advertisement seeking a Director of Economic Development and Tourism Services shown in Figure 5.52.

a) Identify five key skills that are required by the successful applicant.

b) Outline three things that the Director is expected to do to promote tourism in the city.

c) Make one suggestion as to how the Director could expand tourism opportunities in the city.

Figure 5.52 An advertisement for a high-level position in tourism

UNIT 3

three

Tourism and Cultures

NORTH
AMERICA

Chapter 8:
Nova Scotia, Canada.
How has tourism
helped to protect
cultures?

An important part of many tourists' travel is to explore cultures. This unit investigates the attractiveness of culture as a motivator for tourism. It also looks at some of the issues that arise out of tourism's exploitation of culture. The unit deals with how tourism can provide the economic basis for sustaining cultures in many parts of the world.

Destinations You Will Visit

Chapter 6:
South Korea and Japan. In what ways do sporting events contribute to the importance of cultural tourism?

Chapter 7:
Goa, India. What are some problems that arise out of tourism for cultural purposes?

EUROPE

ASIA

AFRICA

Chapter 8:
Vietnam. What roles do governments play in shaping cultural tourism?

SOUTH AMERICA

AUSTRALIA

Chapter 7:
Makkah, Saudi Arabia. How is travel for religious reasons important for cultural tourism?

Chapter 8:
Australia. How has tourism helped to protect Aboriginal cultures?

CHAPTER SIX
Tourism and Culture

FOCUS ON THESE KEY QUESTIONS AND . . .

1. What is the relationship between culture and travel and tourism?
2. What are the different kinds of cultural tourism?
3. What are the positive and negative impacts of cultural tourism?
4. What are the positive and negative impacts of sports tourism?

KEY WORDS & TERMS

alternative tourism
cultural tourism
cultural transmission
culture
democratization
fully independent tourist (FIT)
heritage conservancy
high culture
mass tourism
popular culture
soccer hooligans
sports tourism
transculturation

Geography and Culture

When geographers talk about **culture**, they are referring to the various characteristics of life shared by a group of people in a particular community or nation. What you eat for dinner, how you spend your leisure time, what you learn in school, how the streets and roads in your city or town are organized, and what kinds of jobs you might hold in the future are all considered to be aspects of culture. The way that people in Asia grow their rice in terraced paddies and the way the Haida in British Columbia carve their crests on totem poles are also aspects of culture.

What aspects of culture are shown in the photographs in Figures 6.1 and 6.3?

Figure 6.1 An Inuit tent, Baker Lake, Nunavut; subway rush hour, Tokyo, Japan

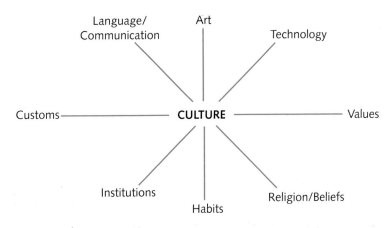

Figure 6.2 Copy this diagram in your notebook. Add branches to each of these characteristics to describe your particular culture. Compare your diagram with that of a classmate. How are your culture webs similar? How are they different?

Language/Communication — Art — Technology — Values — Religion/Beliefs — Habits — Institutions — Customs — **CULTURE**

Figure 6.3 Carpet makers at work, Agra, India; a street in Jaipur, India

Travel that focusses on learning about different cultures is known as **cultural tourism**. Many people travel to experience cultures that are different from their own. To learn more about cultural destinations, geographers study the reasons why cultures have developed differently.

This chapter examines some aspects of cultural tourism, focussing on the universal appeal of music and sports.

EXPECTATIONS

In this chapter, you will have the opportunity to

- demonstrate an understanding of the need to respect the cultural and religious traditions of others
- research and report on the economic, environmental, and cultural impacts of travel and tourism associated with international sporting events
- research and report on the role played by international organizations in encouraging interaction among peoples of the world
- classify different types of travel and tourism and explain the reasons why people travel
- explain how tourism-related development can have important impacts on human systems
- identify significant global tourist attractions
- identify recent trends in travel and tourism
- evaluate the impact of government policies on travel and tourism in a selected region
- explain how changes in technology cause change in travel and tourism patterns

Isolation and Integration

Geography has an impact on cultural development. Sometimes a culture is isolated from other cultures owing to geographic location. Many people in the rural mountain areas of Bolivia have little or no contact with people of different cultures. The cultural behaviour of these people is based on available natural resources for food and housing. Transportation is limited because they have few roads and even fewer cars. Electricity is scarce, and access to international radio and television is almost nonexistent. Their only exposure to international media might occur in Bolivian urban centres. For the most part, the Bolivian people maintain the traditions established by their ancestors.

Another culture may be situated so that the people have frequent contact with many people of different cultures. This group may *adopt* some aspects of culture from these different groups. The Caribbean represents a region that has had many cultural influences. The earliest inhabitants were Amerindians from South America. European colonists arrived in the fifteenth century. They, in turn, transported slaves from Africa. The cultural behaviours from these different ethnic groups have been integrated to create the new cultures we see in the region today.

In cases where one country has taken over another country by force, the people often must change the way they live. They must *adapt* to a new way of life or new culture. This change might occur over time, as in the case of Aboriginal peoples in Canada or the Aborigines in Australia. These people were forcibly moved onto reserves. Adoption of another culture might also occur over a shorter period of time, for example, when a country is defeated in a war.

Figure 6.4 How does this scene reflect cultural integration?

Figure 6.5 Cathy Freeman, an Olympic gold medallist in track-and-field, is an Aborigine. Why do you think she was chosen to light the Olympic flame in Sydney, Australia, at the 2000 Olympics?

The Grand Tour

Today, cultural tourism usually takes the form of either mass or alternative tourism, depending on personal preference. Have you ever heard the expression, "If this is Tuesday, this must be Rome"? **Mass tourism** involves organized movements of large groups of people to specialized tourist areas. An example would be a Mediterranean cruise with stops at designated ports. **Alternative tourism**, on the other hand, is individually planned activity to gain first-hand knowledge about local cultures and environments. People who arrange their own flights and accommodation according to their interests and schedules are engaging in alternative tourism.

VIRTUAL TRAVEL

www.irwinpublishing.com

To learn more about the sites in Figure 6.7, visit the Student Page for *Canada Travels*. Select one site and report to the class on why people would want to visit it.

High impact on the environment

Packaged tours

Little emphasis on local culture

Experiences and knowledge

MASS TOURISM OR ALTERNATIVE TOURISM

Souvenirs

Spontaneous decisions

Tourist impact on local culture

Careful preparation and research

Little or no planning

Figure 6.6 In your notebook, categorize these characteristics under the correct tourism heading.

Cultural tourism is not a recent phenomenon. In the eighteenth century, European aristocracy took the Grand Tour of Europe to "enrich the mind with knowledge." These travellers visited art galleries and historic sites, and attended lectures and concerts. They were a privileged few, travelling as much to increase their knowledge as to return home with tales to entertain their friends.

Figure 6.7 Which of these sites would you like to visit? Why?

Cultural Stops on the Grand Tour

Paris, France	Vienna, Austria	Rome, Italy	Lisbon, Portugal
Notre Dame Cathedral	St. Stephen's Cathedral	Vatican City/Sistine Chapel	Praça dos Restauradores
Pantheon	Hofburg	Arch of Tiberius	National Theatre
Hôtel des Invalides	Church of the Augustinian Friars	Colosseum	São Jorge Castle
Eiffel Tower	Central Cemetery	Roman Forum	Jerónimos Monastery
Bastille	State Opera House	Pantheon	Chapel of São João Baptista
Arc de Triomphe	Schönbrunn Palace	National Museum of Rome	Church of Santo Antonio da Sé
Louvre Museum	Rathaus	Trevi Fountain	Belém Tower
Paris Opera House	Ringstrasse	Campo dei Fiori	Sintra/Paço Real

Travel for All

The Industrial Revolution brought great improvements in transportation technology. With increased salaries and union-negotiated holidays, the ever-expanding middle class had more disposable income. Like the aristocracy, they, too, could begin to travel to distant countries.

Supporting businesses were established to help tourists on their journeys. Guidebooks produced by British travel agent Thomas Cook were specifically designed to help these new tourists make the most of their vacation time. Guidebooks are still a popular resource for travellers who want to know more about their destination before they arrive.

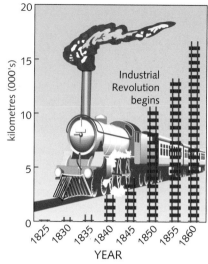

Source: The Peel Web, "Railway expansion," http://ds.dial.pipex.com/mbloy/peel/expans.htm (March 5, 2001).

Figure 6.8 Railway expansion in Britain, 1825–1860 increased tourism.

Figure 6.9 a) Excerpt from *Frommer's Guidebook*

a)

Juneau (JUNE-oh) hustles and bustles like no other city in Alaska. ... Even bears and eagles don't seem able to leave the place alone. Bears have always been a problem, wandering into town to dig through garbage and terrorize neighbors. And every couple of years an eagle makes off with a tourist's Chihuahua, making a snack of Fifi and reigniting a civic debate between those who laugh at the news and those who are outraged at such insensitivity to the tragedy.

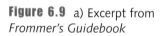

Attractions
- ⑫ Alaskan Brewing Company
- ④ Auke Bay Fisheries Laboratory
- ② Chapel by the Lake
- ① Mendenhall Glacier Visitor Center
- ⑪ Mendenhall Wetlands Refuge
- ③ University of Alaska-Southeast
- ⑭ To Ferry and Shrine of Ste. Thérèse

Accommodations
- ⑤ Best Western Country Lane Inn
- ⑥ Grandma's Featherbed B&B
- ⑦ Juneau Airport Travelodge
- ⑧ Super 8 Motel

Dining
- ⑩ Canton House
- ⑪ To Mike's
- ⑨ Vintage Fare Café

0   2 km

Source: Charles Wohlforth, Melissa Rivers, and Peter Oliver, *Frommer's Alaska*. New York: Simon and Schuster MacMillan Co., 2000, pp. 177, 179.

b)

Alaska's state capital has an air of modernity and progressiveness usually not found in the rural fishing villages of Southeast Alaska. It has always been on the cutting edge, starting out as one of the first major Alaskan gold mining centers. Accessible only by water and air, Juneau has happily avoided the urban sprawl that plagues Anchorage. The tourist industry, however, has had no problem establishing its presence: Juneau is the second busiest cruise ship port in the U.S., after Miami.

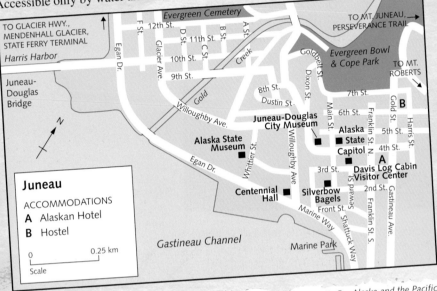

Source: Douglas Rand, ed., *Let's Go: Alaska and the Pacific Northwest 1999.*
New York: St. Martin's St. Press, 1999, pp. 498–499.

Figure 6.9 b) Excerpt from *Let's Go*. Which type of tourist might be attracted to Juneau by the description in a? By the description in b?

With the advent of flight in the twentieth century the number of tourists skyrocketed. For young people living in North America in the 1960s, the lure to Europe was strong. Many young people were curious about the homelands that many of their parents and grandparents had left as emigrants. Another draw was the fact that many of the top recording artists of the day, notably the Beatles and the Rolling Stones, were from Britain. With lower travel costs and an increase in the number of international flights, swarms of young people converged on London, England, and other European countries in search of the exotic.

Cultural Awareness

Dressed in blue jeans and T-shirts and carrying backpacks, North American youth flocked to icons of **popular culture**, such as Penny Lane and Carnaby Street in London, England, and the Latin Quarter and Left Bank in Paris, France. Popular culture or "pop culture" refers to the current cultural practices and activities of a society's general public. Examples include top hits on the recording charts, top television shows, and latest fashion fads.

***Travel* FACT**

In 1968, Lester B. Pearson International Airport (formerly Toronto International Airport) handled 200 800 aircraft movements. By 1999, the number of movements at the airport had more than doubled to 427 315.

These young people were also drawn to the British Museum, Royal Albert's Hall, and Buckingham Palace in London and the Uffizi Gallery in Florence, Italy. These are traditional places of **high culture** and include such activities as opera, ballet, and theatre.

Top Pop Singles, 1964	
"I Want to Hold Your Hand"	Beatles
"She Loves You"	Beatles
"A Hard Day's Night"	Beatles
"Love Me Do"	Beatles
"Do Wah Diddy Diddy"	Manfred Mann
"Please Please Me"	Beatles
"Little Children"	Billy J. Kramer and the Dakotas

Figure 6.10 Compare this list with today's top pop singles list. Does any one artist or group dominate the list today?

Figure 6.11 La Scala, the most important opera house in the world, is located in Milan, Italy. The museum attached to La Scala contains artifacts such as a collection of the works of composer Giuseppe Verdi.

While travelling in Europe, many young Canadians were introduced to the idea of staying at youth hostels. Hostels are low-cost lodgings that were first introduced in the 1930s by Richard Schirmann, a German teacher who recognized that the price of accommodations limited travel opportunities for many of his students.

In today's more affluent society there are even more travel opportunities for young people. Youth from around the world continue to follow pop cultural pursuits, from Pearl Jam concerts in Denmark to helicopter skiing in the Andes.

A developing trend in world tourism today is the growth in numbers of the **fully independent tourist (FIT)**. Hostelling International has responded to this market niche. Hostels provide reasonable accommodation for people of all ages. They promote cultural awareness and interaction among their guests. Many backpackers of the 1960s and 1970s remember the freedom of their youth. Personal connections made at hostels are often the essence of these memories. This demographic group, known as baby boomers, have raised their families and now have more leisure time and money. Rather than booking tour packages of 15

Figure 6.12 The Knappen House Youth Hostel in Winnipeg, Manitoba, was renamed the Ivey International Hostel in 1991, to honour the contributions of Grace Ivey, the founder of hostelling in Manitoba.

cities in 21 days or Caribbean cruises, these travellers want to renew their earlier experiences of travel freedom.

The **democratization** of travel, or travel for all, has resulted in more people visiting cultural destinations. Sharing a cup of coffee at a local restaurant, asking for help at a market, staying at a local hostel, or visiting a museum helps to break down cultural barriers. As we understand more about one another's culture, acceptance and respect are sure to follow.

Figure 6.13 Backpackers in Bangkok, Thailand, and the Tassili Plateau, Algeria. What characteristics do these travellers have in common?

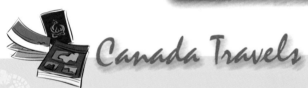

Canada Travels

In the 1970s, young people were also travelling to Canada. In response to their demand for inexpensive accommodation, the International Youth Hostelling Federation recruited Grace Ivey to establish summer hostels at the University of Manitoba. By 1980, the need for a permanent year-round hostel was evident.

Through the efforts of volunteers and grants, Knappen House Youth Hostel was opened. Today, budget travellers can choose from over 70 hostels across Canada, from modern downtown Vancouver to historic Halifax Heritage House.

" One of the many paths to enlightenment is the discovery of ourselves, and this can be achieved whenever one truly knows others who are different. "

– The Dance of Life
by Edward T. Hall

Dollars & Sense

Inexpensive ways of travelling in Europe include purchasing a Eurail pass before you leave home. This pass allows unlimited travel through 17 countries for a fixed period of time. By booking a sleeper at no extra cost, you can save money on accommodation and get to your next destination while you sleep.

Travel FACT

Today, the University of New Hampshire offers family hostel vacations. These learning vacations for families offer an assortment of programs aimed at those with special interests, an adventurous spirit, and a willingness to learn new things. Your itinerary might include the ancient cities and modern culture of Spain or learning vacations in England, the Netherlands, Wales, Austria, or France.

CHECK IN

1   In your own words, define cultural tourism.

2   a) What is the difference between mass and alternative tourism?
    b) List two examples of mass tourism and alternative tourism as they apply to cultural tourism.

3   a) How has the Grand Tour of the 1800s affected cultural tourism patterns today?
    b) How did technological improvements affect tourism?

4   Describe two tourist sites that reflect popular and high culture.

5   Under what category would you find a fully independent tourist – mass tourism or alternative tourism? Why?

VIRTUAL TRAVEL

www.irwinpublishing.com

Discover more about hostels and about travelling in Europe by visiting the Student Page for *Canada Travels*. Find out about the routes and times and costs between two major European cities. Try to compare rail and bus costs.

TECHNOLOGY and Tourism

"Virtual travel" presents one view of a country's culture. Tourist operators and governments want to inform, attract, and sell their product. Glossy versions are posted on the Internet. Critical analysis of these Web sites is important.

High Culture Appreciation

What do you think of when you hear the word "museum"? Do you think of artifacts, dinosaurs, mummies, paintings, or sculptures? Actually, all these things can be found in museums. The world is full of museums – art museums, community museums, and history museums, to name a few. Tourists of all ages and from all countries visit them. They also visit other cultural sites, such as temples and historic buildings around the world. The desire to explore the culture of the past by viewing timeless works of art and by visiting and appreciating great buildings is at the heart of cultural tourism.

Figure 6.14 The Parthenon in Athens, Greece. The temple for the goddess Athena on the Acropolis was completed in 432 BCE. It is considered the finest example of Doric architecture in the world. Why do you think tourists might want to visit this site?

VIRTUAL TRAVEL

www.irwinpublishing.com

Take a virtual tour of the Louvre or the Hermitage museum by visiting the Student Page for *Canada Travels*. Report on a specific work of art that appeals to you.

Culture Promoters

Art galleries and museums around the world have responded to the demands of visitors to improve their facilities and present unique shows. More than $1.1 billion was spent on refurbishing the Louvre in Paris, France, while new art galleries have been opened recently in Hong Kong, China, San Francisco, California, and Bilbao, Spain. The introduction of blockbuster shows, such as Monet at the Chicago Art Institute, the Egyptian Art of the Pyramids at the Royal Ontario Museum, and the Monet/Renoir and the Impressionist Landscape at the National Gallery in Ottawa, has increased the number of visitors to these venues. Selling high culture has led to the development of short-stay cultural tourism. People are attracted to an exhibit through packages offering reduced ticket prices, discounted hotel rooms, and other attractive offers. The tourism industry in any location supports these shows due to the economic benefits for hotels, restaurants, and stores.

Critics of these larger-than-life exhibits believe that the economic aspects have overridden the cultural aspects. Selling tickets for specific time periods allows the optimum number of visitors to see

Figure 6.15 The most popular event was also the event that was open for the shortest period of time. Why do you think Treasures of Tutankhamen attracted so many visitors?

Canada's Top Five Blockbuster Shows

Event	Location	Attendance
Treasures of Tutankhamen	Art Gallery of Ontario (1979)	750 000
From Cézanne to Matisse: Great Paintings from the Barnes Foundation	Art Gallery of Ontario (1994)	600 000
Pablo Picasso: Meeting in Montreal	Montreal Museum of Fine Arts (1985)	517 000
Leonardo Da Vinci, Engineer and Architect	Montreal Museum of Fine Arts (1987)	436 419
Egyptian Art in the Age of the Pyramid	Royal Ontario Museum (2001)	370 000

Source: Adapted from Martin Knelman, "Blockbuster Summer," *The Toronto Star*, June 3, 2001, D10.

Figure 6.16 The Montreal Museum of Fine Arts opened in 1860 as the Art Association of Montreal. Today this world-famous gallery attracts tourists from around the world.

the show. Unfortunately, this practice often results in limiting the amount of time that people can spend at an exhibit. They spend more time in line and less time in the gallery.

Saving the Past

Preservation of important cultural and natural environments is known as **heritage conservancy**. Heritage is a broad concept that includes landscapes, historic places, natural sites, built environments, collections, and experiences. In other words, heritage is the oral and written history and the traditions of a location as well as its buildings and cities. Host communities and visitors alike can benefit from the preservation of important cultural and natural environments.

Acid rain and vandalism are just two of the human activities that can threaten cultural environments. The International Council on Monuments and Sites (ICOMOS) is concerned with safeguarding and conserving important heritage sites and ensuring that people are educated about the importance of maintaining monuments. In the proposed International Cultural Tourism Charter, the ICOMOS states its goal, "to facilitate and encourage the tourism industry to promote and manage tourism in ways that respect and enhance the heritage and living cultures of host communities." The World Monuments Fund lists monuments around the world that are in danger. They collaborate with citizen groups in different countries to save important sites.

Other international groups, such as UNESCO, support the goals of these organizations to ensure the preservation of heritage sites.

Interact

To what extent do you think you have an ethical responsibility to learn about and respect the cultural beliefs and practices in the tourist destinations you intend to visit?

Figure 6.17 (From left to right) The Taj Mahal, Agra, India; historical pageantry at Louisbourg, Nova Scotia, Canada; the Church of the Resurrection of Christ (Saviour on the Blood), St. Petersburg, Russia. Whose heritage do these sites represent? Why would other people be interested in visiting these sites?

Figure 6.18 The Alexander Column in the middle of Palace Square in St. Petersburg, Russia, is a monument to the Russian military victory against Napoleon.

www.irwinpublishing.com

Take a virtual tour of St. Petersburg and visit the Alexander Palace by going to the Student Page for *Canada Travels*. What aspects of heritage would attract tourists to this city? Write a short descriptive paragraph of your favourite rooms in the Alexander Palace in St. Petersburg.

Figure 6.19 What impact might these statistics have on choosing Russia as a place to visit?

Conserving Russia's Past

In Russia, years of neglect following the Russian Revolution, two world wars, and the cold war left most palaces and heritage buildings in a state of disrepair. Since the formation of the Russian Federation and the opening of borders to tourism in the early 1990s, there have been extensive renovations to these buildings in an effort to attract more visitors. International agencies such as the World Bank have approved a US$31 million loan to rehabilitate the central core of St. Petersburg, Russia, to boost the economy of that city. Alexander Palace in St. Petersburg was renovated with assistance from the World Monuments Fund.

Past versus Present   Many Russian citizens question the expenditure of funds that focus on the past. In a country where many people are struggling to make ends meet, they believe the present is more relevant. They consider their greatest problem to be receiving a regular salary. Many key workers – for example, bus drivers, doctors (bus drivers earn more), and other government employees – often are not paid for months at a time. Even those people who are concerned with heritage conservation and work full time in state-owned galleries and museums grumble about large capital expenditures when they have not received a paycheque for several months.

Statistics for Russia, 2001
• Population – 148.3 million
• Range of annual salaries – Can$1135 to Can$10 726
• Average annual salary – Can$3191
• Percentage of population that live below poverty level – 33%
• Infant mortality rate per 1000 live births – 16.5
• Access to clean water – 50%
• International aid per capita in 1995 – Can$16.51
• International aid per capita in 1998 – Can$10.45
• Number of children in orphanages – 600 000
• Number of street children – 600 000

Source: Adapted from World Bank, World Development Indicators Database <www.worldbank.org>

Figure 6.20 The Winter Palace in St. Petersburg, Russia, is a UNESCO World Heritage Site.

TECHNOLOGY and Tourism

What do actor John Travolta, sex therapist Dr. Ruth, singer Mick Jagger, and former South African President Nelson Mandela have in common? All have travelled in the luxury of a Cunard liner. *Queen Elizabeth II*, Cunard's flagship, carries on the tradition of Grand Tour luxury cruising established in the 1830s. Today, clients can improve their cultural knowledge by booking a "themed voyage," with programs that educate people about what they will see on their shore excursions.

CHECK IN

1 a) List one argument in support of and one argument against blockbuster shows at galleries and museums.
   b) How do these shows have an impact on the tourist industry?

2 What role does heritage conservation play in attracting tourists to a location?

3 Identify a cultural environment in your community that you feel qualifies for heritage conservancy. Explain why.

VIRTUAL TRAVEL

www.irwinpublishing.com

Visit the Cunard theme voyages by going to the Student Page for *Canada Travels*. Record two types of themed voyages and suggest who might want to book each cruise.

The Music of Cultures

Music may not be the international language, but it is an aspect of culture that most people can recognize readily. They may not appreciate the sounds of a Caribbean steel band, Indian classical sitar, Chinese jiangnan sizhu (chamber group of winds and strings), or the latest hip-hop star, but they do recognize that it is music.

Figure 6.21 Try to identify regions of the world where each instrument might have originated.

Every culture has a unique music that is related to its development. The music of a culture can be an attraction for tourists to visit various world regions.

Music and Travel

We experience a wide variety of musical styles owing to improved communications, technology, and travel. Satellite technology brings us the current Chinese pop stars and the music of Iran. North American popular music influences many African, Asian, and European styles.

When we travel, our exposure to different sounds is as significant as what we see. Whether you are sitting around a swimming pool in Cancun, Mexico, listening to the sound of a mariachi band, or vacationing at the Mozart Festival in Salzburg, Austria, music has a strong connection to tourism. Music festivals around the world have multiplied in recent years and have become an integral part of cultural tourism.

Figure 6.22 What type of music would you expect to hear if you were attending these events? What does the music tell you about the culture?

These festivals provide the host community a chance to share its identity with visitors as well as to reinforce the existence of different communities within a country. In turn, visitors may photograph the concert and buy recordings to take home. Friends may listen to this music, look for the same type of music at a local music store, or book a holiday to the country of origin.

We may also influence the music of a country that we are visiting. There is no faster way to meet people than to play a few tunes around a campfire or at a coffee shop. Even if your musical talent is restricted to being able to put a CD in a player, you are able to share your music with the people in the countries you visit.

Cultural transmission refers to the meeting of different cultures. Read the letter in Figure 6.24 on the next page to find out how cultural transmission is reflected in Paucartambo's festival.

World Music

One result of increased tourism and the intermingling of cultures is the growing interest in world music.

The term **transculturation** is used to describe the integration of different styles of music. Transculturation occurs when an exotic form of music, usually from a developing country, is processed and sold in the developed world. The globalization of the music industry has led many people to be concerned about maintaining traditional styles of music as well as wanting to ensure that local musicians can benefit by selling their work.

Supporters of world music say that we all benefit from this globalization of music. The development of innovative techniques, cross-fertilization, and integration of musical styles help to improve the art form and appreciation of other cultures.

Figure 6.23 *Cape Verde* is a CD that represents the globalization of music.

Figure 6.24

July 15–18

Hi, Olga and Dan —

You cannot believe how relieved we are finally to have arrived at Paucartambo, Peru. You know how anxious we were to attend the festival for the town's patron saint, Virgen del Carmen.

It is crowded here, with many visitors from nearby Quechua-speaking indigenous communities who have come to watch. The town looks freshly whitewashed and is very clean. The festival participants are from the town itself and are mestizos, people of mixed Spanish and indigenous cultural heritage. It seems during the colonial period, missionaries used music and costumed dances to attract the indigenous peoples to Christianity. This festival seems to combine the celebration of the Catholic saint and the indigenous harvest ritual. I also have to add that the shopkeepers were an integral part of the festivities with their brightly coloured signs.

I think there were about 12 different dance ensembles that represented the stories of the town and its people. It was hard to keep track! The "home team" was the Chunchos, the rich, powerful, and civilized jungle Indians. They wore feathered headdresses and carried spears. The "uncivilized" outsiders were the Qollas, who were traders from the Peruvian high plateau. They were a riot. They led (symbolically, of course) their llamas in and out of stores, upsetting goods, and were generally very unruly. I heard that according to one legend the Qollas tried to steal the statue of the Virgen del Carmen. Of course, their plans are stopped by the Chunchos, the heroes.

Other characters are also central to the meaning of the fiesta. The Saqras (devils) wore blond wigs and their clothes represented the colonial Spanish. Their monster masks were scary. Do you think that they were trying to tell us something about the devils who arrived in ships in the 1500s? The Doctores represented the corrupt government officials and lawyers. As they moved through the streets, they frequently tried to capture and beat visitors from the local indigenous communities with their large law books. Other dancers played the parts of the slaves who were brought during the colonial period, the Chuk'chus or malaria carriers from the jungle, and the Majenos, exploitive liquor traders from a local city.

One group that I was totally shocked to see were those dancers dressed up like young tourists with their backpacks and floppy hats. They were always trying to stick their toy cameras into people's faces as they moved through the crowd. It seemed like everyone turned and laughed with us when they passed by.

All through the procession, different kinds of music were being played. The European colonists introduced the violin and brass instruments. These, along with the traditional Andean flutes, were all played during the fiesta as each dance ensemble had its own band. A few younger musicians also had electric guitars. You cannot believe the overall sound impact!

Cheers,
Barry

Source: Adapted from Bruno Nettl, et al., *Excursions in World Music*, 2nd ed. Upper Saddle River, NJ: Prentice Hall, 1997, pp. 223–229.

1. a) Explain how geographic location affects the development of musical styles.
    b) How are differing musical styles a tourist attraction?

2. a) How has tourism led to an interest in world music?
    b) Do you think this development is positive or negative? Give reasons for your answer.

3. Sketch a diagram that shows cultural transmission of different groups on the Peruvian festival described in the letter in Figure 6.24.

Interact

Is culture just another commodity to be bought and sold by the tourist industry?

Sports Tourism

Sports are considered to be the world's largest social phenomenon. In many countries, travelling to watch or to participate in sporting events is open to all levels of society.

Sporting events help us to

- be entertained
- show and feel emotions
- learn about cultural beliefs and values
- feel part of a group
- express national pride
- participate with people of different interests and social classes

Sports are a part of culture. They reflect values and lifestyle. Many tourist activities are related to sporting events.

Canada Travels

Active Canadian sports tourists are usually
- males and females 20–34 years of age
- university educated
- earn $40 000+
- from Ontario and British Columbia

Figure 6.25 What do these photographs tell you about these sports fans?

More Than Just a Game

Many sporting events attract large numbers of spectators, media, technical personnel, coaches, and officials from a variety of locations. Travel that focusses on these types of sporting events is known as **sports tourism**. The Olympic Games, the Pan-American Games, and the World Cup are some diverse examples of sports tourism opportunities. Sports tourists are individuals who spend their vacations to participate in or attend a sports event. In 1998, 37% of the world's 73.7 million travellers were sports tourists.

The Benefits   Political and economic leaders from around the world have embraced this interaction between sports and tourism. As hosts to the world, political leaders see the chance to show their guests what their country or city has to offer. A smoothly run event offers visitors a positive experience. They might return to that location or encourage their friends to visit. Most of the money used to build infrastructure projects, such as swimming pools and arenas, comes from taxes. If the citizens of an event site believe they have benefited from a sporting event, they may vote for a particular politician again. Popularizing the event and getting people to support such events are essential. International events help to put a country on the world map and can lead to other economic and cultural partnerships.

Economic leaders support large-scale sporting events to provide economic stimulation. Often, large-scale facilities must be constructed or existing facilities upgraded. Construction stimulates growth because of the large number of "ingredients" required and the number and variety of tradespeople that need to be hired. Owners of offshoot businesses, such as accommodation, restaurants, theatres, and concert halls, can all benefit. New markets can also be developed.

www.irwinpublishing.com

Visit the Olympic site on the Student Page for *Canada Travels* and view the Olympic Charter. Select one other fundamental principle that supports the Olympic holistic view of sports.

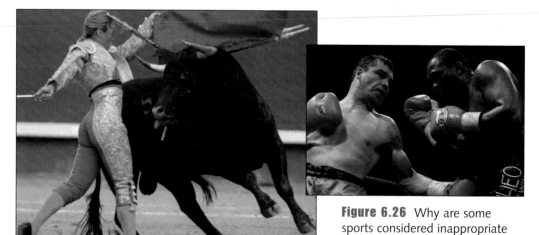

Figure 6.26 Why are some sports considered inappropriate by members of some cultures and attractions for others?

Figure 6.27 The Ski Jump Complex of Canada Olympic Park was built for the 1988 Winter Olympics held in Calgary, Alberta. The complex operates year round and actually gets more use in summer than in winter.

CHECK IN

1 Why is sports tourism a growing trend?

2 Explain the demographic of the "sports tourist."

LOOKING AT ISSUES

South Korea/Japan – 2002 FIFA World Cup

Issue: What action should the government of a host country take to protect fans and tourism from soccer hooliganism?

In 2002, for the first time in history, two countries will co-host soccer's most prestigious event. The 17th World Cup will be held in South Korea and Japan. The opening match will be played in Seoul, Korea; Yokohama, Japan, will stage the final match of the competition. The World Cup, which is held every four years, is so popular that countries bid on hosting the event, much as they do for the Olympics.

On February 15, 2001, ticket applications began for World Cup 2002. For the matches to be played in Japan, alone, about 1.35 million tickets were available. About half of these were allotted to official sponsors and the Japanese public. It is not easy to get a ticket for a World Cup match. You cannot just walk up to a kiosk and buy a ticket. Fans, both in the host countries and overseas, must apply for tickets. The lucky winners are then decided in a lottery.

In 1998, the event was held in France. During the eliminations, 32 teams played 62 matches in 10 cities. Imagine the number of francs that sports tourists must have spent for accommodation, transportation, food, and beverages. There was another bonus for the French when their team beat Brazil, the reigning champions, 3–0, to win the World Cup for the first time. The World Cup will be held in Germany in 2006.

Figure 6.28 Location of Korea and Japan

VIRTUAL TRAVEL

www.irwinpublishing.com

After the 2002 FIFA World Cup has taken place, visit the Student Page for *Canada Travels* for an update on the actual events.

Figure 6.29
French soccer fans celebrate in July 1998 after the French team defeated Brazil 3–0 in the final match of the World Soccer Cup in Paris.

Figure 6.30 This is the official trademark for the 2002 World Cup. Do you think this design is appropriate? Explain.

The Good News

During the four-year period between World Cup matches, teams from 201 countries in the six divisions of FIFA (Fédération Internationale de Football Association) compete to qualify for the big event. The six divisions are Europe, Oceania, South America, Asia, Africa, and CONCACAF (Canada's division). Many Canadians, whose heritages lie in nations from around the world, have renewed their nationalistic spirit through watching television coverage of these matches.

In June 2000, globalization of the communications industry benefited Canadian soccer fans. TSN and CTV's sports network amalgamated and were able to televise 31 matches live with half-hour preview shows. During Euro 2000, a mini World Cup, for the UEFA division, soccer fever was as obvious in some Canadian neighbourhoods as it was in the countries that had teams playing.

With increased mobility, soccer fans are also able to see games live. They can keep up with team rivalries in the news, visit the Web sites of their favourite athletes, and join chat rooms to talk about the games with people from around the world.

Figure 6.31 A Canadian soccer fan shows support for the Iranian team during an exhibition match in Toronto in 1997; Indian workers in New Delhi take time off to watch a live broadcast of the World Cup finals via satellite, 1998.

The Bad News

Soccer also has a negative side. In addition to the violent incidents listed in Figure 6.33, other tragedies, such as hailstorms, fires, and air disasters, have cost fans and players their lives.

When British fans stampeded at a soccer game in 1989, people around the world were disgusted. The press and security forces began to use the term **soccer hooligans** to describe those people who use soccer matches as an excuse to commit acts of violence against fans of other teams. European soccer experts explain that the fans feel so nationalistic and so intense about their teams that they cannot control their emotions. Many fans agree that they are very proud of their teams, but they deny that they are the problem. Nonetheless, soccer fans in some countries are considered "fanatics" in other countries.

Before the 1994 World Cup was held in the United States, law enforcement and other emergency planners in that country held training simulations for riot and crowd control. Some security and counter-terrorist experts were concerned that with its past history of violence, the World Cup presented an opportunity for planned terrorist activities. Police and emergency officials prepared for such situations. Although fan violence did erupt, no one was killed.

In an attempt to maintain order at Euro 2000, the authorities took early precautions. The German government advised citizens not to attend the event. British police forces shared information about the movements of British fans who had criminal records with Dutch and Belgian authorities, but did not ban these individuals from leaving the country. Riot police in Belgium and the Netherlands prepared for the worst.

> **"**These people who engage in these appalling acts of hooliganism and violence – they have no place in our national way of life at all. They disgrace our national way of life.**"**
>
> – Tony Blair,
> British Prime Minister

Figure 6.32 Greek riot police officers stare at a fire set by fans during a soccer game

Soccer Violence		
Date	Location	Incident
October 20, 1982	Moscow, USSR	• 340 people killed at a European Cup match; police forced fans down an icy staircase before the end of the match; exiting fans tried to re-enter when a late goal was scored
May 29, 1985	Brussels, Belgium	• 39 people killed at European Champions Cup Final when riots broke out, collapsing a wall that separated rival fans of England's Liverpool and Italy's Juventus of Turin teams
March 10, 1987	Tripoli, Libya	• 20 people killed when panic-stricken fans fleeing knife-wielding ruffians collapsed a wall
April 15, 1989	Sheffield, England	• 95 people killed and 170 injured when police opened gates and the rush of people onto already filled sections trapped fans against riot control fences around the field
January 13, 1991	Orkney, South Africa	• 42 people trampled or crushed to death along riot-control fences when panicking fans tried to escape brawls in the grandstand
June 16, 1996	Lusaka, Zambia	• 12 fans crushed to death and 52 injured in stampede following World Cup qualifying game
October 16, 1996	Guatemala City, Guatemala	• 84 killed and 180 injured trying to squeeze into stadium; 50 000 fans had tickets for a stadium designed to hold 35 000; forgery was suspected
July 10, 2000	Harare, Zimbabwe	• 13 trampled to death and many injured when police responded to crowd violence with tear gas
April 11, 2001	Johannesburg, South Africa	• 43 killed in stampede during a soccer match as 30 000 fans outside tried to push into the stadium already filled to capacity with 70 000 fans

Figure 6.33 Soccer-related violence occurs all the time. These incidents represent only the most major incidents. How might this information affect tourists' views about attending soccer matches?

Source: Adapted from No Violence, "The World of Violence," <http://www.noviolence.com/Archives/engl_mundo.html> (February 24, 2001) and Jamie Fellrath, "A History of Major Disasters and Tragedies", <http://worldsoccer.about.com/sports/worldsoccer/library/weekly/aa022100b.htm> (February 24, 2001).

The Dilemma

The violence associated with soccer matches also affects cultural tourists. On February 15, 2001, in Rome, Italy, Liverpool fans tossed a Japanese tourist and two Bangladeshi street vendors into the Trevi Fountain, one of Rome's most-visited tourist sites. In that same incident of hooliganism, four fans were stabbed, and a gang of about 30 people kicked and punched a cameraman and a reporter for an Associated Press Television News crew.

Cultural tourists, if they are aware that a World Cup is being held in a particular country, may hesitate to visit that country while the matches are ongoing. Nonetheless, tourism dollars and future promotional opportunities that are tied to soccer victories are substantial. Before a country bids to stage the next World Cup, perhaps it should compare the revenue that cultural tourism generates with the potential revenue from sports tourism to determine which benefits the country more.

Travel FACT

A digital photo scan was taken of every fan entering the stadium for the 2001 Super Bowl. Anyone who was recognized as having a criminal background was refused entry, even if that fan had a ticket.

Figure 6.34 French riot police take position moments before the end of a match between Iran and the United States, Paris, 1998. Iran won 2–1.

Figure 6.35 Buildings in Seoul, Korea, use room lights to form "2002," celebrating the co-hosting of the 2002 World Cup soccer finals with Japan.

CHECK IN

1 a) What actions would you recommend that a host country take to protect fans and tourists from soccer hooliganism?

2 a) Identify the stakeholders involved in this issue.
   b) How might one of these stakeholders regard soccer hooliganism?

3 Why would countries or cities compete to host major soccer competitions knowing the security costs and the potential for violence?

- apply geotechnologies to a study of regional geography
- produce and interpret different types of maps, graphic organizers, and diagrams
- communicate effectively in written, oral, and visual forms
- identify selected factors that influence travellers' destination choices
- demonstrate an understanding that the travel and tourism industry consists of many interconnected components

Hostelling It Through Canada's Maritimes

Purpose: To use ArcView to take a virtual bike trip through Canada's Maritime Provinces, staying at hostels along the way.

Files: province.shp, roads.shp

Functions: View Properties, Create a Table, Add an Event Theme, Convert to Shapefile, Legend Editor (Symbol Edit), Geoprocessing (Merge Themes), Query Builder, Legend Editor (Unique Value), Create a Theme, Legend Editor (Graduated Symbol), Table Edit, Calculate a Field, Layout.

Every year over 4 million people see the world through youth hostels under the auspices of Hostelling International. In Canada alone there are over 70 hostels coast to coast that are members of Hostelling International. In this activity, you will be creating a map showing the location and features of the hostels found in the Maritime Provinces of Canada. For more information on hostelling and/or on hostelling in Canada, refer to the Student Page for *Canada Travels* at <www.irwinpublishing.com>.

1. Your first step will be to create a blank View, name it "Hostelling in the Maritimes," and change the Map Units to "decimal degrees" and the Distance Units to "kilometres."

2. Next, create a new Table, called "Hostels.dbf," containing the fields and records shown in the table on the next page.

3. Create a new View and add the table you have just created as an Event Theme. Turn on Hostels.dbf theme.

4. Add a provinces theme to your View, c:\esri\esridata\canada\province.shp. Turn on the Province.shp theme and make it active. Using the Select Feature tool and Shift key, select New Brunswick, Nova Scotia, and Prince Edward Island. Convert these to a shapefile called "The Maritimes." Delete the original Provinces.shp theme and turn on The Maritimes.shp theme.

5. Use the Legend Editor to make the Province.shp theme transparent.

6. Add a New Brunswick roads theme to your View: x:\nb\roads.shp. Convert this theme to a shapefile, naming it "NB Roads," then delete the original Roads.shp theme. Repeat this step for the Nova Scotia roads (x:\ns\roads.shp) and the PEI roads (x:\pe\roads.shp).

Place	Latitude	Longitude	Name	Open	Cost	Beds	Kitchen	Laundry
Alma, NB	45.59	–64.95	Alma–Fundy National Park Hostel	summer	12	20	yes	no
Annapolis Royal, NS	44.74	–65.51	South Milford–Sandy Bottom Lake	summer	8	9	yes	yes
Barrington, NS	43.57	–65.58	Barrington Hostel	summer	10	10	no	yes
Campbellton, NB	48.00	–66.68	Campbellton Lighthouse Youth Hostel	summer	12	20	yes	yes
Charlottetown, PEI	46.24	–63.14	Charlottetown Hostel	summer	14	50	yes	no
Fredericton, NB	45.94	–66.66	Fredericton International Hostel at Rosary Hall	all year	16	40	yes	yes
Halifax, NS	44.60	–63.60	Halifax Heritage House Hostel	all year	18	75	yes	yes
Miramichi, NB	47.00	–65.56	Governor's Mansion	all year	18	9	yes	no
Nelson, NB	46.99	–65.55	Nelson–Brebeuf Manor	all year	15	24	yes	yes
Nova Scotia's South Shore	44.28	–64.35	LaHave Marine Hostel	summer	11	8	yes	no
Saint John, NB	45.26	–66.07	YMCA-YWCA	all year	20	13	no	yes
South Central NS	44.56	–65.39	Raven Haven Hostel	summer	12	6	yes	no
St. Peters, PEI	45.66	–60.89	St. Peters–Summer Joyce's Motel and Cottages	summer	12	6	yes	yes
Wentworth, NS	45.63	–63.55	Wentworth Hostel	all year	11	24	yes	no

7. Turn on the Geoprocessing Extension, then use the Geoprocessing Wizard to merge the NB roads.shp, NS roads.shp, and the PEI roads.shp themes into one theme called "Maritime Roads." Delete the original Roads.shp themes and turn on the new Roads.shp theme.

8. Use the Query Builder to highlight all roads that are "Multilane Expressways," "Principal Highways," or "Secondary Highways." Convert these to a shapefile called "Highways." Delete the original Roads.shp theme and turn on the new Highways.shp theme.

9. Using the Legend Editor, apply a "Unique Value" legend type to the Highways.shp theme. Change the symbol for "Multilane Expressway" to a width of "2" and the colour red, "Principal Highway" to a width of "2" and the colour orange, and "Secondary Highway" to a width of "1" and the colour yellow.

10. In the View Properties, change the Map Units to "Decimal Degrees" and the Map Units to "kilometres."

11. Assume that you have flown to Halifax, Nova Scotia, and are planning to experience the Maritimes by biking to each hostel. Create a new line theme to represent the route you will follow, starting and ending in Halifax. Select an appropriate line type, size, and colour to represent your route. Note the distance in the bottom left-hand corner of the line theme you have just digitized. How far did you travel?

12. Using the Legend Editor, apply a "Unique Value" legend type using "Open" field to show which hostels are open only in the summer. Repeat for the "Kitchen" field, then the "Laundry" field. How could these maps be useful to you when you are taking this bike trip?

13. Using the Legend Editor, apply a "Graduated Symbol" Technique using the "Cost" field. Repeat for the "Beds" field. How could these maps be useful to you when you are taking this bike trip?

14. Assume that you spend two nights in each hostel. Add a new field called "Total Cost" to the Hostels.shp attribute table. Use the Calculate function to calculate the values for this field (i.e., Total Cost = Cost × 2). Call up the Field Statistics and record the sum of this field. This is the total amount of money that you will spend on accommodations for the entire four-week trip! What a great deal!

15. Return to your View. Using the Legend Editor, change the legend type for the Hostels.shp theme to "Single Symbol." Then, change the symbol of the Hostels.dbf theme to an appropriate type, size, and colour. (You may want to load another palette to find an appropriate symbol type.)

16. Create a layout of your map, complete with an appropriate title, north arrow, legend, and scale bar.

Extension:

Visit the Student Page for *Canada Travels* at <www.irwinpublishing.com> to locate pictures and descriptions of the various hostels. Download the pictures and create text files of the descriptions. Create hot links from the hostels to the pictures and to the text files.

Create a virtual tour of the Maritimes! Visit various tourism Web sites and/or consult various tourism publications. Download or scan pictures of features that you would encounter along your bike route and capture the unique culture of the region. Hot link these to the map. Also, write a colourful reflection or a daily journal that highlights the unique attractions, events, and people that you encountered on your bike trip. Create a text file and hot link it to your map.

Add the places theme to your View again and select an appropriate site for a new hostel. Create a text file describing why you feel that a hostel is necessary at this site and hot link it to your map.

Figure 6.36 Lunenburg, Nova Scotia, is a designated UNESCO World Heritage site. The streets as they were laid out in 1753 still exist today. The same craftspeople who built the town's fishing ships also built many of its houses and commercial buildings.

REVISIT THE chapter 6
Looking Back

Understanding the Concepts

1. Explain how important themes in geography such as location, movement, and interaction influence cultural development. Give an example of each.

2. a) Explain the difference between popular and high culture.
   b) List two challenges for the tourist industry related to each aspect of culture.

3. Describe the factors that contributed to the democratization of travel.

4. Describe how a destination might benefit from sports tourism.

Figure 6.37 A dance performance in Kuala Lumpur, Malaysia

Practising Your Skills

5. Plan an itinerary for a two-week vacation in three cities. Include activities that reflect high culture, pop culture, and sports tourism. Remember to include travel time to and from your destinations.

6. Select a cultural event in your area. Find out how the promoters plan to attract tourists to the event. Present your findings in a report.

7. Sketch a flow chart showing the effects of hosting a large-scale sporting event on human systems, such as transportation, and travel patterns.

Applying Your Skills

8. What aspects of Canadian culture would you like visitors to know? Prepare a photo essay on Canadian culture by collecting a number of images either from magazines or from your personal collection to answer this question.

9. Select a site that reflects your community's culture. Design an advertising flyer to promote this site that will include a map showing the location and route to the site, a slogan, and a logo.

10. Stampedes resulting in deaths and injuries have also occurred at rock concerts – in Cincinnati, Ohio, in 1979, in Minsk, Belarus, in 1999, and in Roskilde, Denmark, in June 2000. Research one of these incidents, or another of your choosing, and compare the economic impact of rock concerts and World Cup events.

Thinking Like a Tourist

11. Part of the fun of travelling is telling people about your adventures either as you move around by sending postcards, by e-mail, or by telephone. Assume that you are on holiday and have just heard some great live music. You want to tell your friends how the music affected you. Your task is to prepare a three-minute audiotape describing where you are. Some examples might be a musical campaign for human rights in Chile, a hip-hop song encouraging young people to stay in school in New York City, or an early music festival held as a fundraiser at an archaeological dig in Riga.

Follow these steps in preparing your audio report:

- Research the country to find out basic geographical information so you can describe your location.

- Research a musical group. Start by visiting the World Music section in a music store and listening to programs like "Global Village: The News of the World in the World of Music" on CBC Radio.

- Write a short script for your report. In your script, identify yourself and your location, and describe what you see and the focus of your experience.

- Provide some ambiance with props, background noise, or a short clip of the music to engage the listener.

JOB SKILLS

Figure 6.38 Being able to collaborate with others on special projects is an essential skill in today's work world.

The tourist industry requires that employees be able to "recognize and respect people's diversity, individual differences and perspectives." Being proficient at asking questions to clarify others' ideas, developing a project plan, and following through on your assigned tasks are ways to ensure success. Work with a partner to develop and carry out an interview with a travel professional. Develop a checklist of positive behaviours that people could use to show respect for individual differences.

CHAPTER seven 7²
Cultural Differences

FOCUS ON THESE KEY QUESTIONS AND . . .

1. What factors influence destination choices?
2. Why does the demonstration effect occur?
3. What factors contribute to the clash of cultures?
4. How do tourist activities contribute to the exploitation of people?

KEY WORDS & TERMS

commodification
demonstration effect
pilgrimage
proximity
socio-cultural characteristics
tourist arrivals
trickle down

Global Destination Patterns

People choose to travel to particular locations for a variety of reasons. As you have seen, some people prefer natural environments, while others like to visit urban centres. There are other factors that have an impact on the destination choices of travellers. One of these factors is **proximity**, or closeness.

Travel costs and the time involved to reach distant destinations make proximity a consideration for some people in choosing a destination. Did you know that 80% of all international tourists are citizens of just 20 countries? Since the majority of global tourists live in North America and Europe, destinations on these continents are more likely choices for these tourists than destinations on continents such as Africa or Asia (see Figures 7.1 and 7.2).

		World's Top 10 Tourist Destinations		
Rank 1990	Rank 1999	Country	1999 Arrivals (millions)	Market (%) of Share
1	1	France	73.0	11.0
3	2	Spain	51.8	7.8
2	3	United States	48.5	7.3
4	4	Italy	36.1	5.4
12	5	China	27.0	4.1
7	6	United Kingdom	25.7	3.9
10	7	Canada	19.6	3.0
8	8	Mexico	19.2	2.9
17	9	Russian Federation	18.5	2.8
27	10	Poland	17.9	2.7

Figure 7.1 According to rank, which country has had the greatest increase in arrivals since 1990? Which countries have decreased?

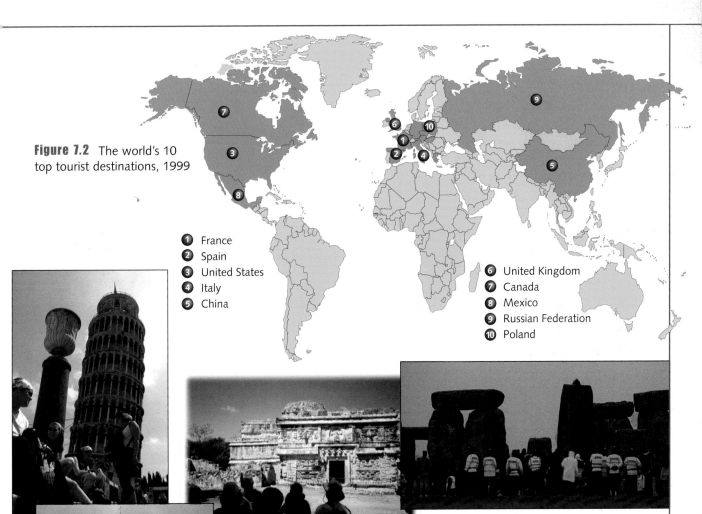

Figure 7.2 The world's 10 top tourist destinations, 1999

1. France
2. Spain
3. United States
4. Italy
5. China

6. United Kingdom
7. Canada
8. Mexico
9. Russian Federation
10. Poland

Figure 7.3 Identify the countries in which each of these photographs was taken.

EXPECTATIONS

In this chapter, you will have the opportunity to

- analyze global tourist flows and explain the reasons for the observed patterns
- analyze the effects of cultural, economic, and political motivators and barriers on travel and tourism patterns
- explain how a tourist activity may contribute to the exploitation of people
- explain the demonstration effect, in which tourists' values and practices replace local values and practices
- identify significant global tourist attractions
- demonstrate an understanding of the need to respect the cultural and religious traditions of others
- demonstrate an understanding that cultural conflicts may result from the interactions of people around the world
- identify recent trends in travel and tourism
- produce a case study analyzing the impact of the demonstration effect in a selected tourism region

Identifying Patterns

The most straightforward way of identifying patterns of tourist destinations is to count the number of tourists who enter a country. This is a measurement called **tourist arrivals**. Figure 7.1 on page 180 shows that European countries dominate the list of top destinations. These places have enviable combinations of interesting and exciting natural environments and historical and cultural attractions. France, which has long held the top spot, is a popular vacation destination for Europeans from across the continent, as well as for North Americans and others.

Figure 7.1 also points out that the United States, Canada, and Mexico are popular destinations for tourists. You may have noticed that China is the only Asian destination in the Top 10 in 1999. China has had rapid growth in arrivals in recent years, moving from twelfth to fifth place.

With the advent of charter flights, packaged tours, and all-inclusive resorts, modern mass tourism has increased dramatically. With this increase in travellers, host countries experience considerable pressures, as described in Figure 7.5.

Figure 7.4 Tourists wait in line to enter the Louvre Museum in Paris, France, June 1999.

Interact

Why is considering only tourist arrivals an imprecise way of measuring the size of the tourist industry?

THE GLOBE AND MAIL

Tourism Growth Threatens World

World tourism is booming with Europe's best-known monuments groaning at the seams and tropical islands at risk of being spoiled, the head of the World Tourism Organization says.

The most urgent task for the organization, which has 138 countries as members, is to put into practice a code of ethics to protect sensitive environments and shield remote cultures from the onslaught of tourists, Secretary General Francesco Frangialli said in an interview.

Things are going to get worse. The organization's forecasts show that by 2020, 1.56 billion tourists a year will be roaming the world – more than double this year's forecast of 668 million.

"The pressure on the environment and on [travel] infrastructure will be high, even based on these conservative forecasts," Frangialli said. Countries just opening to tourism are particularly vulnerable because their roads and airports are ill prepared for the hordes and their people are unused to Western customs.

Europe can just about cope with its 400 million tourists a year now, but not if they all come at the same time and want to go to the same places, he said.

Source: Reuters News Agency, Madrid. Reproduced in *The Globe and Mail*, July 12, 2000.

Figure 7.5 Identify the threats that growing world tourism poses.

Canada Travels

The Calgary Stampede began as a "wild west extravaganza" in 1912. The annual ten-day event now draws over a million tourists from around the world and contributes over $100 million to the city's economy. People concerned about animal rights do not approve of some stampede events.

Figure 7.6 First Nations dancers perform a traditional dance before a huge crowd at the Calgary Stampede. The annual Stampede is a popular holiday destination for many Canadians because of its proximity and familiarity.

CHECK IN

1 Think about the tourism experiences of your family. Give an example to show how proximity to destinations has been a factor in your choices. Have you had a situation where proximity was not a consideration in making a choice? Explain.

2 France has consistently been the most popular tourist destination. Brainstorm reasons for its popularity. Then, list the three factors that you think are most important. Give reasons to justify your three choices.

3 Why would tourists all coming at the same time and wanting to go to the same places be a problem?

Travel FACT

China is predicted to become the world's top destination by 2025.

Socio-Cultural Influences

Socio-cultural characteristics also play an important part in the destination choices people make. **Socio-cultural characteristics** deal with history, culture, and social organization. These characteristics include things like language, religion, food preferences, clothing styles, types of housing, and so on. Socio-cultural characteristics also include much more subtle aspects, such as the way you greet a stranger or the respect that you show someone who is of the opposite gender or older or younger than you. We learn socio-cultural characteristics as we grow up in a society.

Figure 7.7 Tourists relax at a typical inn along the Annapurna mountain trail in Nepal. Travellers who make a point of going to places where the culture is different, so that they can experience new ideas, are still the minority.

Culture Comfort

Most tourists choose destinations where the people have socio-cultural characteristics similar to their own. They feel more comfortable in a place where they know the "rules" for getting along with others. This, of course, is a generalization. But, in general, most tourists come from a European-influenced culture and travel to places with European socio-cultural characteristics. Cultural comfort helps explain why European and North American destinations make up 9 of the top 10 tourist destinations.

Religious Travel

Religion is an important socio-cultural characteristic that influences destination choices. People of different religions make **pilgrimages**, devotional journeys, to places that have special significance for their faith. Christians journey to the Holy Land to visit the birthplace of Jesus, Hindus travel to bathe in the sacred waters of the Ganges River and wash away their sins, Jews journey to Jerusalem to pray at the Western Wall, Buddhists travel to Bodhgaya, India, where they believe Buddha attained enlightenment, and Muslims travel to their holy city of Makkah, Saudi Arabia.

Figure 7.8 Pilgrims bathe in the Ganges River during a religious festival in Allahabad, India.

Figure 7.9 (Below) Jewish worshippers pray at Jerusalem's Western Wall during the Passover holiday; (right) Christian pilgrims wait outside the gate of the Basilica of the Annunciation in Nazareth, the town of Jesus's birth.

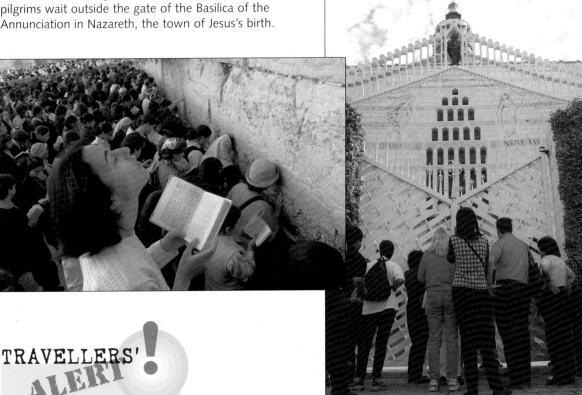

TRAVELLERS' ALERT!

You are subject to the laws and regulations of any country that you visit. Take the time to learn about the culture, customs, languages, and laws of your destination. In some countries, you can be charged for just being with a person suspected of a crime. Depending on the country, once accused, a person may be presumed guilty until proven innocent.

Some of these people regard themselves as tourists on vacation; others see themselves as travellers on a religious pilgrimage. The generally accepted definition of "tourist" includes people who travel for religious reasons.

CHECK IN

1 Identify three socio-cultural characteristics that might influence your travel destination choice, and explain how.

2 Does culture comfort play a role in your destination choices? Explain how.

3 Do you think people on a religious pilgrimage should be considered tourists? Explain why or why not.

4 To what extent do you think that you as a tourist should learn about the cultures of places you visit?

CASE STUDY
Makkah: The Centre of Islam

Figure 7.10 Location of Makkah

The Islamic religion's most holy city, Makkah, is located in the Kingdom of Saudi Arabia. The city, known as Mecca in the English language, has long been identified as an ideal destination or sought-after goal for Muslims.

Makkah was the birthplace of the prophet Muhammad in the year 571. During their daily prayers, Muslims face Makkah no matter where they are in the world, an indication of the reverence that they have for the city and the religious values it symbolizes.

The City

Makkah (population 550 000) sits in a valley surrounded by low hills. The city's location on several trade routes made it commercially important in ancient times. It was also a religious centre before the time of Muhammad, and several holy sites within the sacred grounds of the Great Mosque, called al-Haram, had religious significance in pre-Islamic times.

Figure 7.11 The Great Mosque of Makkah is at the centre of religious activities as Muslims perform the *hajj*.

The Obligation

Male Muslims are required by their faith to undertake a pilgrimage to the holy city of Makkah at least once, no matter where they live in the world, if they can afford the journey. This pilgrimage is known as *hajj*. The performance of *hajj* leaves the adherent to Islam free from sin. The *hajj* is distinct from other pilgrimages that can occur at various times of the year. This pilgrimage takes place only once each year during the twelfth lunar month of the Islamic calendar. The actual dates of this ten-day period known as *Dhu al-Hijja* are established through astronomical observation.

Hajj involves a set of rituals, which have their primary focus around a cubical structure called the Ka'abah. The Qur'an, the sacred book of Islam, provides detailed descriptions of various parts of the rituals of *hajj*, such as purification, prayers, and invocations.

When the *hajj* ends, pilgrims must leave Makkah and Saudi Arabia. The government of Saudi Arabia forbids pilgrims remaining in the kingdom.

> **"** ... and pilgrimage to the House [the Ka'abah] is a duty that people owe to God, those who can afford the journey. **"**
>
> – Al-Qur'an, Surah 3 (Al-Imran), verse 97

Figure 7.12 (Below) Pilgrims circling the Ka'abah at the Great Mosque; (left) relaxing before the start of the *hajj*

The words "Islam" and "Islamic" refer to the religion. A Muslim is a practitioner of the Islamic religion. The root of the word "Islam" comes from the Arabic word for peace.

Figure 7.13 (Left) Pilgrims perform afternoon prayers in the shadow of a minaret, Makkah; (below) a fruit seller attempts to steer his cart through a crowd of pilgrims in Mina, north of Makkah.

The Challenge of Hosting Pilgrims

The pilgrimage provides an opportunity for Muslims from diverse racial and ethnic backgrounds and geographical locations to come together to share their faith. They have an opportunity to feel united as one community. More than a million Muslims travel to Makkah annually for the *hajj*. This is 66% of the total number of pilgrims arriving in Makkah in a year. In spite of a great deal of planning by the Saudi government, this huge influx overwhelms the local infrastructure, including roadways, hotels, and airports. Services are stretched to the limit. Overcrowding reaches epic proportions. In an attempt to deal with the problem of shortage of capacity, the government asks that Saudi pilgrims stay home during *hajj*, to allow foreign visitors to participate.

TRAVELLERS' ALERT

Overwhelming numbers can lead to tragedy. On the last day of the *hajj* in April 1998, 180 people died and 250 were injured. They were crushed when the crowd surged during the ritual known as "stoning the devil." About 35 people died in a similar incident in 2001.

CHECK IN

1 In what ways is Makkah not a typical tourist destination?

2 What two suggestions might you make to the government of Saudi Arabia to improve the comfort and safety of pilgrims while they are in Makkah?

3 Investigate another religious pilgrimage. In what ways is this pilgrimage similar to and different from the *hajj* in Makkah?

Interact

Should governments control very large gatherings for religious or other purposes?

Countries with Cultural Differences

Although North America and Europe are the most popular destination choices, tourism to other parts of the world is growing. In 1999, the Asia-Pacific region had a growth rate of 7.5% and a record total of nearly 94 million international tourists. Arrivals to other areas also increased – Central America: 23%, the Middle East: 17.5%, South America: 10%, and Africa: 9%.

Visiting Developing Countries

People have different expectations when they plan their vacations. Some people want to stay in hostels or small hotels, eat in local restaurants, and use public transportation. These people are often called *travellers*. Other people want to get away, but they still want the comforts of home. This latter group, often called *tourists*, provides the market for the luxurious accommodation found in foreign-owned resorts and five-star hotels.

People have different views about these foreign-owned hotels. Developers, local governments, and some local businesses applaud their construction and operation as an economic injection for the people of the area. They claim that every hotel room creates one to two jobs, directly or indirectly, for the local people.

Local people may see things differently. For many of them, new hotels mean land eviction, pollution, and low wages. Their culture may be exploited and turned into a commercial product or a commodity, a process called **commodification** in the tourism industry. Some local people resent the fact that their history and traditions are reduced to commodities and are no longer appreciated for their intrinsic value.

Figure 7.14 (Below left) Children play on a garbage mound in a slum on the outskirts of Santo Domingo, Dominican Republic; (right) a typical beach resort, Punta Cana, Dominican Republic. Hotels and resorts built for tourists often reflect the difference in standard of living between visitors and local residents.

Statistical Indicators for Selected Countries					
Country	Birth Rate (per 1000 population)	Death Rate (per 1000 population)	Infant Mortality (per 1000 live births)	Life Expectancy at Birth in Years (male/female)	Literacy (%)	GDP (per capita)
Canada	11.41	7.39	5.08	76.02/83.00	97.0	$23 000
Colombia	22.85	5.73	24.70	66.43/74.27	91.3	$6 200
Dominican Republic	25.15	4.72	35.93	71.12/75.38	82.1	$5 400
Guatemala	35.05	6.92	47.03	63.53/68.96	55.6	$3 900
India	24.79	8.88	64.90	61.89/63.13	52.0	$1 800
Mexico	23.15	5.05	26.19	68.47/74.66	89.6	$8 500

Source: *The World Factbook 2000*, Central Intelligence Agency, 1999.

Figure 7.15 How do the indicators of these developing countries support the idea that the trickle-down theory is not a reality?

Local governments counter arguments about commodification by claiming the country needs the foreign currency to boost its economy. They argue that the money that tourism generates will **trickle down** to the people to help them maintain their culture and become part of the global economy.

The reality may be that those people who are most affected by tourism are the ones who benefit the least. Sometimes control of local decision making shifts to powerful corporate executives of foreign-owned companies, and a large percentage of the profits from tourist stays may not reach the host country. Instead, it may end up in the bank accounts of major hotel chains headquartered in the developed world, where it cannot trickle down to the people in the host country.

Negative Influences   Tourism often has other disruptive influences on developing countries. As tourism development continues, workers migrate from other countries in search of jobs. This creates competition for positions that local people had expected to fill.

Traditional family ties often disappear as young people, who are influenced by the lifestyles of tourists, begin to value contact with tourists more than being with their families. This phenomenon of valuing other cultures more than your own is known as the **demonstration effect**.

Figure 7.16 A teenager drinks from a bottle of Coca-Cola in downtown Cairo, Egypt. How might this reflect the demonstration effect?

Figure 7.17 A costumed "devil" at a fiesta, La Vega, Dominican Republic

Traditional clothing styles change as consumer goods are imported for the tourist trade or when factories are established to produce tourist T-shirts and sarongs. In Africa, many local hand-made clothing enterprises were forced out of business when cheaper, factory-made imports were seen as superior by the local residents.

Tourist Behaviour Evidence that some tourists are insensitive to the cultures of other countries is displayed by their failure to learn what is acceptable and what is not in the countries they have chosen to visit. Customs, manner of dress, and social behaviours of one culture are often quite different from other cultures. As distance increases between countries, differences may intensify. Wearing shorts or sleeveless shirts may be the norm in one country, but in Vietnam, for example, arms must be covered before entering a temple. In Iran, where Muslim women wear chadors, Western women must cover their heads with scarves. Failure to conform to strict observances of another culture is insulting at best and may be illegal.

Interact

Do governments have a responsibility to force tourists to conform to the social and cultural behaviour of the people in the countries they are visiting?

Travel FACT

The Dominican Republic boasts the greatest number of hotels in the Caribbean region with over 32 000 rooms, making that country a premier travel destination.

CHECK IN

1 Explain how the process of commodification affects cultures of host countries.

2 Design a graphic organizer such as a Venn diagram to highlight the differences between travellers and tourists.

3 How do local governments justify foreign development to attract tourism?

4 a) Explain the demonstration effect.

   b) Have you seen examples of this phenomenon in Canada? Explain.

CASE STUDY
Goa, India – Tourism, a Necessary Evil

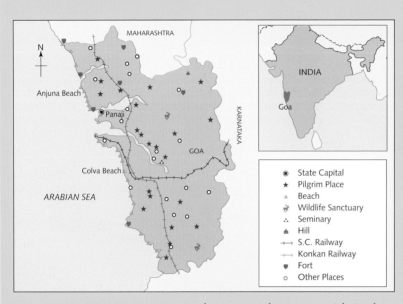

Figure 7.18 Location of Goa

State Capital
★ Pilgrim Place
▲ Beach
Wildlife Sanctuary
∴ Seminary
▲ Hill
⊢⊣ S.C. Railway
⊢⊣ Konkan Railway
▼ Fort
○ Other Places

Cdn$1 = 30.0014 Indian rupees

Figure 7.19 What aspects of Goan culture are shown in these photos?

A Traveller's Diary

October 26, Goa, India
We enjoyed our three-day journey to the Taj Mahal and Jaipur. I can't believe how beautiful the Taj is. On our way to Goa, we were fogged in at the Delhi airport. There we struck up a conversation with Daniel, an American tattooist, and Jooles, a Canadian ski instructor-tree planter-trekker. About 6:30 a.m. we were bused to the Hotel Centaur for a wonderful breakfast. We shared stories about our adventures with Jooles and Daniel. Jooles had been on a 25-day hike in the Himalayas. Daniel was heading for a rave scene in Anjuna Beach, which is in northern Goa. Apparently, it is party-city for travellers. Mixing drugs and being in a foreign country where they can throw you in jail indefinitely seems downright dangerous to me.

The tourist office at the airport was able to book us into the Longhuinos Beach Resort in Colva. It is moderately priced at 850 rupees, breakfast included. Our balcony overlooks the garden, the ocean, and the palm trees that fringe the beach. Awesome! There are a variety of places to stay in this area. These range from the Fisherman's Cottage to some really large chain

Location	Southwest coastal state of India Latitude: 15°N Longitude: 74°E
Population	1.3 million
Area	3701 km²
Capital	Panaji
Major religions	Roman Catholic, Hindu
Main languages	Kokani, Marathi, English, Hindi
Best time to visit	October to May
Historical influences	Portuguese 1510–1961
Economy	Farming, fishing, tourism, iron ore

Figure 7.20 Things to know about Goa

Figure 7.21 Restaurant shacks not only serve tasty food, they also have beach chairs for rent.

hotels in Panaji and along the northern coast, which is one reason we wanted to stay in Colva. The Taj Group operates a complex of three five-star deluxe resort hotels. One has a water sports centre, which seems very weird since it is located right on the Arabian Sea! Prices at these places range from Cdn$325 to Cdn$750. How many rupees is that?

We will be in Goa during Diwali, the five-day Hindu "festival of lights." Apparently, there will be processions, fireworks, and lots of sweets to enjoy. We are really looking forward to it. Before the festival starts, though, we plan to enjoy some beach time.

November 5

We've settled into quite a routine here. Breakfast at the hotel, then a short walk to Sea Sun Sand Restaurant, one of the many huts located right on the beach. We have made friends with Ganesh, our server, Craig from Calgary, and numerous other people, ranging from an Indian oil tanker navigator to a New Zealand nurse.

The restaurant shacks serve the best seafood, spring rolls, and noodle dishes that I have ever tasted. Goaneses food is excellent, especially the popular pork dish, vindaloo. Xacuti is a specialty made from chicken or meat, and sanna are rice cupcakes. Delicious!

In general, it seems very quiet here. Sometimes we are the only people in a restaurant shack for dinner.

There are a number of vendors on the beach who work for a percentage of what they sell. We've bought some jewellery for gifts, and we buy fruit from the same girl every day. When the tourist police arrive, the vendors scatter. It seems ridiculous that they are not allowed to earn a living in an area that caters to tourists.

Swimming in the ocean is beautiful. Very few people – tourists and Goans included – actually swim in the ocean, and we've had more than a few onlookers as we take our daily swim.

Yesterday we took the local bus to Margao, then on to Panaji. We passed many small farms and coconut groves. Old Goa has a strong Portuguese influence, which is not surprising since the Portuguese occupied the area for 450 years.

An Open Letter to Tourists

The following article appeared as a letter to the editor of a local newspaper during our stay.

Dear Sir,

I am very concerned about the increase in violence in our beautiful state of Goa. There have been some terrible incidents. I am ashamed that our people threw rotten fish and cow dung at some German tourists, and the rape of two young Swedish women was tragic. Even petty crimes, such as robbery, have increased. As many have said before, the clashes between our citizens and tourists have to stop. We have to work together to solve the issues that have caused the escalation of these incidents.

Although the government promised to develop programs to educate tourists about our culture, they have done nothing. Something must be done, so I am writing this letter to all visitors to Goa.

Be Aware of Our Sensibilities

Our society is a simple one. We have fished and farmed for many centuries. We value our families and our traditions. Ours is a modest culture. While many men wear Western-style pants and shirts, some of us still wear the traditional brightly coloured lungi in Goa. This looks more like a sarong to you, but it is actually sewn up like a tube and the waist is folded over to fit the wearer. Most women in Goa wear the skirts of the Lambadi people, but some wear saris. We are shocked and offended by the shorts, sleeveless shirts, and bathing suits often worn by Western women. Have you not noticed that even in the water, Goan women wear their clothing? We do not expect you to do the same, but at least be aware of our local sensibilities. Our modesty extends to having our pictures taken, as well. Please ask before you snap a shot. Taking pictures at religious ceremonies or in religious buildings is very offensive to us.

Western women probably have a harder time adjusting to our ways than do Western men. I have heard that in your countries, women have equal opportunities in the home and the workplace. You make your own decisions about where you want to go and what you want to do. Goan women are very influential within our family units, but men make all the other decisions. Married women must follow the rules set by their husbands, and in the case of younger women, those set by their mothers-in-law too.

Change – Not Always for the Best!

With increased tourism, our lives have changed dramatically. At one time, Calangute was a sleepy village. People fished and had small farms. Now, we no longer have access to the sea. The area has been reserved for the guests of large hotels and even some beach shack owners. This means we have to pull our boats out several kilometres along the coast. The large hotels occupy the land that was once farmed. In Morjim village, local gangsters forcibly removed some farmers from the land because the landlord had sold it for tourism development.

The schedule of our lives is very different. With fewer farms to work, some men have had to take jobs in the hotels. This can be very demeaning to people who have always worked in a co-operative way with other fishers or farmers. Often we have to live far from our families. Most hotel workers are paid little. Sometimes the hotel owners withhold our salaries if they are not having a good season. We rely on this seasonal work to feed our families. Imagine how you would feel if your employer failed to pay you!

To us, tourists and travellers appear very wealthy. Even the people who budget their travel have more money than we do. Many of us will never be able to travel very far from home. Our needs are immediate – food and shelter. There is no excuse for crime, but it is not surprising that the casual attitude of many tourists toward money tempts some of our people to steal.

Straining Our Facilities

The building boom has put a strain on the limited infrastructure that exists in Goa. Our electricity is uncertain at best, but with the larger hotels now feeding into the system, we often do not have light at night. The water situation is even worse. The water to supply the hotels and fill their huge swimming pools has been siphoned off the underground aquifer, thus reducing the water table. Why do tourists need pools when they have ready access to the ocean? No matter where you stay, could you please remember that we have access to water only a few hours a day, so shower quickly!

Garbage is another problem. There is so much of it now. It has been estimated that in Panaji, the capital city, about 20 million printed plastic bags are used every year. We are trying to reduce the amount of garbage because we do not have the proper disposal systems in place. Please recycle plastic bags.

I hope that you now have a better understanding of our concerns. All we ask is that you respect our ways. Tourism is important to our economy, but we do not want to trade our culture to achieve financial security. We would be honoured to answer any questions that you have about our culture.

Sincerely,
Savio Cardozo

Figure 7.22 The strong Christian influence makes Goa very different from the rest of India.

Women travelling in India should not walk alone at night. Ask your hotel clerk to recommend a reliable rickshaw or taxi driver. Make sure that you agree beforehand on a fair price that includes waiting to drive you home at the end of the evening.

Figure 7.23 Resorts have changed the geography of Goa.

Figure 7.24 How does tourism affect the lives of these fishers?

TRAVELLERS' ALERT

Tourists beware. Drug use is illegal in Goa. Possession of even a small amount of cannabis is a criminal offence, punishable by large fines or prison sentences of up to ten years.

CHECK IN

1 List three activities in which tourists might participate in Goa.

2 What moral obligations to local residents do developers of large hotels have? Explain your view.

3 Develop a chart illustrating four areas where Goan and tourist cultures clash.

4 a) Using information from "A Traveller's Diary" and "An Open Letter to Tourists," explain why Goa might be considered a cultural region.

   b) List examples of how local inhabitants might be exploited by tourist activity.

VIRTUAL TRAVEL

www.irwinpublishing.com

Find tourist information about Goa on the Student Page for *Canada Travels*.

LOOKING AT ISSUES

2001 WTO World Tourism Organization
The 14th General Assembly in Korea/Japan

World Tourism Organization

Issue: Should tourists be solely responsible for bridging cultural differences between themselves and residents of host countries?

In Figure 7.5, Secretary General Francesco Frangialli of the World Tourism Organization (WTO) referred to a code of ethics. Indeed, the WTO adopted a Global Code of Ethics for Tourism at the 13th General Assembly held in Santiago, Chile, in October 1999. This code contains ten articles (see Figure 7.26). It was designed "to promote an equitable, responsible, and sustainable world tourism order, whose benefits will be shared by all sectors of society."

Figure 7.25 The logo of the World Tourism Organization represents two people shaking hands in colours symbolizing Japan and Korea, the countries that hosted the WTO's 14th General Assembly in 2001. The fusion of the colours expresses mutual interaction and understanding of the people of Japan and Korea, hand-in-hand.

Articles of the Global Code of Ethics for Tourism	
Article 1:	Tourism's contribution to mutual understanding and respect between peoples and societies
Article 2:	Tourism as a vehicle for individual and collective fulfillment
Article 3:	Tourism, a factor of sustainable development
Article 4:	Tourism, a user of the cultural heritage of mankind and a contributor to its enhancement
Article 5:	Tourism, a beneficial activity for host countries and communities
Article 6:	Obligations of stakeholders in tourism development
Article 7:	Right to tourism
Article 8:	Liberty of tourist movements
Article 9:	Rights of the workers and entrepreneurs in the tourism industry
Article 10:	Implementation of the principles of the Global Code of Ethics for Tourism

Figure 7.26 This Code of Ethics is meant to guide the behaviour of workers and companies in the tourism industry.

Figure 7.27 Tourists attending a ceremony in Maui, Hawaii, to launch a traditional canoe sit at a respectful distance from the proceedings. Tourism activities that accommodate local customs and beliefs can entertain and educate visitors while promoting the culture of the host country.

TRAVELLERS' ALERT!

If you are planning a trip, contact Canada's Consular Affairs Branch of the Department of Foreign Affairs and International Trade. This department has up-to-date country-specific information. You can find out about general conditions such as entry and health requirements. The department also issues Travel Advisory Reports (TARs), which indicate countries unsafe for travel, as well as weekly Travel Bulletins (TBs) that highlight dangerous situations.

Earlier you read about some of the problems that result when tourists visit countries that have cultures different from their own. Whose responsibility is it to see that situations like these do not occur?

In his letter to tourists, Savio Cardozo asks "that you respect our ways. Tourism is important to our economy, but we do not want to trade our culture to achieve financial security."

Halfway around the world, people hold a similar point of view about tourism. Two concerned Hawaiians, Reverend Kaleo Patterson and Ken Ka'imi Stokes, had this to say in a local newspaper in May 23, 1994:

We recognize the right of all people to leisure and the freedom of travel for recreation in its fullest sense. We welcome those who respect our dignity and who are willing to adapt to our ways of living, thinking, and relating. Our right to reshape and continue traditional lifestyles and to maintain our privacy is, however, of greater importance.

The WTO agrees with these viewpoints. Article 1 of the WTO code says:

Tourism activities should be conducted in harmony with the attributes and traditions of the host regions and countries and in respect for their laws, practices, and customs.

But the article goes on to say,

The host communities ... should acquaint themselves with and respect the tourists who visit them and find out about their lifestyles, tastes, and expectations. ...

Figure 7.28 Tourists who show disrespect for the activities of different cultures offend the sensibilities of local residents, giving tourists and tourism a bad name.

Article 1 concludes with these words:

Tourists and visitors have the responsibility to acquaint themselves, even before their departure, with the characteristics of the countries they are preparing to visit; they must be aware of the health and security risks inherent in any travel outside their usual environment and behave in such a way as to minimize those risks.

Formulating a Global Code of Ethics for Tourism and implementing it are two different things, however. According to Article 10 of the code, it is the responsibility of stakeholders in tourism development to "co-operate in the implementation of these principles and monitor their effective application." The WTO plans to create a World Committee on Tourism Ethics whose members will be appointed for four-year terms of office. However, this committee will not be responsible for implementing the code, but rather for evaluating the implementation and settling disputes that might arise.

The World Tourism Organization is an international institution in tourism development. With its influence, it should share the responsibility for the implementation of its code. This role may mean educating tourists and host communities, or it may mean establishing programs or procedures for tour operators and major hotel chains – the stakeholders who seem to benefit the most from tourism. Whatever action is taken, it will not be an easy task to eliminate the culture clashes that tourism sometimes generates.

Figure 7.29 Soldiers clear land mines along the border between Ethiopia and Eritrea. The two countries have been embroiled in conflict since Eritrea gained its independence from Ethiopia in 1993, making the African region highly unsafe for travel. Tourists should be aware of this hazard before attempting to travel to this area.

Figure 7.30 (Right) A centuries-old Buddhist pagoda provides the backdrop for this view of Vientiane, Laos. There are no highrises in the city. Architects and city planners are set on preserving "old Vientiane" amid increasing tourism and foreign investment. (Below) A woman sells bread at a local street market in Vientiane.

Interact

Can tourism be developed to ensure cultures are protected from outside influences?

CHECK IN

1 On a scale of one to five, with one being the most responsible, rank the following stakeholders according to where you think their responsibility for preventing culture clash should be:
   - tourists
   - local residents
   - World Tourism Organization
   - tour operators and travel agents
   - hotel managers
   Explain your choices.

2 Have you ever experienced objectionable tourist behaviour either in Canada or in a country you were visiting? Explain how you felt.

3 What measures do you think the WTO should take to implement its Global Code of Ethics for Tourism?

- apply geotechnologies to a study of regional geography
- produce and interpret different types of maps, graphic organizers, and diagrams
- communicate effectively in written, oral, and visual forms
- identify selected factors that influence travellers' destination choices
- research and report on the impact of a natural or human-caused disaster on travel and tourism in a selected region
- demonstrate an understanding that cultural conflicts may result from the movement and interactions of people around the world

Global Travel Advisories – Where Is It Not Safe to Travel?

Purpose: To use ArcView to produce an interactive map of current global travel advisories.

Files: cntry_95.shp

Functions: View Properties, Convert to Shapefile, Table Edit, Create a New Field, Legend Editor (Symbol Edit), Legend Editor (Unique Value), Labelling, Hot Link (Text Files), Layout.

The Consular Affairs Bureau of the Department of Foreign Affairs and International Trade (DFAIT) provides: (a) destination-specific Travel Reports and (b) weekly Travel Bulletins highlighting current "hot spots" and time-sensitive information. Current information is available from the Department through the following means: telephone: 1-800-267-6788 or 613-944-6788; visit the Web site on the Student Page for *Canada Travels*.

Prior to beginning the ArcView portion of this activity, you must

1 visit the above Web site

2 record the names of the countries listed under Travel Advisory Reports

3 click on each of the countries listed and summarize the information in the Attention section (This section provides the details of the advisory for prospective visitors. It describes the current situation in the country and why tourists should either avoid visiting this destination or exercise extreme caution when doing so.)

4 categorize the advisory according to the type of situation (e.g., civil war, terrorism, banditry, natural disaster, disease epidemic, etc.)

The above information can be recorded, using the following table format:

Country	Summary of Advisory	Advisory Category

1. Your first step will be to create a blank View, name it "Global Travel Advisories," and change the Map Units to "decimal degrees" and the Distance Units to "kilometres."

2. Next, add the theme x:\world\cntry_95.shp (located on ArcCanada 2.0 Disk #2) to your View.

3. Now, open the theme for the Cntry_95.shp theme. Locate and select (i.e., highlight) all of the countries listed in the table you created at the start of the activity. Close the theme table. Convert the selected records to a shapefile, naming it "Travel Advisories" and adding it to the View.

4. Next, open the theme table of the Travel Advisories.shp.shp theme. Put the table in Edit mode and add a new "string" field called "Advisory Category" with a width of "48." Refer to the table you created at the start of the activity and enter into this field the proper Advisory Category for each of the countries. Stop editing the table, save your edits, and close the theme table.

5. Now, using the Legend Editor, change the legend type for the Cntry_95.shp theme to "Single Symbol," then make the symbol transparent. Again, using the Legend Editor, change the legend type for the Travel Advisory.shp theme to "Unique Value" using "Advisory Category" as the Values field. Apply any colour scheme you wish by either selecting one or by editing the symbol for each category.

6. Next, in the Text and Label Defaults dialogue box, change the defaults of the "Callout Label" to a font type, colour, size (10 recommended), and style of your choice. As well, change the outline and fill as you prefer but deselect the "use drop-shadow" box.

7. Now, using the Callout Label tool, label each of the Travel Advisory.shp countries with the country's name.

8. Next, open a word processor, such as WordPerfect, Word, or Notepad, that allows you to save documents as ASCII DOS text files. Create a file for each of the countries listed in the table you created at the start of the activity containing the information in the "Summary of Advisory" column. Save each file, giving it the same name as that of the country. Make note of the directory and folder into which you are saving these files (e.g., c:\windows\temp).

9. Now return to ArcView and open the theme table for the Travel Advisory.shp theme. Put the table in Edit mode and add a new "string" field called "Hotlink" with a width of "60." Enter the proper directory paths and file names (complete with .txt extensions) into the field you have just created (e.g., c:\windows\temp\angola.txt). Stop editing the table, save your edits, and close the theme table.

10. Next, finish setting up your hot links to the text documents in the Theme Properties dialogue box, then test to see if they are working.

11. Finally, create a layout of your map, complete with an appropriate title, north arrow, legend, and scale bar.

Extension:

Using the Internet and/or recent magazines or newspapers, locate articles that describe the dangerous conditions in the Travel Advisory countries. Download or scan the pictures and/or text contained in these articles and hot link them to your map.

REVISIT THE chapter 7
Looking Back

Understanding the Concepts

1. Explain why countries in Europe, such as France and Germany, are significant global tourist attractions to Canadians.

2. What socio-cultural factors can influence the choice of tourist destinations?

3. In your own words, explain commodification and the demonstration effect.

4. a) Identify three general situations in which cultural clashes might occur due to tourism.

   b) Select one of these situations and explain who should solve this problem and how.

5. Use information from this chapter to identify several specific examples of how tourism contributes to the exploitation of people.

6. In what way could cultural differences be considered both a motivator and a barrier to travel?

Practising Your Skills

7. Select three of the indicators from Figure 7.15 and design appropriate comparative graphs. Suggest reasons why disparities might lead to differing cultural values between hosts and tourists.

8. Analyze global tourist patterns. Make a four-column chart, listing the countries shown in Figure 7.1 with their 1999 tourist arrivals. Use an atlas or an almanac to find the total population of each country, and put those figures in the third column. Calculate the ratio of tourists to residents for each country, and put that information in the fourth column. Which countries do you think are at risk of unsustainable tourism? Explain why.

Applying Your Skills

9. Design a collage to be used in an educational campaign. Compare the quality of living for a visitor with that of a local person employed at the tourist's hotel. Your goal is to bring attention to commodification of the host country.

10. Design a plan to implement Article 1 of the Global Code of Ethics shown in Figure 7.26. Indicate responsibilities for all stakeholders and how they should be implemented.

11. Select a tourism region and produce a case study analyzing the impact of the demonstration effect.

Figure 7.31 Notre Dame Cathedral, Paris, France

Thinking Like a Tourist

12. Working with a partner, choose a country that has a culture different from your own. Research the socio-cultural characteristics of the people who live in your chosen destination, using the following categories: language(s), religion(s), cuisine, clothing, housing, and values and traditions. Write a magazine article or design a travel brochure or a Web site to teach tourists about the location you have selected.

13. Prepare a ten-point "Tourists' Code of Ethics and Behaviour."

Figure 7.32 Market day in Djenné, Mali

JOB SKILLS

Finding the right job to suit your skills and areas of interest is important. You need to think about what it will take for you to achieve your career goals and how you should plan your educational needs. Search the Internet or daily newspapers to find a number of jobs directly or indirectly related to the travel and tourism industry that appeal to you. Narrow this selection to one. Now contact colleges or universities in your region. The Internet usually has their course offerings. Select one institution that has programs and courses that would help you to achieve this goal. Develop a profile on this institution that includes

- the department in which you would like to study
- a possible major course of study
- a list of course descriptions that would help you to pursue your dream job
- possible internships and scholarships

CHAPTER eight 8
Sustainable Cultural Tourism

Making the Right Choice

Most governments and communities around the world recognize that cultural and environmental problems accompany the economic benefits of tourism. For the profits that hotels and resorts generate, the local community usually pays a price. The United Nations General Assembly, the Commission on Sustainable Development, and the World Tourism Organization have adopted resolutions that support the ideals of tourism when the benefits to the local community outweigh the costs in the long term. These organizations also influence other international groups to focus on positive and equitable results of tourism development. The goal is to educate governments, corporations, and tourists in promoting **sustainable cultural tourism**, the subject of this chapter.

a)

Figure 8.1 Many people welcome the opportunity to share their culture with tourists. However, it is important to them that tourists show respect for their cultural traditions and religious practices. (Right and counterclockwise onto next page:) a) a young Buddhist monk escorts tourists atop the tallest temple at Angkor Wat, Cambodia; b) a baker removes special bread from his oven in preparation for Day of the Dead celebrations, Mexico; c) Aborigine women pass a newborn baby through the smoke of a campfire in an initiation rite, Australia; d) Masai warriors pose in traditional costume, Tanzania; e) a children's folk dance troupe performs in Riga, Latvia.

b)

Sustainable cultural tourism requires

- consultation with local residents
- development not occurring too quickly
- development that is not too large for the community
- first choice of employment opportunities for local people
- sensitivity to cultural traditions and religious practices
- protection of the environment

Figure 8.2 Is there much potential for sustainable cultural tourism in your local area?

d)

c)

e)

Tourism Concern, a non-government agency (NGO) in the United Kingdom, has produced videos and educational materials aimed at tourists, who are the consumers of travel products. Through public education programs, this organization attempts to influence consumers to make **ethical travel** choices. Tourists who know how to identify non-sustainable practices are more likely to be selective in the destinations they visit and the facilities they use.

EXPECTATIONS

In this chapter, you will have the opportunity to

- evaluate the impact of government policies on travel and tourism in selected regions
- identify recent trends in travel and tourism
- analyze the economic, political, and cultural effects of tourism-related development on a community or region
- analyze the involvement of indigenous peoples in travel and tourism
- demonstrate an understanding of the need to respect the cultural and religious traditions of others
- demonstrate an understanding that cultural conflicts may result from the movement and interactions of people around the world
- analyze the impact of marketing and advertising on travel and tourism patterns
- produce a case study analyzing the relationship between tourism and level of development in a developing country
- demonstrate an understanding of the need for sustainable development and protection of the resources on which tourism is based
- analyze the major characteristics of selected tourist regions in terms of natural, cultural, economic, and political criteria

Local Responses to Tourism

Residents in many countries around the world have adapted to tourists visiting their attractions. People have responded to the impact of tourism on their cultures in different ways. For example, Buddhist monks in Nepal started charging admission to their monasteries to discourage inconsiderate tourists who had little regard for their culture.

Machu Picchu, the main attraction in Peru, is another example. This World Heritage site is believed to have been an important religious centre of the Inca Empire (circa 1438–1525). About 1000 visitors a day visit the site. To conserve Machu Picchu, the Peruvian government has increased the entrance fee to US$20. The fee to use the Inca Trail that leads to Machu Picchu has been tripled to US$50. To interest visitors in more than just this site, small off-shoot businesses are being developed to provide special tours by local guides to neighbouring villages and historic sites. In this way local people have a chance to show tourists how they live today, leading to greater understanding among cultures.

Bali, Indonesia, has become a sun haven for tourists from Australia, New Zealand, and Europe. Traditionally, most Balinese residents of the village of Ubud were farmers. However, as the number of tourists increased, the available agricultural land decreased. Today many residents operate guesthouses, drive taxis, and sell goods in the marketplace. As well as the economic benefits, tourism has provided access to the rest of the world through television, the Internet, and interaction with tourists. Nonetheless, traditions remain strong. Excitement runs high during the annual Calonarang performance at Ubud's temple, where dancers enact the Balinese religious worldview of the struggle between good and evil: people prefer it to even the most popular television program!

www.irwinpublishing.com

To learn more about the tourism resolutions adopted by various organizations, visit the Student Page for *Canada Travels*. Select clauses that refer to sustainable cultural tourism from one of the charters and post these on cards around the classroom.

Figure 8.3 The Inca city of Machu Picchu, northwest of Cuzco, Peru. In 2000, one of the site's most sacred monuments, a sun clock, was chipped during the filming of a beer commercial. Why would a government allow important cultural and religious sites to be used for commercial purposes? Do you agree with such decisions?

Canada Travels

Making friends on your travels can be easy and fun. Before you leave home, purchase symbols of Canada, such as pins, pens, and postcards. Local people may enjoy receiving a memento of your visit and may share stories with you. Olympic athletes often exchange pins from their countries with one another.

In the Ecuadorian rain forest, the Huaorani people have seen tourism as a development opportunity. Community members receive salaries and perform jobs in maintenance, guiding, and paddling canoes. To reduce the impact of outsiders on their traditional hunter-gatherer society, the Huaorani restrict the number of tourists to their village. They built a cabin that sleeps eight visitors. It is located 45 minutes from the village. Only one group of tourists, for stays of two to six days, is accepted per month. Guides accompany visitors on hikes, explaining forest ecology, the spiritual relationship between the people and their land, and local arts. Because the emphasis is on teaching about their culture, the Huaorani see tourism as a way of ensuring their cultural future.

Developing Cultural Tourism

Community **empowerment**, or control over decision making, is essential for sustainable cultural tourism. The development of a community tourism assessment ensures that differing opinions are heard. When local people have the chance to express their views and to share their ideas, sustainable cultural tourism development is more likely to occur.

Interact

What are some methods for empowering a community to develop sustainable cultural tourism?

What was here before this resort was built?

What job did the server do before working here?

Who owns this resort?

CHECK IN

1 Why are international organizations concerned with educating people about cultural tourism?

2 Write two or three sentences explaining why two of the points in Figure 8.2 are important to sustainable cultural tourism.

3 Work with a partner to list five ways that tourists can make sure they are practising sustainable cultural tourism or ethical travel.

Figure 8.4 How would the answers to these questions help tourists decide if tourist locations are promoting sustainable cultural tourism?

CASE STUDY
Cultural Tourism in Nova Scotia

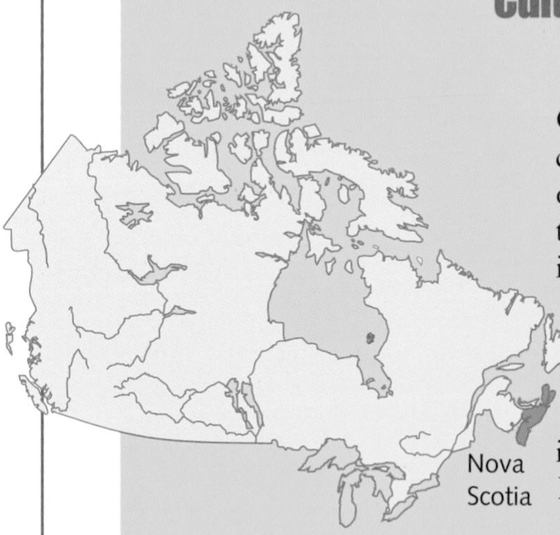

One NGO that wants to participate in the growth of sustainable cultural tourism is the Gaelic Council of Nova Scotia. Gaelic is one of the languages of the Celtic culture whose origins have been traced to the area of modern Argyllshire, Scotland. Scottish immigrants first settled in northeastern Nova Scotia and Cape Breton Island in the late 1700s and early 1800s. Early settlements sprang up in coastal areas, where people survived by fishing. Even as people moved inland to establish farms, they had little communication with the outside world. In these isolated communities, the Gaelic culture remained strong. However, after 1945, people started moving into larger centres for employment. By the 1950s, a dwindling number of Gaelic speakers maintained cultural traditions in a largely English-speaking area.

Figure 8.5 Location of Nova Scotia

Nova Scotia

Figure 8.6 (Left to right) Gaelic games include the caber toss, highland-style dancing, and the hammer throw. While language is important, most cultures also like to preserve significant traditions in dress, celebrations, food, and athletic events.

Restoring a Culture

Today, many people think that it is important to remember their heritage. The descendants of the early Scottish settlers are developing a heightened sense of cultural awareness. Nova Scotia is regarded as the cultural centre of the Gaelic-speaking people, or *Gaidhealtachd*. People from around the world visit Nova Scotia to experience Gaelic traditions by attending festivals, dances, and *ceilidhs*. The Gaelic Council of Nova Scotia views the development of Gaelic tourism as essential to ensuring the future of this culture. The Council believes that erosion of the Gaelic language and culture can be stopped through the economic strength that participation in the tourism sector can provide. By developing tourism, monies can be used to support language classes, educational resources, distance education classes, and cultural festivals.

Figure 8.7 How can the breakdown of one part of a culture affect the other parts?

GAELIC TOURIST PRODUCTS

- history
- dance
- story
- poetry
- song

Canada Travels

Originally, a *ceilidh* (pronounced *kay'-lee*) was simply just a visit. In the past, neighbours and families would gather in someone's kitchen. The party that developed involved the rich traditions of the Gaelic culture, including storytelling, singing, poetry, fiddling, piping, and dancing. Today, *ceilidhs* are much larger and more commercialized. They are really concerts, but the same informality draws crowds from at home and abroad.

Interact

What responsibilities do local governments have to try to keep unique cultures alive?

Cultural Tourism Opportunities

In the late 1990s, tourism was a $1.1 billion industry in Nova Scotia. In the past, tourists to Nova Scotia visited during the summer months and participated in outdoor activities, such as hiking, golfing, and boating. In an effort to diversify its tourist products and to attract tourists year round, the Government of Nova Scotia, in its 2000–2001 budget, allotted almost half of its funding to the area of Heritage and Culture. By stimulating the cultural sector, the government hoped to encourage economic growth, develop local communities, and maintain Nova Scotia's heritage. These three factors would benefit all Nova Scotians.

Gaelic tourism in Nova Scotia has two potential markets – the internal market and the external market. The **internal market** are those people who live in the Atlantic Provinces. Many of these people come from locations within Nova Scotia and travel to events around their own province. People from the other Atlantic Provinces make up 43% of the non-resident visitors. In many cases, they have a Scottish or Gaelic heritage and want to learn more about the culture of their ancestors. They may want to learn Gaelic, take fiddling or step-dancing lessons, or just attend performances. The growth of this side of the tourist industry helps to strengthen the Gaelic presence in local communities. For example, Feis an Eilein is a community festival that uses the physical and cultural resources of the community to promote its Gaelic heritage. The profits go back to the community and provide for year-long Gaelic instruction.

Figure 8.8 What do the trends signal about tourism in Nova Scotia?

Nova Scotia Tourist Arrivals, 1997–2000				
Year	Automobile	Bus	Recreational Vehicle	Air	Total
1997	1 005 000	75 000	94 000	329 000	1 503 000
1998	1 163 000	85 000	106 000	445 000	1 799 000
1999	1 460 000	103 000	109 000	531 000	2 203 000
2000	1 436 000	91 000	100 000	533 000	2 160 000

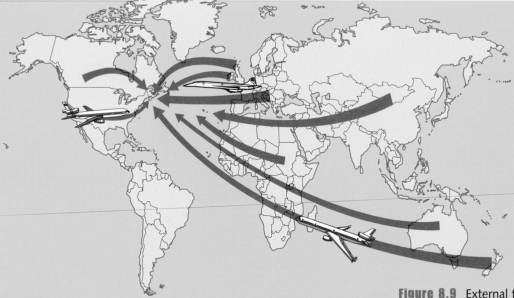

The **external market** for Gaelic tourism is the people who live in the rest of Canada and elsewhere in the world. Visitors from around the world travel to Nova Scotia to experience the Gaelic festivals, dances, and ceilidhs. In part, the international commercial success of music artists like the Rankin Family, the Barra MacNeils, Ashley MacIssac, and Natalie MacMaster has contributed to the resurgence of interest in and curiosity about this culture and helped to attract visitors to Nova Scotia.

Figure 8.9 External tourist flows to Nova Scotia. Why do you suppose people will travel long distances to take part in cultural events?

Benefits of Gaelic Tourism

- shares cultural heritage with all residents of Nova Scotia
- educates tourists about distinctive Gaelic culture
- develops Gaelic landmarks, such as museums
- provides economic benefits through activities such as guided tours
- employs Gaelic singers, musicians, and step-dancers
- promotes Nova Scotia as a distinctive cultural destination

Figure 8.10 In what ways might Nova Scotia promote Gaelic tourism in the rest of Canada? Around the world?

VIRTUAL TRAVEL

www.irwinpublishing.com

Take a virtual tour of Nova Scotia by visiting the Student Page for *Canada Travels*. During your tour, click on Festivals and select two that reflect Gaelic culture. Describe what you see.

Figure 8.11 The broad popular appeal of Gaelic music is reflected in Edmonton's foot-stomping fiddle ensemble, Barrage.

Along with the natural beauty of Nova Scotia and existing Scottish events, truly Gaelic events substantially increase tourism to the province. Cultural tourism is seen as the key to sustainable socio-economic development for the region.

CHECK IN

1 What circumstances helped to preserve Gaelic cultural traditions in Nova Scotia?

2 a) What is the main difference between the internal and external markets for Gaelic tourism to Nova Scotia?

   b) If you were responsible for planning where the province's development monies would be spent, on which sector would you focus? Why?

3 In this case study, how are economic benefits closely tied to cultural sustainability?

LOOKING AT ISSUES

Socialist Republic of Vietnam

Issue: Is central government control of all aspects of tourist activity an advantage to sustainable cultural tourism?

For some people in North America, the mention of Vietnam evokes images of a brutal war that ended decades ago with refugees fleeing a repressive regime. Since opening the country's borders to international visitors in the late 1980s, the officials of the Socialist Republic of Vietnam have worked to dispel these images and to tie the country into the Southeast Asian tourism boom. As a **centrally controlled state**, the communist government controls every aspect of development. It has set up a State Tourism Action Program, which is geared to promote both the natural and cultural resources of the country while enhancing the treasury and providing economic benefits for the Vietnamese people.

Figure 8.12 Location of Vietnam

Travel FACT

The government predicts that the contribution of the tourism industry to the country's GNP will rise from 18% in 2000 to 27% in 2010.

Figure 8.13 Images of Vietnam (clockwise from top): A vendor sells birds in hand-made bamboo cages, Hanoi; a child rests on a wooden boat in one of the many canals of the Mekong Delta; women play traditional drums while taking part in a celebration of Hanoi's 990th anniversary, October 2000. What are some resources that this country can use to develop its tourism potential?

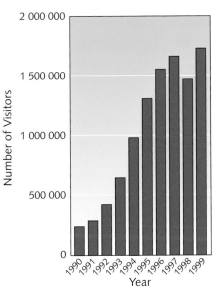

Figure 8.14 Tourism expanded rapidly in Vietnam once the government encouraged the development of a tourist industry.

www.irwinpublishing.com

To learn more details about Vietnam's Strategic Plan, visit the Student Page for *Canada Travels*.

Smiles cost gold

Everybody knows that smiles carry their own meaning and express different shades of feelings. Smiles are unique characteristics of man. "Smiles cost gold" means that smiles bring about happiness, health which cannot be created by any tonic.

Frequently, Vietnamese people show their smiles. When asked, why do Vietnamese often smile, the answer given is that smiles reflect the optimistic spirits of the people despite the 4000-year history of warfare and invasion by foreigners where death and separation prevailed. During the resistance war against the US, a famous foreign female writer spared three pages in her essay about Vietnam to describe and express her feelings of seeing friendly smiles of Vietnamese women when walking in Hanoi streets damaged by American bombardments.

A Vietnamese writer who is an expert in applied linguistics has discovered that the Vietnamese language has about 50 different words that mean smiling.

Friendly smiles are not loud, especially when they are used to express appreciation or agreement. The most important factor is honest and friendly behaviour in communication. That is a greeting more valuable than a banquet.

Source: Adapted from *Tourism Concern About Them*. Nha Trang City, Khanh Hoa Province: National Politics Publishers

Figure 8.15 An excerpt from a government pamphlet. Why do you think the Vietnamese government distributed an article about smiling to tourist businesses in Vietnam?

An important component of the government's Strategic Plan for tourism is the preservation and promotion of the cultural traditions and human dignity of the Vietnamese people, who graciously welcome visitors to their country. To help businesses and citizens adopt positive attitudes toward tourism, Vietnam's National Politics Publishers provided a pamphlet, an excerpt of which is given in Figure 8.15.

Vietnamese entrepreneurs have quickly established a tourism infrastructure based on the identification of specific tourism regions in the government's Strategic Plan. Many small businesses, such as restaurants, hotels, tour companies, and shops, have responded to the opening of Vietnam's borders. As a result, the standard of living for many people has improved. An essential element in the development of tourism is foreign investment in Vietnam. However, the government regulates tourist development by foreign-owned companies to ensure sustainable cultural tourism. Officials control where development will occur, the services that can be offered, and the level of government support available.

Growth of Tourism in Vietnam				
	Number of Visitors in 2000	Revenue in 2000 (US$)	Predicted Number of Visitors in 2010	Predicted Revenue in 2010 (US$)
International tourism	3.5 million	2.6 billion	9 million	11.8 billion
Domestic tourism	11 million	not available	25 million	not available

Preserving Historical Influences

The Vietnamese government has committed funds to restore and renovate buildings and monuments to show the resilience of Vietnamese culture despite earlier cultural influences of the Champa Kingdom from the Indian subcontinent, the Chinese, the French, and the Americans.

The Champa Kingdom flourished from the second to the fifteenth centuries, largely in southern Vietnam. Owing to trade relations with India, these Vietnamese people adopted the Hindu religion and Sanskrit language. The Cham influence is still evident in Indian-style construction techniques, pottery making, and art forms.

The 1000-year rule of the Chinese (from the second to tenth centuries) and their innovations in dike construction and irrigation led to the establishment of a culture based on rice farming that still endures. As well, the curved roofs, bold colours, and intricate outlines that characterize Chinese architecture remain the preferred style in Vietnam today.

Figure 8.16 International tourism is predicted to grow over the next decade. What might be some forces driving this growth?

Travel FACT

Vietnam is the 14th most populated country in the world, with a population of 79 million in 2000. The population density is over 240 persons/km^2. (Canada has 3.1 persons/km^2.)

Figure 8.17 (Left) These ruins at My Son are all that remains of the Cham culture after bombing by the Americans during the Vietnam war. (Right) The main sanctuary of Long Son Pagoda, Nha Trang, Vietnam. Can you identify the Chinese architectural details? The statue shown is Kwan Yin, a female bodhisattva (enlightened being) revered by Chinese Buddhists.

Examples of Hill Tribes	
Tay	1.2 million
Tai	1 million
Muong	900 000
Nung	700 000
H'mong	550 000
Jarai	190 000
Bahner	135 000
Sedang	95 000
Dao	470 000
Ede	24 000

Protecting Cultural Minorities

Vietnam has a large population of cultural minorities. Some cultures have been in the area for a thousand years, others only a hundred. These cultural minorities have a long history of intertribal warfare and independence from the larger population. As a result, many continue to live traditional subsistence lifestyles, such as slash-and-burn farming, and they remain at the bottom of Vietnam's socio-economic ladder.

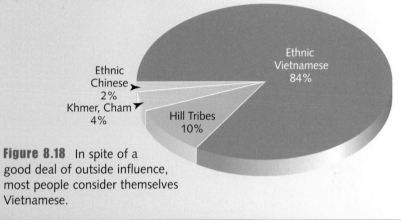

Figure 8.18 In spite of a good deal of outside influence, most people consider themselves Vietnamese.

General Characteristics of Some Hill Tribes

Tribe	Clothing Styles	Housing Styles	Cultural Activities	Agriculture
Tay	Indigo, blue-black clothes	Stilt houses	Buddhism, Taoism, Confucianism; music, songs, poetry	Wet rice, tobacco, fruit, herbs, spices
Tai	Vibrant-coloured blouses, headdresses	Bamboo stilt houses	Fifth-century literature, poetry, songs	Paddy rice
Muong	Long skirts, short blouses; indigo tops and trousers	Earthen mud houses	Gongs, drums, panpipes, flutes, two-stringed violins	Paddy rice
Nung	Black, indigo clothing	Bamboo/mud, separated into 2 sections	Bamboo furniture, basketry, silverwork, papermaking	Vegetables, fruit, spices, bamboo
H'mong	Indigo clothing (almost metallic); skirts, aprons, leggings, cylindrical hat	Bamboo/mud	Jewellery	Dry rice, vegetables, fruit, medicinal plants, pigs, cows, chickens, horses

Figure 8.19 The various Hill tribes are distinguished by differences in language, physical features, traditional dress, and housing styles. They see themselves as Vietnamese, but with a separate culture from the majority of the Vietnamese population.

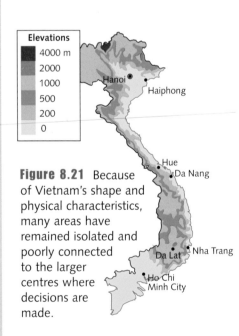

Figure 8.20 (Left) A woman from the Bahner ethnic minority, a Hill tribe from the central highlands, strikes a pose for a photographer; (below) a young H'mong woman carries her rice to market.

The government encourages the Hill people to participate in tourism as a way to develop their economy, which is largely based on agriculture. Tourism is also seen as a way to modernize or bring the Hill tribes into mainstream Vietnamese society. Infrastructure development, such as upgrading roads, establishing new hotels, and improving electrical services, makes it easier for tourists to visit some of the larger communities. Entrepreneurs have begun to offer hiking trips between villages in much the same way as trekking occurs in Nepal and Thailand.

Members of some of the Hill tribes feel threatened by these intrusions into their traditional lands and customs. An example of change is found in the northern town of Sa Pa. In the past five years, Sa Pa has become a major site for cultural tourism. Visitors primarily visit to attend the weekly market to purchase colourful clothing and to observe the "love market." Traditionally, men sang and played their musical instruments and young women sang songs to attract partners. Tourists have become so fascinated with this ritual that today, locals will play the music only for a fee, and there is virtually none of the original market left. The Vietnamese government believes that such changes in cultural practices show a maturation of the culture. Many Hill tribes, however, resent the disappearance of part of their cultural history.

The government has sought to protect more isolated Hill tribes from tourist invasion by limiting the number of permission forms required by tourists in order to stay in private homes. However, it is the government alone that decides what degree of impact on the culture is acceptable. The local people are not consulted.

Elevations	
	4000 m
	2000
	1000
	500
	200
	0

Hanoi • Haiphong

Hue • Da Nang

Da Lat • Nha Trang

Ho Chi Minh City

Figure 8.21 Because of Vietnam's shape and physical characteristics, many areas have remained isolated and poorly connected to the larger centres where decisions are made.

Figure 8.22 The recent history of Vietnam continues the struggle against outside forces.

Remembering Modern Invasions

The 1860s saw the French make forays into Indochina. During the colonial period (1859–1954), the French established an ambitious public works program. Three examples are the construction of

- ports that could be used to export natural resources
- a railway between Saigon (now Ho Chi Minh City) and Hanoi as a way to secure control
- a large number of grand buildings in the French style to house colonial administrators

There is still evidence of the French legacy. The ports and railways remain important for trade and movement of people, while the colonial mansions are used as foreign consulates and museums.

At every opportunity, the government of Vietnam focusses on its victory in what it calls the American War, and the subsequent **reunification** of the communist North and formerly capitalist South. Museums around the country celebrate the efforts of the communist Vietnamese soldiers, farmers, women, and children. The influences of the West – France and the United States – are portrayed as evil and morally wrong.

In efforts to unify the country and to liberalize the economy, the government continues to highlight the successes of its policies. Today, some forms of capitalism are allowed, since it was clear through the 1970s and 1980s that strict communism was not going to lead to a higher quality of life. Propaganda billboards are scattered throughout the countryside and displayed prominently in urban centres. Their message encourages individual economic achievement within a structured social and political setting. Visitors may not agree with these indoctrination tactics. Nonetheless, the massive changes in Vietnamese society today indicate that such policies have had some success in improving the quality of life and the economy.

Criticisms of Vietnam's Tourism Developments

Besides local concerns, opposition to tourism development has largely been voiced by a variety of foreign non-governmental organizations that fear the negative cultural consequences of too much tourism. After forcing the French and Americans out a few decades ago, the Vietnamese are welcoming foreigners back into the country in an effort to promote economic development. While the government points out that it has made efforts to control development and to protect Vietnamese culture, critics argue that the outside influences cannot help but have an impact on Vietnamese society.

A second set of criticisms comes from countries that give official development assistance – sometimes known as foreign aid – to Vietnam. Many donor countries prefer to see their contributions used to promote social development rather than economic development. These countries question the apparent lack of concern that has been shown for minority groups, women, and children in the rush to develop tourism opportunities in the country.

The article in Figure 8.25 deals with the problem of maintaining a strong culture in the face of outside influences. The article focusses on the influence of foreign cartoons on television and what the government has done to promote Vietnamese cartoons. Opponents to increased tourism have argued that more tourism will have a similar impact on the rest of Vietnamese culture.

Figure 8.23 Reminders of Vietnam's colonial past: Leaders of La Francophonie, an international association devoted to closer ties among Francophone nations, met in Hanoi in 1997. Note the more Western appearance of this building, constructed during the French period of Vietnam's history.

Figure 8.24 Vietnam's attitude toward the war has evolved from a propaganda vehicle for the communist party to a lure for tourism. (Left top) Tourists gather around a display of U.S. bombs at a war museum in Hanoi. (Left centre and bottom) A tour of a section of the 250-km long Chu Chi Tunnels used by guerrilla forces is a must see for tourists visiting the northern part of the country.

Figure 8.25 An excerpt from a newspaper article

VIET NAM NEWS

Vietnamese cartoons lose out to foreign productions

Ho Chi Minh City – Cartoon time for many youngsters is a daily afternoon fix they wouldn't dream of missing. But some say the children are missing something, namely Vietnamese cartoons.

Managers of local TV stations and cinemas say that Vietnamese cartoon-makers, with their limited budgets, poor techniques, and boring scripts, are losing out to more sophisticated hi-tech imports.

Any regular TV viewer will confirm that locally produced cartoons are seldom shown.

Meanwhile, television stations opt for slick imports of world-renowned favourites such as *Mickey Mouse*, *Donald Duck*, *Tom and Jerry*, and *Tin Tin*.

Some Vietnamese cartoon companies are making efforts to turn the situation around.

Last year the Central Cartoon Company joined forces with Ho Chi Minh City's Book Distribution Company to produce 10 cartoon videos and sold about 50 000 copies in southern provinces. The company also published some of the more popular cartoons as comic strips.

Other firms are cooperating with social organizations and private companies to make cartoons of fairy tales or stories featuring historical characters.

Together they are asking TV stations to get behind their efforts by reserving time for broadcasting Vietnamese cartoons, many of which, they say, aim to increase children's appreciation for their parents, friends, and country.

In fact, up to 98% of cartoons shown on TV are made overseas, despite state regulations requiring that 50% of films shown on Vietnamese television must be locally produced.

Source: Adapted from "Vietnamese cartoons lose out to foreign productions," *Viet Nam News*, August 7, 2000, p. 19.

Dollars & Sense

Tourist offices in Vietnam offer inexpensive bus trips from North to South or South to North. To save a lot of money, buy a bus pass. Talk to fellow travellers to find out which bus company they liked. Some good questions to ask are how many stops there are, how frequently the buses run, and whether they are air conditioned.

Figure 8.26 Small wooden boats loaded with fresh produce gather along a canal in the Mekong Delta. The delta, Vietnam's "rice basket," is a network of rivers and canals, and often the only route to a village.

CHECK IN

1 Refer to Figures 8.14 and 8.16, which show the growth of tourism in Vietnam. Write three points describing these trends.

2 Explain why the Vietnamese government has identified ethnic minorities and national preservation in its Strategic Tourism Plan.

3 Identify the stakeholders in this issue concerning the central government's control of tourist activity and outline their viewpoints.

CASE STUDY
Aboriginal Tourism

Figure 8.27 Some large corporations such as Air Canada recognize the advantages of building awareness for Aboriginal tourism. This eagle motif, titled "Free Spirit," was created by Iroquois artist Arnold Aron Jacobs. The man shown here is Reg Crowshoe, a Blackfoot from Alberta.

66 Too many times in the past have well-intentioned people forgot to respect their culture in attempts to succeed in the tourism industry. 99

— The Canadian Aboriginal Tourism Association

In the past, the participation of Aboriginal peoples in cultural tourism in places like Australia and Canada was usually quite limited. They were largely assigned roles as performers or as wilderness camp guides. At historical re-enactments their perspectives were usually ignored. Today, conditions in many places are changing. The value of Aboriginal cultures from a travel and tourism perspective is being recognized, and both businesses and governments are eager to capitalize on the economic growth. This activity raises the question whether the unique cultural characteristics of Aboriginal nations can be protected while the people benefit from tourism.

In Canada, interest in Aboriginal tourism is broad and varied. Tourists who want to experience Aboriginal culture fall into two basic groups:

- travellers who want to visit historic sites and are interested in purchasing arts and crafts as a part of their tourism experience
- travellers who have a strong interest in learning about Aboriginal history and want to participate in their customs and their relationship with nature

Both groups seek travel and tourism products that range from spending time in a longhouse on a reserve to eating traditional food at a Haida restaurant to searching for shaggy musk-ox. The challenge for Aboriginal tourism is to find a balance between exposing enough cultural activities and products to attract tourists without exposing so much that their culture begins to change with outside influences.

Level of Interest in Aboriginal Tourism Products in Canada

Tourism Category	Tourist Interest	Aboriginal Examples
Heritage sites	90%	Buffalo jumps, medicine wheels, burial grounds, treaty sites, sweat lodges
Arts and crafts	82%	Beading, moccasins, moose or caribou hair tufting, birchbark-biting
Guided wilderness trips	75%	Canoeing, nature interpretation
Entertainment	70%	Pow-wows, rodeos
Hunting and fishing	60%	Native guides
Gambling	14%	Casinos

Source: Adapted from *Aboriginal Cultural Tourism: The Market* by Bernard Campbell, <cormier.icomos.org/canada/bulletin/vol3_no3_campbell_e.html>.

Figure 8.28 How would you rate your level of interest for each of the categories in this chart?

Canada Travels

In Peawanuck, northern Ontario, Sam Hunter established Hudson Bay Polar Bear Park Expeditions. Visitors can enjoy the pristine wilderness and observe wildlife in their natural habitat, as trained guides escort them from campsite to campsite. Sitting around a crackling campfire, guests can feast on caribou, goose, or freshly caught fish while they listen to Aboriginal tales and legends.

Figure 8.29 Sam Hunter, host and founder of Hudson Bay Polar Bear Park Expeditions, is only one of many Aboriginal people who have established cultural tourism businesses.

Benefits of Cultural Tourism to Aboriginal Nations

Aside from the jobs it creates, Aboriginal cultural tourism gives people the opportunity to explain Aboriginal history, its relationship to the larger community, and the evolution of its political system. By sharing information about how and why lifestyle changes occurred, Aboriginal nations can teach visitors what remains of the old ways, thus safeguarding the past for the future.

Aboriginal people also benefit from involvement in the tourist industry. Learning and teaching about their own culture can help to develop a sense of pride in history and heritage. Business owners learn management skills, giving the local economies greater strength. New Aboriginal partnerships with neighbours and businesses help to build stronger communities.

Because Aboriginal tourism has become so culturally and economically important, some governments have established official groups such as the National Aboriginal and Torres Strait Island Tourism Strategy in Australia, and the Canadian National Aboriginal Tourism Association. These and other groups work with Aboriginal people to develop their tourism strategies. This state involvement in the tourism industry in an advisory capacity is a form of **societal guidance**. Governments provide a plan, training, information services, and advertising for the tourism sector. However, final decisions lie with the Aboriginal tourist operators.

Examples of Sustainable Aboriginal Tourism: Australia

There are a number of examples where sustainable tourism has been implemented in Australia. In Northern Queensland, one Aboriginal community took over the management of a wilderness lodge, turning a losing venture into a commercial success. Hazel Douglas, a member of the Guguyalanji tribe, owns and operates Native Guide Safari Tours and leads tours across the Daintree Rainforest, a World Heritage site. While explaining traditional culture, she teaches visitors how to listen for bird-call warnings about crocodiles, how to fix snakebite with seaweed, and how to eat the thirst-quenching abdomens of live green ants.

To the Anangu Aborigines, Uluru (Ayers Rock) has great spiritual significance. Entering sacred sites around the base or climbing the rock is considered a sacrilege. The Anangu have established a tourism industry by helping outsiders to learn about and respect their culture. Guided walks around the base of Uluru focus on the mythology, cave paintings, and plants used by the Anangu. At the Cultural Centre, cultural and artistic displays have been established to educate tourists.

The Aboriginal arts industry has developed with new galleries and a new marketing approach. This approach emphasizes the cultural distinctiveness of Aboriginal peoples and their ties to the land and natural environment. The Bangarra Dance Theatre of Sydney, the Tjapukai Dance Theatre of Kurnanda, and Dreamtime Culture Centre in Rockhampton are examples of recent successful businesses in urban centres.

Figure 8.30 Two Inuit throat singers demonstrate their skill in the Senate chamber, Ottawa. Throat singing is traditionally a women's game in which two players rapidly alternate producing sounds that together mimic everyday events, such as seagulls in flight or a saw cutting through wood.

Interact

What groups should Aboriginal people consult in preparing their development strategies?

Figure 8.31 Very few of the dancers who performed this dance for the opening ceremony of the 2000 Olympics in Sydney, Australia, were actually Aborigines. In what ways might commercial events like this threaten Aboriginal culture?

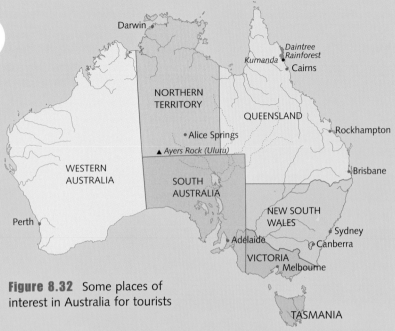

VIRTUAL TRAVEL

www.irwinpublishing.com

To view Aboriginal art from Canada and Australia, visit galleries in different countries by going to the Student Page for *Canada Travels*. The Aboriginal Art and Culture Centre provides two types of tours and explanations for some of their paintings.

Figure 8.32 Some places of interest in Australia for tourists

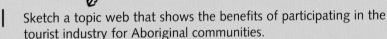

CHECK IN

"Not only does [Aboriginal tourism] offer economic independence, but it does so within the Aboriginal context."

– Sam Hunter

1 Sketch a topic web that shows the benefits of participating in the tourist industry for Aboriginal communities.

2 a) List two ways that culture can be protected.

   b) Explain why it is important to protect Aboriginal culture.

3 Five areas in which Aboriginal people can develop tourist-related businesses are
- transportation/travel and tours
- hospitality
- cultural and heritage products
- adventure tourism
- arts and crafts

Brainstorm a list of businesses for each of these categories. For example, under the hospitality category, you might have restaurants as one business.

4 How have the Anangu protected their culture while still participating in cultural tourism? Suggest two off-shoot businesses that could be developed to support cultural tourism in the area.

- demonstrate an understanding of how a variety of factors are used to define regions
- analyze the major characteristics of selected tourist regions in terms of natural, cultural, economic, and political criteria
- demonstrate an understanding of the need to respect the cultural and religious traditions of others
- apply geotechnologies to a study of regional geography
- produce a plan of action and conduct an independent inquiry that synthesizes concepts, skills, and applications relating to a geographic issue involving travel and tourism either within a region or on a global scale

Cultural Travel in Canada

Purpose: To use ArcView to choose a cultural travel destination in Canada where a large percentage of the population declares a first language of your choice.

Files: cd96.shp, sgc_lang.dbf, prov_bnd.shp, places.shp

Functions: View Properties, Add Table, Join Tables, Legend Editor (Graduated Colour), Zoom, Select Features, Convert to Shapefile, Select by Theme, Query Builder, Label.

1. Your first step will be to select one of the following languages, perhaps one that is significant in your family's ethnic background.

2. Start ArcView, create a blank View and name it "Travel Destinations With a High Percentage of Their Populations Declaring Dutch as Their First Language."

3. Then, add the x:\canada\cd96.shp theme to your View.

4. Now, open the theme table for the Cd96.shp theme. Select "1 Untitled" from the Window menu to return to the project window. Add the x:\tables\sgc\1996\sgc_lang.dbf to your project. Select "Tile" from the Window menu and join the sgc_lang.dbf table to the Attributes of Cd96.shp table using the "sgc" field. Close the Attributes of Cd96.shp table, then maximize your Travel Destinations With a High Percentage of Their Populations Declaring Dutch as their First Language View.

Italian	Filipino	Japanese	Slovak	Slovenian	Dogrib
Chinese	Hungarian	Creole	Macedonian	Turkish	Kutchin
German	Vietnamese	Finnish	Khmer	Bengali	Tlingit
Portuguese	Cree	Czech	Norwegian	Maltese	Serbo_Croa
Polish	Persian	Armenian	Hebrew	Flemish	Dakota_Sio
Ukrainian	Croatian	Yiddish	Estonian	Montagnais	Malay_Baha
Spanish	Gujarati	Urdu	Swedish	Bulgarian	Blackfoot
Dutch	Korean	Inuktitut	Lao	Mi'kmaq	Malayalam
Punjabi	Russian	Romanian	Lithuanian	Gaelic	Thai
Greek	Hindi	Ojibway	Serbian	South_Slav	Kurdish
Arabic	Tamil	Danish	Latvian	Chipewayan	Pashto

Note: The remainder of the instructions will use "Dutch" as the selected language. Wherever "Dutch" appears, please substitute the language that you have selected.

5. Next, using the Legend Editor, create a graduated colour map using "Dutch" in the Classification field and "Pop_96" in the Normalize By field. (Since the populations of the census divisions vary greatly, it is important to "normalize" or divide the number of people declaring "Dutch" as their first language by the total population of the census division. This will produce values that are proportionate to population rather than absolute numbers.)

Figure 8.33 A teacher of Aboriginal languages gives a lesson in Ojibway to a Grade 12 student. Because the use of Aboriginal languages is declining, some experts fear that most of Canada's 50 Aboriginal languages will one day disappear.

6. Now, zoom in on an area of your map that contains census divisions with a large proportion of the population declaring "Dutch" as their first language and that is an area that you would like to visit.

7. Now, using the Select Feature tool, select those census divisions (in the area you have zoomed in on) that contain the highest proportion of people declaring "Dutch" as their first language. Convert the selected census divisions to a shapefile, naming it "Destination Areas" and adding it to your View. Delete the Cd96.shp theme.

8. Next, add a theme containing the provincial boundary of the province in which your destination areas are found: e.g., x:\bc\provbnd.shp. Using the Legend Editor, change the Provbnd.shp symbol to Transparent.

9. Now, add a theme containing the communities found in the province in which your destination areas are found: e.g., x:\bc\places.shp. With the Places.shp theme active, use the Select by Theme function to highlight all places that intercept the Destination areas.shp theme.

10. Finally, using the Query Builder tool, select from the set of communities currently highlighted all those whose population class is greater than or equal to "3" (i.e., greater than 10 000). (Note: If you do not have any communities in your destination areas with a population class greater than or equal to "3," repeat the process using "2." Likewise, if you have too many communities, repeat the process using "4.") Convert the selected communities to a shapefile, naming it "Destinations" and adding it to your View. Delete the Places.shp theme. Using the Callout Label tool, label your destinations.

Extension:

Scan or download photos of the communities, attractions, or cultural events found in the destination areas you have selected in this activity. Hot link these graphics to either the destinations theme or the destination areas theme. Also, create a layout containing both your map and the graphics you have acquired.

REVISIT THE chapter 8

Looking Back

Understanding the Concepts

1. Work with a partner to develop a list of sustainable cultural tourist activities that are found in your community or in a region that interests you.

2. Why do you think that culturally unsustainable practices have continued in the tourist industry?

3. Why is developing authentic cultural experiences for tourists important to the host community? To the visitor?

4. Select one case study from this chapter and explain how it reflects the meaning of sustainable cultural tourism based on the criteria stated in Figure 8.2.

Figure 8.34 An egg vendor in Hanoi, Vietnam. Eggs are considered a delicacy in Vietnamese cuisine.

Practising Your Skills

5. Prepare a one-page report on a Nova Scotia community that has a Gaelic cultural festival. Start by visiting the Student Page for *Canada Travels* to find statistics for Community Profiles.

6. Use information from the text and do additional research to compare the travel and tourism industries of Vietnam and Canada. Use these categories: Opportunities, Challenges, Role of Government, Role of Local People, and The Future.

Applying Your Skills

7. Do research to compile an inventory of three Aboriginal travel expeditions or destinations that are readily available to tourists. In a chart, record information for each about the types of activities that are offered, best season or time of year to visit, travel requirements, and another category of your choice.

8. In countries like Canada and Australia, Aboriginal cultures are often best observed in places that are far from the largest centres, such as in Nunavut, Canada's newest territory. In your opinion, what should Aboriginal groups do to ensure that their tourism developments are successful, given the distances?

9. Create a chart that identifies the various policies, marketing strategies, and initiatives of governments and organizations found throughout the chapter. In the last column of the chart, briefly evaluate the impact of each on travel and tourism.

Thinking Like a Tourist

10. Write a 250-word article for a travel magazine on one of Vietnam's Hill tribes or one of Canada's Aboriginal nations. Include the following:
    - background information on your selected group
    - a sketch map showing their location
    - reference to their traditions
    - travel hints
    - suggestions for sustainable cultural tourism

Figure 8.35 A woman from the Yao Hill tribe, Sa Pa, Hoang Lien Son Province, Vietnam

JOB SKILLS

Georgian College in Barrie, Ontario, offers a six-semester diploma course in Aboriginal Tourism Management. Graduates of this program will have knowledge of Aboriginal culture, traditions, and contemporary issues as well as current government policies and programs as they relate to tourism, and particularly to Aboriginal tourism. The core values of respect and kindness will be evident as students demonstrate competencies in the areas of hospitality and customer service, ecotourism, research, entrepreneurship, business administration, and human resource management.

Conduct research to explain how this program would prepare a graduate for a management position in Aboriginal Tourism Development to ensure that Aboriginal tourism is sustainable.

UNIT 4

four
Understanding and Managing Change

Chapter 11: Florida, United States. What is the value of marketing in keeping a tourist destination's economy strong?

NORTH AMERICA

Chapter 10: Cancun, Mexico. How does careful planning help ensure the economic success of a destination?

Tourism has an enormous economic impact. This unit looks at how tourism can both help places by establishing stable economies and hurt them by creating economic challenges. The difficulties of developing a sustainable economy are examined in a number of issues.

Destinations You Will Visit

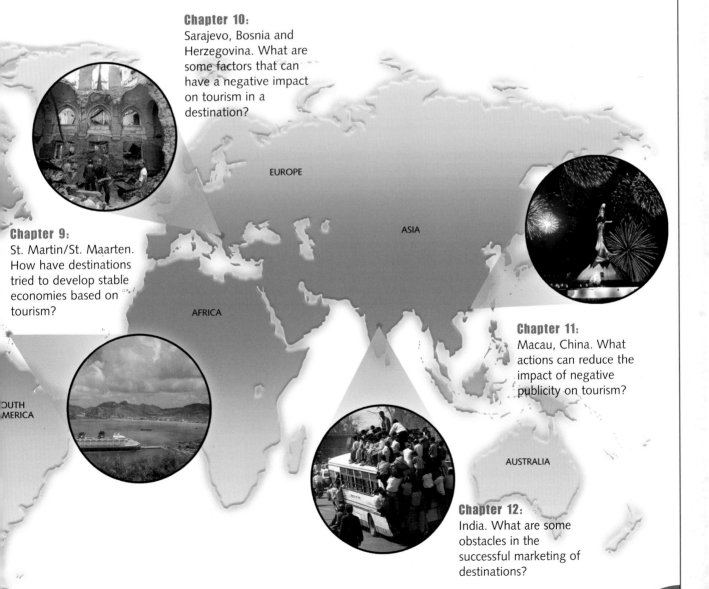

Chapter 10:
Sarajevo, Bosnia and Herzegovina. What are some factors that can have a negative impact on tourism in a destination?

EUROPE

ASIA

Chapter 9:
St. Martin/St. Maarten. How have destinations tried to develop stable economies based on tourism?

AFRICA

Chapter 11:
Macau, China. What actions can reduce the impact of negative publicity on tourism?

SOUTH AMERICA

AUSTRALIA

Chapter 12:
India. What are some obstacles in the successful marketing of destinations?

CHAPTER nine 9

Economic Patterns: The Success of Tourism

FOCUS ON THESE KEY QUESTIONS AND . . .

1. What are important economic trends in tourism?
2. What places are sources of tourists, and what impact do tourists have on the tourist industry?
3. What economic issues arise out of tourist trends and patterns?
4. What important issues do destinations such as St. Martin/ St. Maarten face?

KEY WORDS & TERMS

domestic tourism
hedonism
independent travellers
planned travellers
reluctant travellers
satellite accounting system

An Economic Success Story

The quotation at the top of the next page points to the economic trends of travel and tourism on a world scale. International tourism generates a tremendous amount of wealth and employs ever-increasing numbers of workers around the globe. Add to this the economic value of **domestic tourism**, travel within a country, and we can see the total value of the industry. Clearly, travel and tourism has a large and growing place in the world economy.

Figure 9.1 (This page and opposite) The many faces of tourism: tourists like these contribute to the economic growth of the tourist industry. Check newspapers, Web sites, or travel brochures to find out the cost of a one-week cruise in the Caribbean or Mediterranean seas, or a one-week golf trip in South Carolina or Arizona.

In this chapter, we will investigate the economic impact of travel and tourism. Because the industry is so large and complex, the focus will be on understanding who tourists are, where they come from in the world, and the impact they have on the tourist industry. We need to be clear about what the tourist industry is and how we determine its economic importance.

EXPECTATIONS

In this chapter, you will have the opportunity to

- identify recent trends in travel and tourism
- identify selected factors that influence travellers' destination choices
- demonstrate an understanding that the travel and tourism industry consists of many interconnected components
- analyze global tourist flows and explain the reasons for the observed patterns
- compare rates of tourism and tourist spending for selected countries
- analyze the effects of cultural, economic, and political motivators and barriers on travel and tourism patterns
- identify criteria that planners must consider when planning for tourism development within a region
- explain how tourist-related development can have important impacts on human systems
- produce a case study analyzing the relationship between tourism and level of development in a developing country

Economics of the Travel and Tourism Industry

It is easy to find facts and figures that point to the economic strength of the travel and tourism industry. Here is a sample:

- The travel and tourism industry generates 5.5 million new jobs annually.
- The annual growth rate of the travel and tourism industry is 3.7%.
- Capital investment in the travel and tourism industry is over US$800 billion per year.

These figures seem to indicate that the industry is growing quickly and becoming more economically powerful, contributing to improved qualities of life in some parts of the world. To understand how this growth is occurring and in what sectors of the economy, we need to take a closer look at the industry. We will consider the economic impact of tourism to be the total of all the money spent by people who are engaging in tourist activities.

Figure 9.3 The Ginza shopping district in downtown Tokyo is an economic hub and a major attraction for tourists.

Projections for Economic and Employment Growth, 1996–2006		
	1996	**2006 est.**
Number of jobs worldwide	255 million	385 million
Tourism jobs as a percentage of all jobs	10.7%	11.1%
Total value of all tourism activities	US$3600 billion	US$7100 billion
Percentage of Gross Domestic Product	10.7%	11.5%
Total capital investment	US$766 billion	US$1600 billion
Total taxes paid	US$653 billion	US$1300 billion

Figure 9.2 Calculate the percentage increases for the number of jobs from 1996 to 2006 and for the total value of all tourism activities from 1996 to 2006. Report your findings in a sentence that explains the projections of the industry.

When a person buys a high-priced item like an appliance or an automobile, the transaction is fairly easy to understand. The consumer goes to the retailer, chooses a product, and pays the price for it. The money from the purchase goes directly to the retailer

Characteristics of the Travel and Tourism Industry

The travel and tourism industry is…

- composed of many different products and services
- a 24-hour-a-day, seven-day-a-week industry
- labour intensive, with job opportunities at all skill levels
- composed largely of small businesses
- open to new firms, with few barriers to entry
- private-sector driven

Figure 9.4 In what ways is the travel and tourism industry different from the automobile industry or the banking industry?

Travel FACT

Taxes often take an important part of your travel and tourism dollar. The average tax rate for a hotel room in the United States is 12.36%.

and tax collectors. Indirectly, money goes to the manufacturer of the product and all its suppliers, the retailer's suppliers and advertisers, trucking companies, banks, and so on.

Let's take a look at what happens when a person books a vacation, say to a Caribbean island. First, the consumer makes a choice about destination and type of package (all-inclusive, air only, etc.) and books the vacation, generally through a retailer. The retailer keeps a part of the purchase price as commission, then pays the airline for seats to the destination, the hotel for rooms and meals if included, various governments for departure and other taxes, and admission fees included in the package. These are the direct payments.

Many companies and employees benefit indirectly from tourist dollars. Those who benefit indirectly include the suppliers of goods and services to the hotels and airlines, credit card companies, airport employees, and government officials. At the destination, the vacationer makes other purchases of souvenirs and services that are also seen as a part of the overall industry. The travel and tourism industry is very complex, with many different products and services woven into the economy.

Figure 9.5 For many Canadian tourists, their travel experiences begin with a visit to a travel agency. What is the agent's role? What economic impacts occur when tourists book vacations?

Figure 9.6 The components of the tourist industry. In your opinion, which of these components has the greatest employment in your local area?

Source: Adapted from Hannell et al., *Travel and Tourism: A World Regional Geography*. Toronto: John Wiley & Sons Canada Limited, 1992.

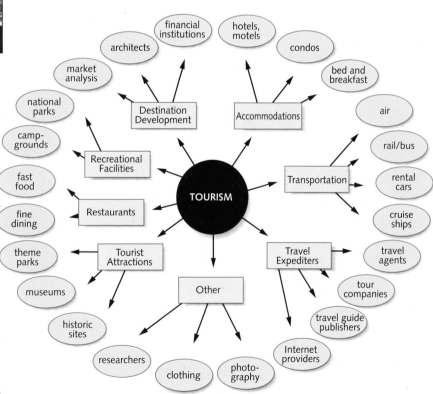

Trying to figure out the best ways to measure total economic value has been a challenge because of the diversity of the industry. Having an accurate accounting method in an industry experiencing both rapid growth and rapid change is seen as crucial. Both governments and businesses need to have accurate measurements to identify trends, forecast growth, plan effectively, and avoid costly failures. Because of this, international government agencies like the World Tourism Organization (WTO), private sector groups including the World Travel and Tourism Council (WTTC), and various governments have worked to set up an international accounting system for the industry. This **satellite accounting system** links to national accounting systems to give up-to-date, accurate information about travel and tourism.

Interact

Why is it important that there be an international accounting system for the travel and tourism industry?

Terrorist attacks hurt travel and tourism

- Quebec City faces a tourism loss of up to $40-million after 25 000 hotel room nights are cancelled to the end of the year.
- Cruise ships are still making calls to ports in Nova Scotia, but many of the ships carry only half the normal number of passengers.
- BC's $10-billion-a-year tourism industry is down 50 percent since the attacks.
- Business at the Casino Windsor in Ontario, where Americans usually make up 80 percent of the business, has been cut in half.
- Theatre ticket sales at Niagara-on-the-Lake's Shaw Festival in southern Ontario have been cut in half.
- Canada's travel agents ask the federal government for $25-million in compensation.
- Typically one-third of people who eat out are travelling. Since the attacks, restaurant owners have been hit hard.
- Carpet stores in Islamabad, Pakistan, which depend on tourists, are almost empty.

Figure 9.7 The effects of the September 11, 2001, terrorist attacks on the World Trade Center and the Pentagon, emphasized just how interconnected the travel and tourism industry is. Direct participants in the industry such as airlines, hotels, and travel agencies all suffered dramatic losses. So, too, did more indirect beneficiaries of the travel and tourism industry, such as hotel bellhops and hairdressers, small store owners, café owners, and companies that prepare food for airlines.

CHECK IN

1 Identify five different ways that we might use statistics to show growth in the tourism industry.

2 a) Choose one of the bulleted points in Figure 9.4 on page 232 and demonstrate that it is true, using examples from your local area.

   b) In your opinion, which of the bulleted points least applies to the travel and tourism industry in your local area? Explain your answer.

3 Use examples to explain how the travel and tourism industry is based on interconnected components.

4 Using Figure 9.6, identify three parts of the industry which it might be relatively easy to enter, and three parts which it might be more difficult to enter. For each, give reasons to support your choices.

Economic Patterns

In this section of the chapter we investigate who tourists are and, in particular, where they live in the world. The locations of tourists and their travel to tourist destinations create movements or flows, pointing to economic patterns.

Who Are the Tourists?

The economic value of the tourist industry is determined by the total amount of money spent by those people classified as tourists while at home, en route, and at their destinations. Therefore, we should be clear about who is considered to be a tourist. In general, tourists are people who travel to places other than their homes for longer than 24 hours, but less than a year. This definition includes not only people who are on vacation seeking rest and relaxation, but also people travelling for business reasons and for other purposes such as attending conferences. There are some exceptions. Migrants (including refugees and nomadic people) are not considered to be temporarily away from their homes and so are not designated as tourists.

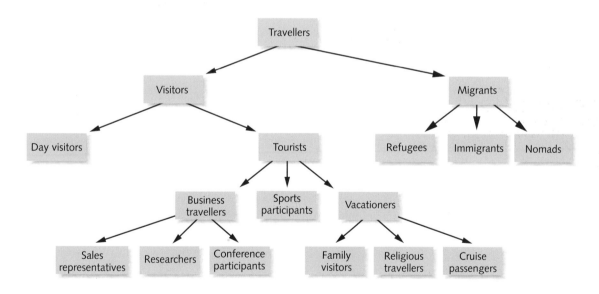

Figure 9.8 Classification of travellers. Why do you suppose day visitors are not considered to be tourists?

Source: Adapted from Hannell et al., *Travel and Tourism: A World Regional Geography*. Toronto: John Wiley & Sons Canada Limited, 1992.

An Elite Activity

Only a small share of the world's people can afford to be tourists. Tourism is a service that people consume. We pay for this service with money that remains after our basic needs are met for food, clothing, and shelter. Unfortunately, for two-thirds of the world's population, spending on tourism is just a dream. The world's tourists are, by and large, residents of the richest nations. Many of these people have money to spend on discretionary activities, including leisure and travel.

The reality is that people from Canada and the United States and from the 15 nations of the European Union spend two-thirds of the world's tourist dollars. If Japan is added to the list, these 18 countries account for almost 80% of global tourism. This concentration of demand for tourism very much shapes the nature of the industry. The industry must respond to the desires and demands of a small proportion of the world's people who largely share the same socio-economic characteristics.

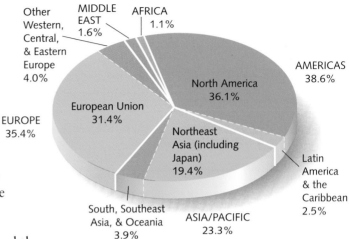

Figure 9.9 Personal tourism expenditures by region as a percentage of world, 2000. Personal tourism expenditures are a measure of how much individuals spend on tourism and do not include what governments and industries spend. The graph shows how much each region of the world spends as a percentage of the world's total.

Figure 9.10 The regions shown on this map are the same as those shown in the graph in Figure 9.9. Generally, which areas have the greatest expenditures on tourism?

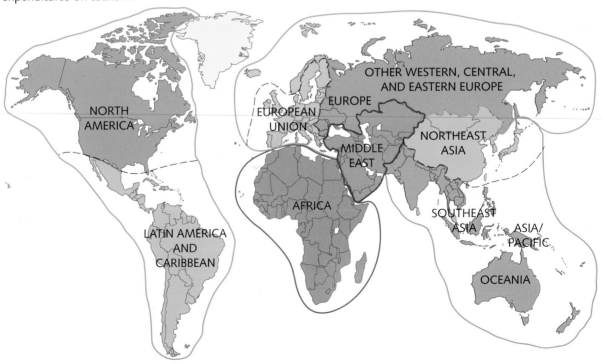

Figure 9.11 Local residents selling candied mangoes walk past a sunbathing tourist on the beach at Acapulco, Mexico. Most Canadians can afford to travel, at least within their own province or country.

A number of Internet sites offer planning tools to help you get the kind of vacation that you want. You answer a number of questions about likes and dislikes, activities that you want to engage in, regional preferences and, of course, how much you are prepared to spend. The site searches its database to provide options that best meet your specifications. You can connect with these sites by visiting the Student Page for *Canada Travels*.

New Trends in Tourism

While there is no doubt that North Americans and Europeans dominate the tourist industry, the picture has changed somewhat over the past few years. Rising incomes in the rapidly growing economies of Asia – particularly South Korea, Taiwan, Singapore, and Indonesia – have resulted in expansion of the tourist industry in many parts of Asia. Also, freedoms that came after the collapse of communism in Eastern Europe ignited a growing trend to international tourism in countries like Poland, the Czech Republic, and Russia.

Who Wants to Be a Tourist?

It would be incorrect to paint a picture of the people of rich countries as tourists one-and-all. In fact, every society, including our own, has people who cannot afford to travel and people who do not care to travel, preferring to remain at home. Studies of Canadians show that about 30% of adults have not engaged in tourism within the preceding five years. Two factors that seem to shape interest in tourism are

- income levels, with more travel corresponding to higher incomes
- levels of education, with more years of school tied to greater amounts of travel

Even when we look at recent travellers, 18% of Canadian tourists do not see travel as integral to their lives, and claim that they do not enjoy it. These people travel as little as possible.

Travel FACT

On April 28, 2001, California millionaire Dennis Tito became the first space tourist. The 60-year-old former NASA engineer-turned-investment manager paid Russia US$20 million to take him to the International Space Station. Tito spent four days in flight, round trip, and six days on the station.

Characteristics of Tourists

Those people who do value travel and are prepared to spend their money on tourism are not all alike. Industry analysts talk about three groups of travellers, each with its own preferences and wants.

Planned Travellers   **Planned travellers** make up 37.5% of all tourists. These people

- use travel agents and make all arrangements before starting their vacations
- purchase vacation packages that include both accommodations and transportation
- prefer all-inclusive packages
- take guided tours

Independent Travellers   Globally, 33.5% of tourists would be considered **independent travellers**. These travellers

- make their own arrangements for vacation trips
- arrange their activities as they go during their trips
- prefer to travel on reduced airfares

Travel FACT

According to surveys conducted by the travel and tourism industry, 91% of North American tourists spend less than 30 minutes making financial preparations for their vacation.

Reluctant Travellers While **reluctant travellers** are not enthusiastic about travel, they do travel to some extent. These people make up about 29% of tourists globally. They

- delay making travel arrangements
- would prefer to spend their money on other things
- return to places that they have visited before
- prefer to remain in one spot once they get to their destinations

Figure 9.13 Planned travellers are the market for advertisements like this one.

EGYPT

LAND OF THE PHARAOHS

GRAND TOUR—Visit Egypt with the experts!

5 nights Cairo • 4 nights deluxe Nile cruise
• 4 nights in the exclusive Red Sea resort of Sharm-el-Sheikh
Breakfast and dinner daily at hotels • Travel within Egypt via air
• Visa cost & tips included

Extensive sightseeing including Temple of Ramses II at Abu Simbel
Max. group size 26 • Can$4949 including air from Toronto

TRAVELUXE LTD.
Toll free: 1-800-987-6543
www.traveluxe.com

Figure 9.14 (Bottom left) A group of tourists on a package tour arrive at the National Museum, Cairo, Egypt. About one-third of tourists make all their travel arrangements before they leave home. (Bottom right) Independent travellers cycling through Nepal. What are the advantages of travelling in a relatively independent fashion?

Travel Philosophy Segments by Country (percentage of travellers)			
Country	Planned Travel	Independent Travel	Reluctant Travel
Australia	33	35	32
Brazil	43	26	31
Canada	38	33	29
Germany	39	22	39
Italy	41	35	25
Japan	34	27	38
Singapore	44	24	32
South Korea	19	44	37

Figure 9.15 Do the figures shown for Canada reflect the attitudes of your friends and family members?

Travel Preferences

One factor that may influence attitudes about travel is the average age of the population. More mature tourists may prefer packages, while younger travellers, probably with less money to spend, may choose less structured vacations. This might explain why, in Figure 9.15, 41% of travellers from Italy, a country with a relatively large population of seniors, preferred planned travel. The degree of the development of the tourist industry in a country is likely another factor. As an emerging economy, South Korea's travel and tourism industry is not as well established as the industry is in places like Canada or Germany. This may explain why South Korea's planned travel rate is low. A third factor might be the degree to which a country is connected by family ties to other parts of the world. Canada's relatively low rate for reluctant travellers may well be a product of our strong immigration, with Canadians travelling to visit family and friends in other parts of the world.

Figure 9.16 Eight out of ten Canadian seniors want to travel now or in the near future. Seniors, on average, can expect at least 20 years of active life after retirement.

Figure 9.17 A tour group of Canadian students visits the Lion's Gate at Mycenae, a city of ancient Greece.

The travel and tourism industry recognizes the differences in travellers and has separate products and services that are designed to accommodate the different ways that the three groups vacation.

Canada Travels

In 2000, globally, more travel services were sold over the Internet than any other consumer product. Canadians, as leading users of this medium, are expected to spend $4.2 billion on travel over the Internet by 2004. Within the next few years, experts suggest that fully half of all travel arrangements made by Canadians will be booked online.

Looking for Experiences: Reasons for Tourism

Understanding who is engaging in tourist activities – and therefore contributing to the economic value of tourism – is important for the travel and tourism industry. As a way of helping to plan and develop facilities and services for tourists, industry analysts have developed a number of tools for analyzing tourists' needs and wants. One interesting approach tries to plot tourists' characteristics, using two important dimensions:

1. freedom and independence versus stability and security

2. recreation versus social/cultural awareness.

These opposing characteristics are illustrated in Figure 9.18 on the next page.

Tourists who fit at the left side of the horizontal axis would prefer to engage in activities such as backpacking through the Rockies or bicycling through Europe. Generally, 46% of tourists want some degree of independence while on vacation.

If you value stability and security, you might book your vacation with a guided tour where you were confident that you would be safe. You would look for a facility that offered no surprises. This quality is valued to some extent by 54% of travellers.

Tourists who make recreation their priority search out vacations at beach resorts with plenty of "fun and sun" activities. The fact that 63% of tourists seek this characteristic explains the popularity of resort vacations.

At the bottom of the vertical axis are tourists who plan on visiting museums and art galleries and touring battlefields and places of historic interest. Studies show that about 37% of tourists rate these activities as desirable on a vacation.

The two-dimensional diagram can be used to categorize the kinds of activities that people are searching for when they engage in tourism.

Travel FACT

In 2000, 6.7 million consumers used the Internet to make travel reservations.

Recreation 63%

Freedom/Independence 46% ← → Stability/Security 54%

Social/Cultural Awareness 37%

Figure 9.18 A technique that plots tourists' attitudes toward travel experiences. What impact might changing attitudes and characteristics have on the tourism industry?

Canada Travels

Tourism analysts in Canada have picked up on a growing trend for vacationers in their 40s, 50s, and 60s. Rather than seeking beaches and adventure, this segment of the travelling public is exploring museums, architecture, and art galleries. They generally stay longer in one spot than other groups and tend to be more affluent.

CHECK IN

1 a) Write a definition for "tourist" using the information in Figure 9.8 on page 235.

   b) Why it is necessary to distinguish between visitors and migrants? Between same-day visitors and tourists?

2 a) According to Figure 9.9 on page 236, people who live in Africa and the Middle East spend only small amounts on travel and tourism. Explain why this is so.

   b) If you were part of the travel and tourism industry in Africa, what might you do to try to stimulate interest in travel to boost the tourism industry?

3 What type of tourist do you suppose would be attracted to space tourism? Why would someone pay so much for this type of travel adventure?

4 Think about one tourist facility familiar to you. Describe the type of tourist that it seems to target, using the categories discussed in this chapter. Or, if the facility is large, such as a theme park, describe the ways that it tries to meet the needs of different types of tourists.

Figure 9.19 Tourists visiting the Lincoln Memorial, Washington, DC

LOOKING AT ISSUES

St. Martin/St. Maarten

Issue: To what extent should local residents of a travel destination have to financially support the tourist industry?

Many Caribbean islands have developed travel and tourism industries in an attempt to build stronger, more stable economies. Competition is strong among these many tourist destinations, as each location tries to attract a major share of tourists. Each place attempts to meet the diverse needs of the travelling public by offering a range of facilities and activities that appeal to planned, independent, and reluctant travellers. One island that demonstrates the efforts of Caribbean destinations to attract tourists to strengthen their economies is St. Martin/St. Maarten.

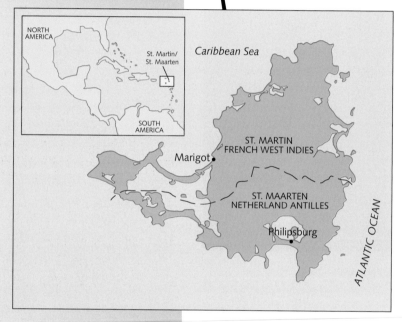

Figure 9.20 Location of St. Martin/St. Maarten

A Divided Island

St. Martin/St. Maarten is a small island, only 96 km². It is located in part of the Caribbean Islands referred to as the Lesser Antilles. The island is home to two separate governments. The southern part of the island is the Dutch colony of St. Maarten (Sint Maarten), with its capital at Philipsburg. St. Maarten is part of the Netherland Antilles, a possession of the Kingdom of the Netherlands. The northern part of the island is St. Martin (Saint Martin). This territory is within the subprefecture (a small political unit) of Guadeloupe, one of France's overseas departments. The capital of St. Martin is Marigot.

St. Maarten is home to 39 000 people, and St. Martin to 34 000 people.

Figure 9.21 At Princess Juliana Airport, the largest airport on St. Martin/St. Maarten, signs are posted in Dutch, French, and English. The benefits of living in European dependencies have helped to keep demands for independence to a minimum.

Interact

In what ways might tourism help to preserve the natural environment of the island?

Economic Conditions

Island residents have few economic resources besides tourism. The volcanic island has steep hillsides and shallow soils that make agriculture an unproductive venture. Farmers cannot produce sugar cane the way farmers on other Caribbean islands do. There are no mineral deposits of consequence. In the past, residents extracted salt from shallow lagoons. That activity ended when salting fish was replaced by freezing them. Businesspeople on St. Martin/St. Maarten have not had the resource base to develop distinctive products like rum or coffee that have made other islands famous. Because shipping is expensive, manufacturing of goods is not a viable option.

With few other economic options, the businesspeople of St. Martin/St. Maarten developed the island's travel and tourism potential. Now, 95% of all economic activity is directly or indirectly tied to tourism. This industry has allowed island residents to earn per capita incomes of about US$11 800 and US$9000 on the Dutch and French sides, respectively. This is substantially higher than the per capita incomes of many of the island's neighbours. For example, on average, residents of St. Kitts and Nevis earn US$6000 and residents of Antigua and Barbuda earn US$6800. The lack of other economic opportunities and the seasonal nature of tourism mean that unemployment rates are stubbornly high at 15% in St. Maarten and 28% in St. Martin.

Marketing Hedonism

St. Martin/St. Maarten's tourism industry is built on marketing **hedonism,** or pleasure, within a distinctive cultural setting. Activities are designed to pamper tourists and make them want to see and do more while on the island.

The island has 37 beaches facing both the Caribbean Sea and the Atlantic Ocean. Some of the beaches are isolated and seldom visited by tourists, while others have been developed into extensive resort properties. Orient Beach, in the northern part of the island, is the most developed and has a wide variety of activities, including snorkeling, wind surfing, and kayaking. These activities employ many local and migrant tourism workers. Parts of this beach are designated "clothing optional." Topless bathing is popular on all the beaches.

The interior of the island offers rugged hillsides for hiking and horseback riding. Other attractions include the famous Butterfly Farm, which allows tourists to walk freely about enclosures with rare and exotic butterflies from around the world.

Figure 9.22 Some beaches on the island have had little tourist development.

Figure 9.23 Large resorts like this one attract visitors from North America and Europe.

Selling Culture

The blending of two distinct European cultures with the Caribbean cultural influence has helped to create a draw for North American and European tourists. The French part of the island is particularly well known for its French-Caribbean cuisine. The tiny village of Grand Case is considered to be the gourmet capital of the Caribbean, with its main street lined with fine restaurants to serve tourists and sailors who moor in its harbour. A number of these restaurants are owned by non-residents who operate them only during the busier times of the year.

The Dutch side of the island bears the distinctive architectural styles of the Netherlands, transplanted to the Caribbean. The shops and homes of Philipsburg are painted in bright pastels that are much admired by tourists who day-trip off the cruise ships that make the village a port-of-call.

On both sides of the island, duty-free shops and boutiques catering to wealthy tourists feature garments by top French and European designers. All of these attractions employ local workers, although the seasonal nature of the industry means that many jobs are of short duration.

Travel FACT

Over 400 restaurants on the island represent the more than 50 distinct nationalities living there.

Figure 9.24 (Right) The cultural impacts of a European heritage are clearly obvious in this street scene in Philipsburg, on the Dutch side of the island. (Above) A shop on Front Street, Philipsburg

TRAVELLERS' ALERT!

St. Martin/St. Maarten has a high crime rate. Tourists visiting the casinos should be especially vigilant.

Selling Excitement

The Dutch side of the island is famous for two activities that appeal to tourists – casinos and duty-free shopping. Large and small casinos cater to people who enjoy the challenge of slot machines and games of chance. They are found throughout the Dutch side, while specialty shops are mostly located in the commercial centre of Philipsburg. Jewellery, perfume, linen, and cigars are popular duty-free purchases. Many of the outlets are owned by large international chains or by people of Asian extraction who have been drawn to the island by its economic opportunities.

Industry Challenges

The island has strong tourist attractions that have allowed it to be competitive in the region. Nonetheless, it does face significant challenges that may limit its appeal to tourists in the future. Tourists may regard these challenges as barriers to their travel to the island. Let's look at some of these challenges.

Costs Are High   Services offered by the island's tourist industry are relatively high priced. Eating in the fine French restaurants of Grand Case costs roughly the same as fine dining in a large urban centre in Canada. Rates for accommodation are above the average for hotels on other Caribbean islands, and renting a car is a must if you want to tour the island. These factors make the total price for a vacation on St. Martin/St. Maarten greater than a vacation in other parts of the region. For people travelling on a budget, this is an important factor. Higher prices on the island also make it difficult for local residents to afford the services offered to tourists.

Infrastructure Improvement Driving on the roads of the island can be a challenging experience. Potholes and washouts are spectacular, and repairs are slow by Canadian standards. Also not up to the standards most tourists are used to are the water supply and sewage systems. The small island has few streams, and generating enough fresh water to meet the needs of the tourist industry is a problem. Notices in hotel rooms ask guests to avoid wasting water. Expanding the infrastructure of the island to include such things as desalination plants is expensive, and efforts are barely keeping ahead of new developments. The island's governments are already experiencing high levels of debt as they try to pay for improvements. To some extent tourists pay through such means as airport departure taxes. However, additional tourist taxes could very well create hard feelings among the people whose spending supports the whole economy. Hiding the taxes through increased business or gasoline taxes would raise prices in a highly competitive market. These costs of infrastructure improvements, it seems, must be paid through local taxation.

Figure 9.25 This new pier in Philipsburg was built especially to handle cruise ships carrying tourists. Upgrading of infrastructure is a costly endeavour, but necessary for expansion of tourism.

Hurricane Damage The hurricanes of November 1999 had a devastating effect on tourist revenues for 2000. Many resorts and hotels were forced to cancel bookings, and travel agencies discouraged tourists from travelling to the island while rebuilding was taking place. Millions of dollars of business was lost. Unemployment rose sharply for hotel and restaurant workers. There was one group of workers who did benefit: the extent of the damage meant that tradespeople were overloaded, and progress on repairs was slow.

The Future

Despite challenges and intense competition in the region, the continued popularity of St. Martin/St. Maarten suggests that its travel industry has a future. To remain competitive, however, the island must continue to improve and modernize its infrastructure, which will increase taxation for local residents.

Figure 9.26 Hurricanes are a fact of life in the Caribbean, and can have devastating impacts on tourism.

Figure 9.27 (Upper right) The flamboyant tree is among the distinctive vegetation of St. Martin/St. Maarten. (Above) Cruising yachts are a familiar sight off the coast of the island.

CHECK IN

1 All of the Caribbean islands can offer sun, surf, and sand. What distinctive characteristics has St. Martin/St. Maarten attempted to market to potential tourists?

2 a) What kinds of tourists are likely to be attracted to vacation on this island? Explain.

   b) What types of tourists are not likely to book trips to this island? Why?

3 Identify features or conditions of St. Martin/St. Maarten that you think act as "barriers" or discouraging factors for tourists vacationing on the island.

4 Suppose you were asked to recommend changes that the travel industry in St. Martin/St. Maarten could make to improve their prospects. What three improvements would you recommend, and who should pay for them? Give reasons to support your opinions.

5 How might the following groups of people feel about paying for improving, expanding, and modernizing the infrastructure of St. Martin/St. Maarten?

   a) residents through increased income taxes

   b) foreign owners of shops and services through increased business taxes

   c) tourists through increased prices and user fees

- apply geotechnologies to a study of regional geography
- produce and interpret different types of maps, graphic organizers, and diagrams
- communicate effectively in written, oral, and visual forms
- compare rates of tourism and tourist spending for selected countries
- analyze the causes and effects of economic disparities between selected world tourism regions
- use statistics effectively to analyze travel and tourism patterns

Personal Travel Expenditures: Who's Spending All the Money?

Purpose: To use ArcView to produce a series of maps illustrating variations in the amount of money spent by various peoples throughout the world on tourism.

Files: cntry_95.shp

Functions: View Properties, Convert to Shapefile, Table Edit, Create a New Field, Legend Editor (Graduated Colour), Legend Editor (Chart), Labelling, Layout.

1. Your first step will be to create a blank View, name it "Personal Tourism Expenditures as Percent of World," and change the Map Units to "decimal degrees" and the Distance Units to "kilometres."

2. Next, add the theme x:\world\cntry_95.shp (located on ArcCanada 2.0 Disk #2) to your View.

3. Now, convert the Cntry_95.shp theme to a shapefile, naming it "Countries" and adding it the View. Delete the Cntry_95.shp theme.

4. Next, open the theme table for the Countries.shp theme and place the table in Edit mode. Create a new "string" field called "Region" with a width of "48." Close the Attributes of Countries.shp window to return to the View.

5. Now, using the Zoom, Pan, and Select Feature tools, select all of the countries that belong to Africa. (Using click, hold, and drag, you can select several countries at once. Also, by holding down the Shift key and clicking you can select and deselect records without deselecting those already highlighted.)

   Another option for selecting countries is to open the theme table and select records (i.e., countries) by locating and clicking on the names of the countries. (Again, you can hold down the Shift key and click on records to select and deselect them without deselecting those already highlighted.)

6. Next, open the theme table for the Countries.shp theme. Promote all of the selected records to the top of the table. Click the Edit button and enter "A" into the "Region" field for all of the highlighted records. Remember to hit Enter after keying in the last entry. Click the Select None button before proceeding.

7. Now, close the Attributes of Countries.shp window to return to the View. Repeat Steps 5 and 6 for the remaining regions shown in the table on the next page. (You may have to consult an atlas, or another appropriate source, to determine the countries that belong to each region.)

Personal Tourism Expenditures as Percent of World, 2000		
Region	Region Name	Personal Tourism Expenditures (% of world)
A	Africa	1.1
B	North America	36.1
C	Latin America and the Caribbean	2.5
D	Northeast Asia (including Japan)	19.4
E	South, Southeast Asia, and Oceania	3.9
F	European Union	31.4
G	Other Western, Central, and Eastern Europe	4.0
H	Middle East	1.6

8. Next, perform a Sort Ascending on the theme table using the "Region" field. Toggle down to the bottom of the table to see the records that you missed. Determine the region to which each belongs by either looking at the country's name or by selecting it, returning to the View, and performing a Zoom to Selected. Complete the remaining entries, save the edits, then close the Attributes of Countries.shp window to return to the View.

9. Now, turn on the Geoprocessing extension, start the Geoprocessing Wizard, then dissolve the Countries.shp theme using the "Region" attribute, and naming the output file "Regions." (Do not include any additional fields and operations to be included in the output file.)

10. Next, open the theme table of the Regions.shp theme and place the table in Edit mode. Change the names of the regions to their proper names (e.g., "A" to "Africa"). Add a new "number" field called "PTE_% World Total" with decimal places

set to "1." Enter the values as shown in the table above. When complete, save the edits, then close the Attributes of Regions.shp window to return to the View.

11. Now, using the Legend Editor, apply a "graduated colour" legend type to the Regions.shp theme using an "equal interval" classification type.

12. Next, cut the Countries.shp theme, then paste it into a new View.

13. Now, open the theme table for the Countries.shp theme and place the table in Edit mode. Add two new "number" fields to the table, naming them "Tot_Per_Expend" (decimal places set to "1") and "PerCap_Per_Expend," respectively. Locate the countries shown in the table on the next page and enter the appropriate data into the two new fields you have created. (To make this step easier, you can open the Table Properties dialogue box and uncheck all the fields that you do not need visible in your table.)

Remember to hit Enter after keying in the last entry. When complete, save the edits, then close the Attributes of Countries.shp window to return to the View.

 14. Next, using the Legend Editor, apply a "chart" legend type to the Countries.shp theme, adding only the "Tot_Per_Expend" field, and setting the Size Field in the Properties dialogue box to "Tot_Per_Expend." Experiment with different minimum and maximum sizes and set the background symbol to transparent. Label each of the 15 countries using callout labels.

15. Now, name the View "Total Personal Expenditures on Tourism, Top 15 Countries."

16. Next, copy and paste the Countries.shp theme into a new View. Repeat Step 14, except this time use the "PerCap_Per_Expend" field.

17. Now, name the View "Per Capita Personal Expenditures on Tourism."

18. Finally, create a layout for each of your three maps, complete with an appropriate title, north arrow, legend, and scale bar. To each layout, add a text box that describes and accounts for the patterns illustrated in the map.

Total Personal Expenditures on Tourism, 2000		
Country	Total Value (US$ millions)	Per Capita Spending (US$)
United States	725 914.3	2686
Japan	350 374.2	2783
Germany	168 277.4	2050
United Kingdom	135 857.7	2303
France	106 397.1	1810
Italy	98 333.9	1731
Canada	53 396.4	1739
Spain	53 257.3	1362
China	39 945.6	32
Australia	28 315.9	1576
Netherlands	28 289.9	1836
Switzerland	23 904.9	3275
Brazil	23 599.0	139
Austria	20 055.5	2476
Belgium	19 503.3	1912

Download or scan pictures of tourists involved in activities for which they have had to spend money. Create a new View containing the Cntry_95.shp theme and link these pictures to their appropriate countries.

Create a series of scatter charts to test for correlations between "Per Capita Personal Expenditure on Tourism" (i.e., PerCap_Per_Expend) and other variables that you think might be related. Create a layout for each scatter chart containing it and a text box that describes and attempts to account for the relationship.

Figure 9.28 In Fort-de-France, Martinique, tourists look for bargains on high-priced designer items such as perfume.

Understanding the Concepts

1. The quotation that opens this chapter says, "Tourism is one of the most remarkable success stories of modern times." What evidence is there to support such a bold claim?

2. On a global scale, identify the sources of tourists and their characteristics.

3. St. Martin/St. Maarten tries to encourage tourism by appealing to quite different types of tourists. Summarize the tourism potential for this destination.

Figure 9.29 Cupecoy Beach, St. Martin/St. Maarten

Practising Your Skills

4. Think about a specific tourist experience. As much as possible, identify the ways that money would be spent, either directly (buying souvenirs, staying in hotels, etc.) or indirectly (suppliers of food to restaurants, workers at the airport, etc.). Explain the total impact that this particular tourist experience would have on the economy of the destination.

5. As a travel agent, how would you determine the best vacations for your customers? Describe a process that you might use to figure out individual preferences.

6. Sketch a poster or newspaper advertisement that could be used to promote the tourist industry in St. Martin/St. Maarten. On the back of your sketch, explain why you selected each element.

Applying Your Skills

7. Explain which components shown in Figure 9.6 have the greatest impact on the people and economy of St. Martin/St. Maarten.

8. Collect five maps published for use by tourists while on vacation. Compare these maps with those found in high-quality atlases or those that are available from cartographic Internet sites. Which of the tourist maps most accurately display the geographic qualities of the places? Which provide the most useful information for tourists? Use your maps to prepare a report or display on the characteristics of helpful tourist maps, giving examples from your collection.

9. Choose a developing country and produce a case study analyzing the relationship between tourism and level of development.

Figure 9.30 What features would make a Caribbean destination desirable to you?

Thinking Like a Tourist

10. The economic value of domestic tourism is important to many Canadian regions, but it may also be important to your wallet. Choose two ski resorts, one in the United States and one in Canada, where you would enjoy vacationing. Compare the costs at both locations. Include transportation, accommodation, lift tickets, and money for meals. Do not forget to include the exchange rate for converting Canadian dollars to cover the U.S. costs. Prepare an oral presentation to convey your findings about domestic versus international destinations.

11. It is time to book your winter vacation, and you have decided on a Caribbean destination. The problem is that you cannot decide which island is best for you.

    a) Make a checklist of those qualities that you would most prefer in a Caribbean destination.
    b) Rate three destinations according to your checklist.
    c) Write a letter to a friend explaining why you made your particular choice of winter vacation destination. Include any ethical concerns you considered in making your decision.

JOB SKILLS

More than 700 000 executive positions exist in the tourism industry on a global scale, and these jobs are expected to grow at a faster rate than the overall economy. It has been predicted that, between 1998 and 2005,

- amusement/recreation executive jobs will grow by 40%
- food and beverage executive jobs will jump by 31%
- hotels and lodging executive jobs will climb by 28%
- air transport executive jobs will expand by 16%

Work with a partner to decide on three actions that young people could take to improve their chances of getting into the executive level with a large travel and tourism company.

CHAPTER ten 10
Tourism and Economic Development

1. What are some of the economic impacts of tourism on a destination?

2. How can global and regional forces have an economic impact on tourism in a region?

3. What are some economic issues that result from the development of the tourism industry?

KEY WORDS & TERMS

commercialism
direct impacts
ethnic cleansing
foreign investment
indirect impacts   invisible export
leakages   life cycle
multinational corporations
multiplier effects
superstructure
travel and tourism economy
travel and tourism industry

The Challenge of Development

Suppose you are a member of Parliament for a developing island nation in the Caribbean Sea. Your country has not done well in recent years, and you have been put in charge of economic development. One way to improve would be to increase sales of your country's commodities to other countries. These sales would bring in more foreign income, increasing the overall wealth of your country. Working with your team, you examine all the possible ways of expanding exports. You produce the results in Figure 10.2.

Figure 10.1 Major economic activities in the Caribbean region besides tourism: (a) fishing boats, St. Lucia; (b) banana plantation, Martinique; (c) nutmeg processing, Grenada. Why do you suppose these places have weak economies?

a)

b)

c)

Economic Development Options for Your Hypothetical Country

Possible Exports	Market Status
Sugar	Global prices have been low in recent years because there is less demand from health-conscious consumers.
Coffee	Oversupply has lowered prices and producers barely break even.
Rum and other spirits	Market demand is down given a consumer shift to wines and beers.
Manufactured products	High energy and transportation costs make it hard to compete with Mexico and Asian countries, where costs are lower.
High-tech industrial goods	Workforce does not have the required skills and the country lacks educational infrastructure and capital necessary to make these goods.

Figure 10.2 Most developing countries find themselves with few real opportunities to increase their economic development. Many other factors also affect specific commodities. The weather, import/export regulations (alcoholic spirits), and supply chain pricing (coffee), are examples of other factors.

Further economic development through exporting may be a challenge. The natural resources available on your island are found in many places around the world, and in such large quantities that markets are glutted and prices are weak. Human resources – people with skills and training – are limited. The people who do have skills and training tend to migrate to places that pay higher salaries. Gaining further wealth by producing goods to export does not seem to be the answer. However, the team recognizes a marketable resource that your country has in abundance. The tropical climate, long sandy beaches, and inviting landscapes make your island perfect for tourism.

This chapter will look at how tourism provides an economic base for growth and development.

EXPECTATIONS

In this chapter, you will have the opportunity to

- analyze tourist travel within selected regions and explain reasons for the observed patterns
- explain how tourism-related development can have important impacts on human systems
- research and report on the potential of natural and human factors to attract tourists to your local region
- analyze the causes and effects of economic disparities between selected world tourism regions
- identify the economic, cultural, political, and environmental components of selected issues related to travel and tourism
- demonstrate an understanding of the factors that contribute to the growth of tourism around the world
- analyze the effects of cultural, economic, and political motivators and barriers on travel and tourism patterns
- research and report on the impact of a natural or human-caused disaster on travel and tourism in a selected region

Tourism's Economic Potential

The rapidly growing demand for "sun, sand, and surf" destinations suggests that this industry has long-term potential for making money.

To return to our example, the idea of selling the beauty of your island is just like selling any other product. The only difference is that tourists are bringing their money to you instead of you sending a product to consumers. In effect, tourist spending is an **invisible export**. Your team decides that providing goods and services to tourists can become the basis for a new prosperity in your country.

The foregoing example illustrates the importance that tourism has for many developing countries.

Figure 10.3 What natural resources can you identify in the photograph that might provide a basis for sustainable development in this country?

Figure 10.4 The generation of income through tourism has the same effect as exporting locally made products to other countries.

CHECK IN

1 List the resources that your community or region has for economic development.

2 In one paragraph, explain why developing countries are eager to expand tourism in their economies.

3 Using your atlas, an almanac, and the Internet, choose five Caribbean countries. Look for leading sectors of the economy and organize your information in a chart. Include percentages, if possible. How do the bases of their economies compare?

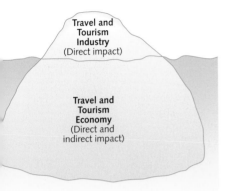

Travel and
Tourism
Industry
(Direct impact)

Travel and
Tourism
Economy
(Direct and
indirect impact)

Figure 10.5 The travel and tourism industry and economy. In some economies that are heavily dependent on tourism, up to 95% of jobs are included in the travel and tourism economy.

Figure 10.6 A delivery scooter zips away from a Pizza Nova store in Havana, Cuba, to deliver food to tourists. Many Canadian businesses have set up in Cuba to cater to the tourist trade. Is this activity part of the travel and tourism industry or the travel and tourism economy?

Travel FACT

Airplanes fly with an average of 33% of seats empty.

Figure 10.7

The Economic Value of Travel and Tourism

Most of the money made from tourism goes to destinations in the developed countries of Europe and North America. Nonetheless, the economic benefits of the industry are felt in other countries as well. Wherever tourists spend money there is an economic impact. Let's see how countries benefit from tourism.

Direct and Indirect Impacts of Tourism

Direct impacts of tourism are created by the dollars tourists spend for such things as airline tickets, hotels, meals, entrance fees to attractions, and souvenirs. These expenditures are easy to identify and count. Economists refer to this direct, straightforward spending as the **travel and tourism industry**.

Indirect impacts occur because of direct spending, but they are less easy to identify. For example, the airline that flies you to your vacation destination must pay for fuel, purchase in-flight meals,

maintain equipment, and rent airport space. The restaurant that you eat in at your destination must buy the food, pay for energy to cook your meals, hire kitchen and wait staff, and dispose of garbage. All of these indirect transactions that occur because of direct spending are part of the broader **travel and tourism economy**.

In a sense, direct spending is like the tip of the tourism iceberg: it is visible, but it is only a small part of the total impact of the tourism economy.

Canada's Travel and Tourism Industry, 2000		
	Travel & Tourism Industry (Direct Benefits)	Travel & Tourism Economy (Direct & Indirect Benefits)
Employment (% of total employment)	4.99%	13.22%
Gross Domestic Product (% of total GDP)	4.58%	12.14%

Multiplying Economic Benefits

Direct and indirect tourist spending lead to greater economic activity and jobs. Let's see how this works. Suppose you went snowboarding on your winter break and purchased a daily lift pass for $50. The resort operator would use part of this money to pay the wages of the lift operator. The lift operator would purchase groceries in a local store, and the store owner would use this revenue to pay the rent. The landowner might use some of the income to pay for dry cleaning, and the dry cleaner might then purchase a bottle of imported wine, in which case the money leaves the local economy. This example illustrates two points:

- In each round of respending, total economic activity is increased because of this **multiplier effect**.
- **Leakages** occur: these remove money from the local economy, release it into the global economy, and reduce economic activity in the local area.

The greater the amount of money kept by the local economy, the greater the respending, and the greater the multiplier effect. Leakages mean that the money is no longer creating wealth in the local economy.

Leakages include money spent on imported products and services, profits that leave the region, and money put into savings accounts, since that money is no longer available for spending.

Figure 10.8 Skiers file up the lift at Canada Olympic Park in Calgary under trailing chinook clouds. Skiing is a typical winter travel and tourism activity in many parts of Canada. Identify five ways that economic benefits of this activity are multiplied by respending.

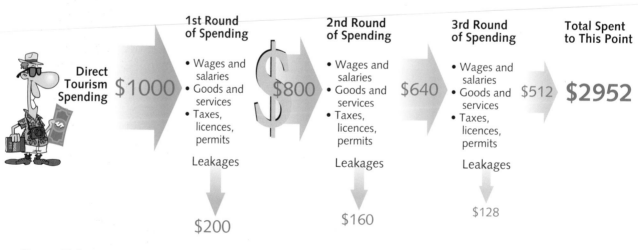

		1st Round of Spending		2nd Round of Spending		3rd Round of Spending	Total Spent to This Point
Direct Tourism Spending	$1000	• Wages and salaries • Goods and services • Taxes, licences, permits	$800	• Wages and salaries • Goods and services • Taxes, licences, permits	$640	• Wages and salaries • Goods and services • Taxes, licences, permits $512	$2952
		Leakages		Leakages		Leakages	
		$200		$160		$128	

Figure 10.9 The multiplier effect at work!

Tourism Income Multipliers for Selected Countries	
Country	**Multiplier**
Fiji	0.7
Bahamas	0.8
St. Lucia	0.8
Antigua	0.9
Bermuda	1.1
Jamaica	1.3
Greece	1.4
United Kingdom	1.7
Ireland	1.7
Turkey	2.0
Typical range for developing countries	0.6–1.2
Typical range for developed countries	1.7–2.0

Source: McGahey, Stan.
Tourism: The Multiplier Effect and Linkage.
University of Guam, 1996.

Figure 10.10 Which three countries benefit the most from tourism? Which three countries benefit the least?

Travel FACT

Globally, tourism accounts for 10.9% of all consumer spending.

Those tourist destinations that are most self-sufficient – that is, those able to supply most of their own goods and services – have the greatest multiplier effects. This is because they can keep leakages to a minimum so that more money can be respent locally. Figure 10.10 shows the income multiplier for some destinations. The higher the income multiplier, the greater the benefit to the economy.

The Multiplier Effect and Jobs

Economic activity generated by the multiplier effect leads to more jobs in the local economy. Studies show that the multiplier in tourism around the world ranges from a high of about 4.0 to a low of close to 0.0. Suppose a country has a multiplier of 2.0. This multiplier means that for every one job directly supported by tourism, 2.0 jobs are indirectly created in the local economy. Because of the multiplier effect, a large resort hotel that employs only 300 local workers can provide up to 600 additional jobs in the local economy. On the other hand, the multiplier effect can work in reverse. If a destination loses popularity and tourist spending drops, indirect jobs will disappear at the same rate as when they were being created. So, it is important for destinations that have been built on tourism to keep up their popularity or face economic hard times.

One advantage of tourism is that this industry can often generate jobs in remote parts of a country where there are few other economic opportunities. A good example in Canada is sport hunting and fishing in northern and mountainous locations. Tourist spending creates jobs and helps to diversify the economy. Figure 10.12 shows the jobs created in California from spending on travel and tourism in a single year.

Figure 10.11 A street busker plays the trombone for passersby in a pedestrian tunnel in Boston, Massachusetts. Explain how this economic activity is connected to other travel and tourism activities in the city.

Jobs Created in California from Spending on Travel and Tourism, 1999	
Sector	**Number of Jobs**
Eating and drinking establishments	211 000
Accommodations	144 000
Recreation	101 000
Retail sales	94 000
Air transportation	54 000
Ground transportation	43 000
Travel arrangement	28 000
Food stores	20 000

Source: California Division of Tourism

Figure 10.12 Of the total jobs created, calculate the percentage that are related to entertainment and recreation.

66 Some communities look to tourism to avoid the 'elephant burial ground' syndrome, places where the young leave and the old return to die. 99

– Phil Alexander, Michigan State University

Figure 10.13 Since the closing of the northern cod fishery in the early 1990s, these Newfoundlanders have made their living by taking tourists out sport fishing instead. But many more young men and women have left the province in order to find work.

Figure 10.14 Paradise Island in the Bahamas plays host to several foreign-owned resorts, including a large and popular Club Med. While foreign-owned businesses such as this provide jobs for local workers, they are responsible for leakages from the economy. Supplies such as food and drink are often purchased offshore, and foreign owners profit.

www.irwinpublishing.com

Analysis of tourism issues is the major role of the Canadian Tourism Research Institute, an arm of the Conference Board of Canada. Visit the Institute's Web page by going to the Student Page for *Canada Travels* and identify a current "hot topic."

Foreign Investment and Leakages

Many smaller, poorer countries simply do not have enough money (capital) to build tourist facilities on their own. Think of how much capital is needed to build an attractive resort in a Caribbean destination such as Turks and Caicos Islands! To spur tourism and create jobs in the country, these nations often encourage large, **multinational corporations**, such as Club Med, to build resorts and other facilities. Profits that these corporations make are paid to shareholders in other countries. These profits – often a significant part of revenues – leave the host nations and go to wealthier countries. These profits are leakages. As we have seen, the greater the leakages, the weaker the multiplier effect. This, then, becomes a dilemma for countries trying to expand tourism: do they encourage **foreign investment** to spur growth, or discourage it to limit leakages from their economy?

Economic Dependence on Tourism

Most of the countries on the list of the most popular tourist destinations are not troubled about foreign investment in their travel and tourism industries. For the most part, these countries have wealth and are developed. They have well-diversified economies, that is, there are many different types of economic activities taking place within the country. Also, investment capital can be found locally to expand tourism.

Travel and Tourism Industry as a Percent of GDP, 2000					
Rank	Country	% of GDP	Rank	Country	% of GDP
1	Maldives	37.3	30	Spain	7.6
2	British Virgin Islands	34.6	52	United States	5.1
3	Anguilla	32.5	53	Austria	5.1
4	Cayman Islands	24.1	54	Italy	4.9
5	Saint Lucia	22.1	56	Greece	4.8
6	Aruba	21.1	58	United Kingdom	4.7
7	Bahamas	20.8	60	Canada	4.6
8	Malta	20.3	69	France	4.4
9	Virgin Islands	20.2	99	Czech Republic	3.2
10	Cypress	17.5	114	Germany	2.6
11	Antigua & Barbuda	16.8	115	Mexico	2.6
12	Barbados	14.6	123	Russian Republic	2.5
13	Mauritius	13.8	125	China	2.4
14	Jordan	12.5	128	Hungary	2.3
15	Belize	12.0	132	Poland	2.2

Source: World Tourism Organization

Figure 10.15 The 15 countries with the highest percentage of their GDP tied to tourism are shown on the left side of the chart. The 15 countries with the highest total earnings from travel and tourism are shown on the right.

The amount of the total economy – measured as the Gross Domestic Product (GDP) – that the travel and tourism industry generates for the 15 most popular destinations is shown on the right side of Figure 10.15. Notice that France, the most popular destination, earns only 4.4% of its income from travel and tourism. While this is a great amount of money – roughly US$69 billion – it is only one industry in a very large economy.

The left-hand side of Figure 10.15 tells a very different story. This is a list of countries and territories that are most dependent on tourism, as shown by the high percentage tourism makes of GDP. The economies of these countries are small. They have few options for economic opportunities. A small change in tourism for these places can have important consequences, either for good or bad. Countries like these are working hard to expand tourism and to use it to create broader, more diversified economies.

Interact

What problems might occur in a region that depends heavily on tourism?

1   a)   Identify three economic activities that are part of the travel and tourism economy.

    b)   Which of these economic activities take place in your local area?

2   a)   Using Figure 10.9 as a model, determine the economic impact of $1000 spent on tourism after five rounds of respending if the leakage rate was 10%. Determine what the economic impact would be if the leakage rate was 40%.

    b)   What three actions might a country take to reduce the leakage rate for its economy? Which of the three do you think is most likely to be effective? Explain your choice.

3   Make up an advantages and disadvantages chart on foreign investment, recording several points in each column. Based on your chart, in your opinion, is foreign investment a good or bad idea?

Dollars & Sense

When planning your trip, check out hotel accommodations on the Internet. Many hotels offer better rates and special discounts (some almost 60%) to people who book online.

Interact

Which viewpoint do you think is most important? Why?

Tourism and Economic Development

Many small countries tie their future economic development to tourism. The travel and tourism industry is viewed as being the best opportunity for generating more wealth and a better living. But the term "development" is used in a variety of ways, and its meaning is often vague, or worse, confusing. Let's look at what development really means.

Impacts of Tourism

The meaning of development is not fixed. It varies from place to place and over time. The conditions that people in an African village might identify as "development" would be different from those identified by residents of a large city in North America. Changes in conditions must be seen from the perspective of who is developing and what is improving.

This approach leads to many viewpoints about the benefits and disadvantages. From some perspectives, economic growth is the single most important outcome of change. Other people hold the view that development should occur only when there are widespread positive changes for society, the environment, the culture, and the economy. They argue that development of this type is sustainable well into the future.

Indicators of Positive Development from Tourism

Aspects for Improvement	Indicators of Change
Employment increases	• direct and indirect jobs created • unemployment levels fall • seasonal work reduced • job satisfaction increases
Incomes increase	• household incomes rise • personal spending increases • tax revenues expand
Migration changes	• out-migration drops • in-migration rises
Services expand	• health care improves • social services become better distributed • recreational activities become more accessible
Cultural enhancement	• cultural facilities become more accessible • events occur with greater frequency
Environmental enhancement	• environmental practices improve • funding for environmental protection increases • pollution levels drop

Figure 10.16 Using the information here, identify one change in your local area that could be considered as positive development.

BIG BAD WORLD   by Polyp

Figure 10.17 People have different opinions about tourism and development.

Source: *New Internationalist*, No. 324, June 2000, page 8.

The Life Cycle of Destinations

Improvements in a society come at different points in the life of a tourist destination. The geographer Richard Butler proposed that tourist destinations go through six stages – something he called a **life cycle** – as they grow and change. The benefits to the society are different at each stage.

Exploration Stage At this stage, tourists have not discovered the destination. It is known only to a few travellers and is considered remote and exotic. Since getting to it is difficult, those who do visit are seen as adventurers. They arrive expecting few amenities. Their economic impact is relatively small, but entrepreneurs see expansion of tourism as a good possibility.

Involvement Stage Because of growing demand from tourists, government agencies and local businesses begin to invest in infrastructure, such as airports and facilities, including accommodations and attractions. Employment in direct and indirect activities expands. The destination is becoming known more widely.

Development Stage The destination experiences a rapid growth in tourism investment, largely from outside sources that want to exploit the site's growing popularity. The number of jobs increases as large volumes of tourists arrive seeking services and amenities.

Consolidation Stage The destination is now established as part of the domestic and international tourist industry. It is well known and popular among tourists for its amenities and attractions. Tourism is the most important economic sector in the destination.

Figure 10.18 Remoteness of a location has advantages and disadvantages. On the one hand, people seeking adventure will value the isolation and challenge of travel. On the other hand, most tourists will not endure the time and effort to reach the place.

Figure 10.19 Construction of the Sheraton Eau Claire Hotel in Calgary, Alberta. Money continues to flow into destinations in the consolidation stage as investment capital. Who benefits from these expenditures?

Canada Travels

Projected growth in travel to the Pacific region by Canadians until 2009 is expected to average 8.8%. This growth is being stimulated by rapid economic growth in Asia and the opening of new destinations in the region. Growth in travel to the United States and Europe is expected to average a more modest 4.3% annually.

Stagnation Stage The destination peaks in its popularity. Facilities and attractions are no longer being planned and built. It is no longer fashionable to go to that destination as tourists take a "been there, done that" attitude.

Decline Stage The destination's accommodations and attractions are aging. Other emerging destinations are seen as more exciting. Jobs are lost and out-migration occurs.

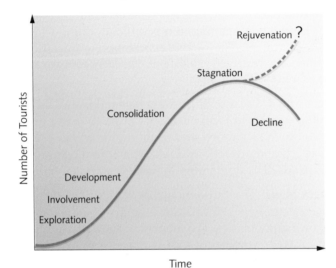

Figure 10.20 Try to identify a destination for one of the stages in this life cycle.

Riding the Destination Life Cycle

Destinations move through the life cycle at different speeds. Those destinations that have a good variety of amenities and attractions may remain popular for a long time. Niagara Falls, Ontario, is a good example of a traditional tourist destination that has been rejuvenated through the addition of attractions such as a water theme park and a casino.

Economic benefits to the destination occur as tourism expands in the location. This is a time for the destination to invest in the infrastructure, such as roads, airports, and electrical grids, and in the

Figure 10.21 Which stage do you think the hotel in this photograph represents?

Figure 10.22 A visitor to Marineland in Niagara Falls, Ontario, watches the Beluga whales through a large underground window in their outdoor tank.

superstructure, including hotels, places for entertainment, shopping centres, and restaurants. With luck, the destination remains popular with tourists long enough for these costs to be recovered and for the destination to show a profit. During the period of decline, there is little investment and the existing facilities decay. That makes them even less likely to attract tourists, and so the decline goes even faster.

Success Factors

Even when local people are enthusiastic about tourism as an economic saviour, some places are still not able to establish vital tourism industries. The differences between successful and unsuccessful regions often have to do with just a handful of key factors, shown in Figure 10.23.

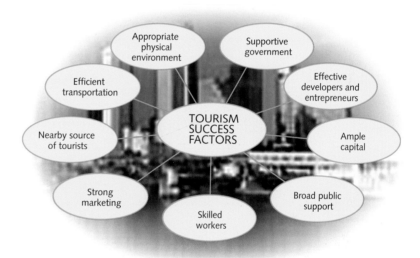

Figure 10.23 Factors for success in tourism. How does your local area rate for three of these factors?

CHECK IN

1 List three ways that residents in a tourist destination might benefit from expansion of tourism in the area. List three ways that they might suffer.

2 In a group, make up a series of cartoons or illustrations with captions to show the stages of the life cycle of tourist destinations.

3 For each stage in the life cycle of destinations, brainstorm opportunities and potential problems of that stage from the perspective of the travel and tourism industry. Record your ideas in a chart.

CASE STUDY
Sarajevo, Bosnia and Herzegovina – Destruction of a Tourist Industry

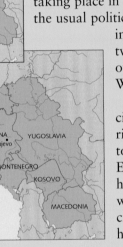

a)

b)

Figure 10.24 (a) Sarajevo, Yugoslavia, 1984; (b) Sarajevo, Bosnia and Herzegovina, 2001

In February 1984, the city of Sarajevo, Yugoslavia, hosted the 14th Winter Olympic Games. Forty-nine nations participated in these Olympics, with over 2500 competitors. A record number of media representatives, 7283, were there, along with tens of thousands of sports fans. The games were watched on television around the world. People hailed these games as a victory for the Olympic spirit, peace, and human cooperation. The games were taking place in a communist country in Eastern Europe, free from the usual political and diplomatic wrangling that had been part of international events in the second half of the twentieth century. Sarajevo became a synonym for overcoming the turmoil and barriers of the Cold War period.

Tourism was not new to Sarajevo. As the capital city of the state of Bosnia and Herzegovina, it was rich in history and culture and had many assets for tourism, including a central location in Eastern Europe and wonderful natural beauty. Some people had even proclaimed it the most beautiful city in the world. In preparations for hosting the Olympics the city's infrastructure and transportation networks had been expanded. The event had also given sports officials experience in running international events.

Interact

In what ways can sports tourism contribute to better relations among peoples?

Figure 10.25 Tourists to Sarajevo were captivated by its culture, architecture, and physical environment. For most people from the West, it broke the stereotype they had of cities in communist countries.

Building on this sports tradition, in the few years following the Olympics, Sarajevo hosted many more international competitions. The city's tourism future seemed to be guaranteed. Then, things fell apart.

Civil War

In March 1992, Bosnia and Herzegovina, the state in which Sarajevo was located, declared independence from Yugoslavia. The people of Bosnia and Herzegovina were largely from three ethnic groups: Bosnians, Muslims, and Serbs. Serbs dominated the whole country of Yugoslavia and held key positions in government and the military. The Bosnians and Muslims resented this control and voted for independence in a referendum. Since together they formed a majority in the territory, independence was achieved. The country of Bosnia and Herzegovina was admitted to the United Nations in 1992. However, the Serb minority in the country refused to give up their ties to Yugoslavia and launched military strikes to weaken the new government. The government of Yugoslavia supported the Serbs. Thus, a five-year civil war began in the new country.

Sarajevo was at the epicentre of the civil war. People from all three ethnic groups lived in the city, and each group sought to control parts of the city for itself. The civil war brought about many instances of **ethnic cleansing**, where one group forced other groups to leave the area. All sides committed atrocities. Shelling, fires, and simple neglect destroyed much of the city, including the sports and tourist accommodation facilities.

Figure 10.26 (Top) In 1984, the gold, silver, and bronze medals for men's figure skating were won by the USA's Scott Hamilton (centre), Canada's Brian Orser (right), and Czechoslovakia's Josef Sabovtchik (left), respectively. The euphoria of the Olympic games pointed to a bright future for tourism in Sarajevo. (Right) In 1997, the Olympic Stadium lay in ruins and an adjacent soccer field had been turned into a graveyard after the siege of Sarajevo because of lack of space to bury all the victims of the civil war.

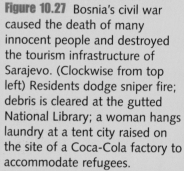

Figure 10.27 Bosnia's civil war caused the death of many innocent people and destroyed the tourism infrastructure of Sarajevo. (Clockwise from top left) Residents dodge sniper fire; debris is cleared at the gutted National Library; a woman hangs laundry at a tent city raised on the site of a Coca-Cola factory to accommodate refugees.

Rebuilding and Revitalizing Tourism

After five years, the civil war ended. However, resentment among the three ethnic groups remains strong, and cooperation is difficult to achieve. Peacekeeping forces maintain a presence in the country to monitor the fragile peace. The ongoing tension has made it difficult to attract foreign and domestic investment in industries and business. Investors simply do not want to make a commitment to a place where ethnic violence may erupt at any time. It has been particularly slow to re-establish tourism.

In spite of the difficulties, there are attempts to reconstruct tourism facilities, such as hotels, parks, spas, and restaurants. These efforts are the result of support for tourism from outside Sarajevo and Bosnia. Trends show a strong growth in tourism demand across the whole of Eastern Europe, particularly in Russia and the Czech Republic. This growth is due partly to the easing of red tape for international travel and partly to growth in the economies of the region. Because of this growth, the prediction is that by 2020 nearly one in every three visitors to Europe will choose central or eastern destinations. Together, these trends point to a predicted average annual growth rate for tourism in Eastern Europe of 4.6% over the next decade or two. This is good news for Sarajevo.

VIRTUAL TRAVEL

www.irwinpublishing.com

Immediately after the 1994 Winter Games, the Peace Flame Foundation invited a group of Olympic and Paralympic winners to Sarajevo to light a "peace flame" as a reminder of the Olympic ideals of cooperation, peace, and human endurance. A further initiative of the Foundation is the establishment of a peace park and community centre in Sarajevo. To visit this site, go to the Student Page for *Canada Travels*.

Figure 10.28 (Top) Canadian peacekeepers pass devastated buildings; (right) children play in a wrecked bus amid the ruins of Sarajevo. The destruction of the city's sports, transportation, and tourist facilities put the whole future of tourism in Sarajevo in question.

So, in spite of its recent troubles, Sarajevo may have the support to rebuild and revitalize its travel and tourism industry. But will tourists be enticed to return? The key to getting them back is to invest in tourism in the city. This means refurbishing hotels and accommodations, building new attractions, and rekindling Sarajevo's sports legacy. This, of course, will happen only if peace is assured and investors are confident about the future. In a real sense, peace, tourism, and economic prosperity are closely tied together in Sarajevo's future.

CHECK IN

1 At what stage in the destination life cycle model is Sarajevo? Explain your answer.

2 a) In a chart, analyze the positive or encouraging aspects of Sarajevo's situation as a tourist destination under the heading "Motivators" and the negative or discouraging aspects under "Barriers." For each column, consider cultural, economic, and political conditions.

   b) What conclusions can you draw from your chart?

3 Explain why rebuilding and revitalizing the tourism industry in Sarajevo is a problem even with an end to the civil war.

4 Suggest three actions that the tourism industry in Sarajevo might take to strengthen its chances of successfully rebuilding. Give reasons to explain why your ideas are useful.

LOOKING AT ISSUES

Figure 10.29 Location of Cancun, Mexico

Cancun, Mexico

Issue: Should jobs and other aspects of economic development for tourism outweigh sustaining the cultural and natural environment of an area?

Prior to 1970, most of Mexico's tourism was concentrated on the Pacific coast along what is known as the Mexican Riviera. This region includes the centres of Acapulco and Mazatlán. In 1967, the Mexican government realized the potential for tourism and started a detailed search for alternative sites on the Caribbean side of the country. The characteristics that the government sought were

- kilometres of sandy beaches
- suitable areas for swimming
- appealing climate
- sites of cultural interest

The top candidate that emerged was a remote sandbar off the eastern shore of the Yucatan Peninsula on Mexico's Caribbean coast. This island is a slender, 22.5-km long ribbon of smooth, sugar-white sand shaped like the number seven. The only existing economic activity was a small fishing village, home to 12 families. Construction of the Cancun resort zone began in 1974.

Figure 10.30 The attractions of Cancun's natural environment are obvious. But many places have similar characteristics. What other qualities made Cancun an excellent site for tourism?

Cancun's Hurricane History		
Year	Date	Wind Speed (km/h)
1887	July 25	152
1887	September 17	152
1888	September 7	128
1922	October 19	128
1933	September 22	168
1938	August 15	144
1942	August 28	152
1966	October 7	200
1988	September 14	248
1995	October 9	184

Figure 10.31 Research the 1966, 1988, or 1995 hurricane and prepare a report describing the damage that resulted in the Cancun area. Share your report with the class.

A Threat from the Natural Environment

One potential threat that had to be taken into account in developing the Cancun site was the risk of hurricanes. The Cancun area had experienced destructive hurricanes in the past that had destroyed property and killed residents and travellers. There was a high probability that hurricanes would occur again, so tourism developments had to incorporate the latest technological advances, giving them better chances of surviving major hurricanes. These developments included breakwaters and specially designed marinas, hurricane-resistant buildings, and water and sewage systems capable of functioning through torrential rainfalls. Also important were advances in hurricane tracking and prediction. These preparations were put in place to reduce the economic disruption caused by hurricanes.

Development of Cancun

By the mid-1980s, Cancun was still relatively small and undiscovered, with only a dozen or so hotels. Investment by multinational corporations in the late 1980s and effective marketing vaulted Cancun into the global tourism arena during the 1990s. Today there are over 25 000 hotel rooms accommodating about 1.5 million tourists a year. Besides resort hotels, facilities include convention centres, sports complexes, golf courses, and shopping malls. There is also a 1500-slip marina complex. Cancun generates about 20% of Mexico's tourism income.

Figure 10.32 The resort zone of Cancun. Notice the modern buildings that suggest a "high end" destination.

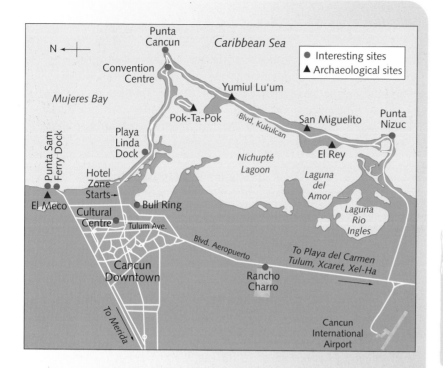

Figure 10.33 Cancun and surrounding area

Map labels:
N
Caribbean Sea
Punta Cancun
Convention Centre
Mujeres Bay
Yumiul Lu'um
Pok-Ta-Pok
Blvd. Kukulcan
San Miguelito
Punta Nizuc
Playa Linda Dock
Punta Sam Ferry Dock
Nichupté Lagoon
El Rey
Laguna del Amor
Hotel Zone Starts→
El Meco
Laguna Rio Ingles
Cultural Centre
Bull Ring
Tulum Ave.
Blvd. Aeropuerto
To Playa del Carmen Tulum, Xcaret, Xel-Ha
Cancun Downtown
Rancho Charro
To Merida
Cancun International Airport

● Interesting sites
▲ Archaeological sites

Travel FACT

Did you know that 20% of hotel guests never unpack their suitcases? They simply take out items when they are needed. About 40% of travellers only unpack clothing that will wrinkle.

Cancun was designed to have three distinct zones. Facilities in the City of Cancun – known as *El Centro* by the locals – house about 400 000 people, mostly workers in the tourist industry. The city is also popular among tourists for shopping and dining and offers less expensive tourist accommodations. A small ecological reserve, with lagoons and mangrove swamps, is the second zone. This area separates the city from the third zone, the resort area. From the beginning, the layout of the island was planned to minimize conflicts among the different activities.

Urban designers laid out the city well before construction began. A modern infrastructure was put in place before building started, eliminating many problems that come with rapid growth of communities. The city has efficient water-supply and sewage systems, as well as good roads and communication equipment. Because of this strong infrastructure, Cancun's resort zone boasts more luxury hotels than any other resort in the Caribbean, and none is older than 20 years.

Figure 10.34 Many of Cancun's hotels were constructed using the most up-to-date styles in architecture and resort design.

Figure 10.35 (Right) Snorkelling and scuba diving are popular among the reefs around Cancun. (Below) Chac Mool, a Mayan statue, seems to stand watch over Cancun's beach.

Selling History

One of the attractions of Cancun's site was access to the cultural resources of the Yucatan. This area was home to the Mayan culture that flourished for centuries before the Spaniards arrived in 1519. Within a few hours' drive from Cancun there are over 1200 archaeological sites, some fully restored and some still covered by jungle vines. Vacationers can take day tours to ruins at places like Tulum, Coba, and Chichen Itza.

What Price Success?

Cancun does have its critics. Many people do not like its **commercialism**. The town's whole reason to exist is to extract dollars from tourists, and to do it in such a way that the tourists will want to return. The buildings and layout of the destination are decidedly un-Mexican in appearance. In fact, they look much the same as large hotels and resorts that can be found in most places that attract tourists. And while the Mayan sites are authentic, vacationers on optional day excursions learn little about the culture and people of the region.

Critics argue that Cancun is typical of the homogenous packaging of tourist resorts. Resorts are designed to be predictable, to deliver a charming mix of sun, sand, and surf in a safe, socially entertaining manner. They are constructed, packaged, and marketed to achieve maximum business efficiencies. For most visitors, the location of this mixture of products and services is generally irrelevant. Cancun looks and feels like most other large resorts in the world, whether on the Mediterranean, along Australia's coast, or on a Caribbean island.

Figure 10.36 (Top) Crowded discothèques like this one are typical of Cancun's nightlife. (Below) Tourists in speedboats have been criticized as a threat to the region's aquatic plants and animals.

Interact

Which do you think is more important: the environment and culture, or jobs?

Another criticism is that the tourist traffic in the region is threatening the sensitive reef and lagoon environments around Cancun. The boat traffic, complete with sewage and fuel spills, has lowered the quality of the water and disturbed the habitat for reef dwellers. Divers and snorkellers have been known to knock off pieces of the reef as souvenirs.

Some tourists do not like the approach to development that has been used in Cancun. These people prefer destinations where development has respected the natural and cultural characteristics of the location. In these destinations, visitors encounter the natural environment and the people of the area in ways that are mutually rewarding. The tourists have the experiences that they seek, and the local area is improved through the industry.

Dollars  & Sense

While still at home, find a "meal in a bar" product that you like. Carry some when travelling so you are not forced to eat in airport restaurants or snack stands where prices are high and cleanliness uncertain. Also, when driving in an unfamiliar country, it may take time to find a restaurant that appeals to you. These meal bars can be a lifesaver.

a)

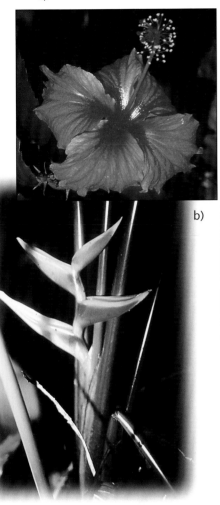

b)

Figure 10.37 (a) Hibiscus and (b) bird of paradise are two of the many flower species native to the Caribbean region.

Cancun's Success

In spite of these criticisms, Cancun is a huge economic success. Thousands of jobs in construction and tourism were created in a part of Mexico that was remote and undeveloped. Over 1.5 million visitors come annually to enjoy its attractions.

CHECK IN

1. a) What attributes were responsible for the selection of Cancun as a site for the development of tourism resources?

   b) If you had been in charge of selecting a new site for tourism, what additional attributes would you have added to the list? Would you have removed any? Explain your answers.

2. The hurricane in 1988 resulted in huge damage to Cancun. How does an event like this affect tourism in the region? What might the tourist industry do to reduce the impact of such disasters?

3. Where is Cancun on the destination life cycle model? According to the model, what changes are likely to occur to this area in the next few decades?

4. a) If you could go on only one winter vacation, would you choose to visit Cancun? Explain your answer.

   b) If you were to vacation in Cancun, what attractions would you consider most interesting? What steps would you take to ensure that you got the most enjoyment out of your experience?

5. a) In a chart, analyze the positive or encouraging aspects of Cancun's tourist industry under the heading "Motivators" and the negative or discouraging aspects under "Barriers." For each column, consider cultural, economic, and political conditions.

   b) What conclusions can you draw from your chart?

This activity will enable you to

- analyze tourist travel within selected regions and explain reasons for the observed patterns
- analyze the major characteristics of selected tourist regions in terms of natural, cultural, economic, and political criteria
- analyze global tourist flows and explain the reasons for the observed patterns
- compare rates of tourism and tourist spending for selected countries
- analyze the causes and effects of economic disparities between selected world tourism regions
- use statistics effectively to analyze travel and tourism patterns

Where Do People Travel?

Purpose:

To use ArcView to illustrate global variations in tourist arrivals. You will produce two maps: (1) showing variations in the absolute number of tourists visiting destinations of the world, and (2) showing the same data except expressed as a percentage of the destination's population. The final part of the activity involves creating a series of scatter graphs to test for correlations between tourist arrivals and a host of social and economic indicators.

Files:

cntry_95.shp

Functions:

Convert to Shapefile, Legend Editor (Graduated Colour), Table Edit, Field Calculation, Chart (Scatter Chart), Hot Link

 Your first step will be to create a blank View and name it "Global Tourism."

 Next, add a theme containing data on tourism and measures of development: x:\world\cntry_95.shp. Convert the theme to a shapefile, naming it "World," and delete the original theme.

 Now, using the Legend Editor, create a graduated colour map illustrating variations in the annual number of tourists arriving in countries throughout the world. In doing so, use the "Tourists_k" classification field ("k" means that the data is expressed in thousands), choose a "natural breaks" classification, set the Null Value to equal "–99" (for countries in which data was not available), and display a "No Data" using a partial fill symbol. Lastly, rename the theme "Annual Tourist Arrivals (000s)" in the Theme Properties window.

 Next, copy and paste the theme into the same View. Again, you will create a similar map, except this time you will express the data, i.e., number of tourists, as a percentage of the country's total population. However, since this statistic is not available in the theme table, you will have to add a new field and perform the calculations. To do so, open the theme table of the theme you have just pasted, put the table in Edit mode, add a new (number) field called "Tourists_%Pop," and calculate this field using the following equation:

(([Tourists_k] * 1000)/ [Pop_cntry]) * 100

Examine the equation carefully and understand why you performed each of the operations it contains. Now, perform a sort ascending on the new field, then change all of the negative values at the top of the column to

Figure 10.38 Egypt has long been a popular destination for tourists. (Right) One of the many columns of the vast Hypostyle Hall at the Temple of Karnak, near Luxor, the site of ancient Thebes; (far right) a cruise down the Nile River in a felucca (traditional sailboat) offers a panoramic view of the Temple.

"–99" and all of the "100 000s" at the bottom of the table also to "–99." (These values occurred because there was no tourism and/or population data available for many of the countries, and so a value of "–99" was assigned.) Remember to hit Enter after making the last change. Save the edits you have made to the table and return to the View.

5. Now, using the Legend Editor, create a graduated colour map illustrating variations in the number of tourists per population arriving in countries throughout the world. In doing so, use the "Tourists_%Pop" classification field, choose a "natural breaks" classification, set the Null Value to equal

"–99" (for countries in which data was not available), and display a "No Data" using a partial fill symbol. Lastly, rename the theme "Annual Tourist Arrivals (% Total Pop)" in the Theme Properties window.

6. Next, with the Annual Tourist Arrivals (000s).shp theme active, use the Select Feature tool to highlight three countries in each of the data classes for a total of 15. Open the theme table and create a series of scatter charts using the following pairs of variables. (Note: select the scatter chart type that will apply a logarithmic scale to the "Tourists_k" variable. Name each chart appropriately.)

Tourists_k vs. Grwrate	(Population Growth Rate)
Tourists_k vs. Lifexpct	(Life Expectancy)
Tourists_k vs. Infmortrt	(Infant Mortality Rate)
Tourists_k vs. Safe Water	(Percentage of Population with Safe Water)
Tourists_k vs. Sanitation	(Percentage of Population with Sanitation)
Tourists_k vs. Humandev	(Human Development Index)
Tourists_k vs. Litrate	(Literacy Rate)
Tourists_k vs. Yrsschl	(Years in School)
Tourists_k vs. Inc_pcap	(Income per Capita)
Tourists_k vs. Exportm	(Value of Exports)
Tourists_k vs. Energyus	(Energy Use per Capita)

Congratulations! You have just completed a spatial analysis of tourist destinations as well as a comparative study of tourist arrivals and a variety of development indicators.

Map and Interpretation and Analysis

1. a) Study the two graduated colour maps you have created by turning each on and off. What similarities and what differences do you notice between the two?

   b) What are the advantages of expressing this data in absolute terms (i.e., total number), and what are the advantages of expressing it in relative terms (i.e., as a percentage of the total population)?

2. a) For each of the scatter charts you have created, indicate which of the following best describes the relationship shown:

   - strong positive correlation
   - weak positive correlation
   - strong negative correlation
   - weak negative correlation

For each of the noted correlations, attempt to explain the relationship. Remember, correlations are measures of tendencies (i.e., positive correlations are when one variable is high, the other also tends to be high; negative correlations are when one variable is high, the other tends to be low). Correlations, then, are not necessarily cause-and-effect relationships. They may, in fact, have no impact on one another at all.

   b) What other measures can you think of that are directly related to the annual number of tourist arrivals? What about those that are indirectly related?

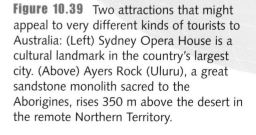

Figure 10.39 Two attractions that might appeal to very different kinds of tourists to Australia: (Left) Sydney Opera House is a cultural landmark in the country's largest city. (Above) Ayers Rock (Uluru), a great sandstone monolith sacred to the Aborigines, rises 350 m above the desert in the remote Northern Territory.

Extension:

Create ASCII DOS .txt files containing detailed descriptions of attractions found in the countries that are popular tourist destinations. Then, hot link these text files to the appropriate countries on the world map by entering their directory paths in the respective theme tables.

Extension:

Locate data on annual tourist arrivals in the world's popular cities. Attach this data to a cities theme. Then, display the data statistically using a circle chart technique.

Extension:

Scan or download photos of attractions found in the countries that are popular tourist destinations. Then, hot link these to the appropriate countries on the world map by creating new Views and adding the .jpeg photos as image data. (Hint: Don't forget to turn on the JPEG Support extension and name the Views appropriately!)

Extension:

The activity you have just completed involved displaying data on the destinations of tourists. Locate data on the origins of these travellers, attach it to a countries theme, then display it statistically using a graduated colour technique. As in the activity, discover correlations between the number of tourists leaving their country and other variables.

Understanding the Concepts

1. Explain why developing countries find it difficult to experience real development based on the following economic activities:
   a) manufacturing
   b) international trade

Figure 10.40 A farmer carries tobacco leaves in Pinar del Rio Province, Cuba. After sugar, tobacco is Cuba's chief agricultural crop.

2. In what ways might a government use the multiplier effect to stimulate economic growth in a region?

3. Use the destination life cycle model in Figure 10.20 to evaluate a tourist facility in your area. Produce a description of the facility, its stage of development, and reasons for your assessment.

Practising Your Skills

4. Figure 10.23 on page 269 lists a number of factors that are important in the success of tourist destinations. Compare the successes of both Sarajevo and Cancun, using the factors in Figure 10.23 in your analysis. In cases where the factor is not strong or is proving to be difficult, identify the consequences. Organize your information in a chart with the following headings: Factors, Sarajevo, Cancun.

5. Make a diagram or a visual display that clearly shows the differences between direct and indirect impacts of tourist spending in an economy.

Applying Your Skills

6. Consider the tourist industry in your local region. In a chart, identify the strengths and weaknesses of natural and human factors to attract tourists to the area.

7. Examine Figure 10.15, a table showing the 15 countries that are most dependent on tourism. Compare the characteristics of these countries using a table with the following headings: Population, GDP per Capita, Growth Rate of Economy. Use a world almanac or an Internet search to find the information for the chart. When your chart is complete, note three observations that you can make about this group of countries.

8. Using an atlas and the Internet, compare the Cancun tourist region on the Caribbean Sea with tourist facilities on Mexico's Pacific coast,

such as Acapulco or Mazatlán. Use the following categories:
- natural and cultural factors that attract tourists
- motivators and barriers to tourism
- the impact that tourism has on each region
- future prospects for development for tourism

9. As a government official, what strategy might you use to try to attract foreign investment in tourism to Sarajevo?

Thinking Like a Tourist

10. Compile information on Cancun using the Internet and travel resources. Make a list of resorts showing price, location in Cancun, and facilities. Identify the resort you would like to book and explain why.

11. You have a week to travel in Eastern Europe and want to spend two days in Sarajevo. Decide on other cities or sites that you could see during your week. Create an itinerary for your week, describing travel methods and routes.

JOB SKILLS

An important employment skill is to be able to interpret statistical information and then communicate important conclusions to others.

Examine the data in Figure 10.41 and write three conclusions that are suggested by the data.

World's Top Tourism Earners			
Country	International Tourism Receipts (US$ billions)		% Change 1998–1999
	1998	1999	
United States	71.3	74.4	4.5
Spain	29.7	32.9	10.7
France	29.9	31.7	5.9
Italy	29.9	28.4	–5.1
United Kingdom	21.0	21.0	0.0
Germany	16.4	16.8	2.4
China	12.6	14.1	11.9
Austria	11.2	11.1	–0.9
Canada	9.4	10.0	6.7
Russian Federation	6.5	7.8	19.4

Figure 10.41

CHAPTER eleven 11
The Sinister Side of Tourism

Image Isn't Everything

When you pick up tourism magazines or travel agency catalogues, you usually see pictures like those below, showing attractive, energetic people enjoying fun activities. Most likely, the photographers' models will appear to be under 30 years of age, unless older travellers are the target market. Then, the advertisements will show mature people who are fit and well dressed. The models are always good-looking. The underlying message, of course, is that if you travel to the destination or use the products, then you too can have the same experiences as the models in the photographs.

The travel and tourism industry is built on providing services and products to satisfy consumers' desires for interesting leisure and travel experiences. Marketing, or selling a destination, is simply one aspect of the industry. It is marketing's job to create a positive,

Figure 11.1 Tourism is mostly about people having fun, relaxing, and enjoying life, but that is not all there is to it, as the pictures on the next page show.

Figure 11.2 Travel and tourism also has a sinister side that is tied to greed, poverty, exploitation, and suffering. (Counterclockwise from top right) The family of a person with the Ebola virus waits outside a hospital ward wearing protective masks in Gulu, Uganda; on crowded buses in downtown Rome, Italy, professional pickpockets prey on residents and tourists alike; two teenage Nepali prostitutes wait for customers in the red light district of Calcutta, India.

pleasing image of a place so that people will want to travel there to spend their money, rather than to some other location. Tourism functions best when consumers feel good about their travel experiences.

Unfortunately, there is a down side to the travel and tourism industry that should not be ignored. Some problems, such as overcrowding of facilities, destruction of historic, cultural, and ecological sites, and harassment of wildlife have already been discussed in earlier chapters. Some specific economic problems that have been explored are the impact of change as economies shift from traditional activities to tourism, seasonality of employment, and the vulnerability that tourism-dependent economies feel in the face of tourists' changing choices.

In this chapter, we will focus particularly on child-sex tourism, the spread of global diseases, and criminal activity.

EXPECTATIONS

In this chapter you will have the opportunity to

- identify recent trends in travel and tourism
- analyze the effects of cultural, economic, and political motivators and barriers on travel and tourism patterns
- explain how a tourist activity may contribute to the exploitation of people
- produce a case study to investigate the future of tourism for a selected region or destination
- evaluate the impact of government policies on travel and tourism in a selected region
- analyze the impact of marketing and advertising on travel and tourism patterns

Child-Sex Tourism

Child-sex tourism involves people who travel to other countries with the intention of seeking sex with children. This is an important component in the sexual exploitation of children. An estimated 1 million children worldwide enter the sex trade annually, with many destined to serve tourists. Experts suggest that the child-sex trade generates US$20–23 billion per year.

Children Involved in the Sex Industry, Selected Locations	
Location	**Estimated Number**
Brazil	500 000
India	400 000
Nepal	200 000
Taiwan	100 000
Thailand	200 000 to 850 000

Source: These figures were reported by the non-profit organization End Child Prostitution in Asian Tourism (ECPAT). Estimates were based on UNICEF studies.

Figure 11.3 Children are involved in the sex-trade all over the world. Often their clients are tourists from other countries.

Figure 11.4 (Left) The Shinjuku district of Tokyo, Japan, houses many peep-shows and sex shops; (below) The red light district in Bangkok, Thailand, has been linked to the child-sex industry as well as to several murders of prostitutes and tourists.

Why Does Child-Sex Tourism Exist?

It is hard to believe that a child-sex industry exists. Unfortunately, it does exist in most countries, and child-sex tourism is expanding rapidly. People who do not engage in this deviant behaviour at home travel to other countries with the intention of having sex with children. Three reasons seem to explain this pattern.

First, people who travel outside their home country often experience a sense of freedom from the legal and social constraints of their own society. This is a part of the appeal of tourism, in general. For a week or two, we can have fun, experience new cultures and ideas, and generally do things that we would not do normally. Most tourists enjoy this freedom within the legal and moral limits of their own society and those of their destination. Unfortunately, people interested in having sex with children exploit this sense of freedom and end up supporting the child-sex industry.

Second, some tourists who travel to developing countries consider the people, especially the children, to be inferior to themselves. Such tourists do not value the culture they are visiting, and see the social characteristics of their destination as less worthy than their own. This view is known as **ethnocentrism** – the valuing of one's own culture above others. People use this attitude to justify their exploitation of children in a developing country. They feel that their acts do not have the same harmful impact as they would have in their home country.

Third, police and governments in some destinations do not have or do not enforce laws against the sexual exploitation of children. These developing countries are so eager to use tourism as a stimulus for economic development that they overlook its harmful impact. The child-sex industry is often ignored because it generates tourist dollars and creates employment for legitimate enterprises, including hotels, casinos, and restaurants.

Figure 11.5 Children who live in poverty, like these children searching for food scraps in Calcutta, are most vulnerable to sexual predators.

Children as Victims

Poverty is the main reason that children end up in the child-sex trade. In some cases, children are lured away from their families with promises of jobs and places to live. Once removed from their families, the children are forced into prostitution. In other cases, economic desperation encourages parents to sell their children to recruiters. Also, large cities of developing counties typically have populations of street children who have fled abusive homes or who have been forced out of homes by poverty. These children are easy prey for child-sex recruiters and the sex industry.

Figure 11.6 A homeless boy sleeps outside Rio de Janeiro's Central Station as his friends play nearby. These are the type of children that may be recruited for sex.

What Do People Think About the Problem?

A survey conducted in Europe in 1998 revealed the following about people's understanding of child-sex tourism:

- 85% of the respondents were aware of the problem.

- 63% considered it widespread.

- 55% thought that it was increasing worldwide.

- 92% condemned the practice.

- 4% had come in contact with child-sex tourism in some way.

Figure 11.7

What Can Be Done?

Eliminating poverty is the only real solution to child-sex tourism. Poverty is a large-scale problem that can be solved only through social and economic reforms. Two necessary actions are expansions to health care and improved education systems, so that children grow up strong and have the skills to earn reasonable incomes. Before funding becomes available for these expansions, the economies of these countries must be improved. Such improvements might involve eliminating foreign debts, making international trading systems fair, and improving access to investment capital. These changes will take a long time, perhaps generations. In the short term, some practical actions specifically aimed at protecting children are needed.

A strong first step in reducing child-sex tourism is to make it illegal in the home country for a tourist to travel abroad to have sex with minors. With **extraterritorial laws** in place, charges can be laid in the predator's home country for acts that took place in the destination country. For example, in 1998, a German man was jailed in Germany for sexually abusing children in Thailand. U.S. citizens may face penalties of up to ten years in prison for having sex with children in other countries.

Figure 11.8 A young woman cuts a diamond in a gem factory in Bangkok, Thailand. She is a participant in the international project Women of Tomorrow, which seeks to give parents and their daughters financial opportunities through scholarships, vocational training, and jobs to reduce the appeal of child prostitution.

Figure 11.9 Delegates display slogans against sex with children at the first meeting of the World Congress Against Commercial Sexual Exploitation of Children in Stockholm, Sweden, 1996. Delegates from 130 countries attended this global effort to combat child prostitution and pornography.

Another positive step toward reducing child-sex tourism is to inform workers in the travel and tourism industry of the extent and harmful impacts of exploiting children in this way. Airline employees, hotel staff, travel agents, and other workers play key roles in identifying where child prostitution is occurring and reporting it to authorities. Airlines like Lufthansa already include instruction in their staff training on recognizing commercial sexual exploitation of children. Industry workers are in an influential position to detect child-sex tourism and to establish proper procedures for reporting instances of child exploitation.

Other organizations have taken up the cause as well. The United Federation of Travel Agents Association has been working with UNICEF since 1986 and has pledged to combat the prostitution of children. The International Hotel Association has prepared a charter for the hotel industry that includes strong statements on the problem. The World Tourism Organization has taken the step of identifying tour operators who are involved in child-sex tourism. Many other organizations in the travel and tourism industry have also publicly opposed child prostitution and child-sex tourism.

An important step toward stopping child-sex tourism is for all countries to develop and enforce strict laws on child prostitution. Such actions would make child-sex tourism a criminal activity no matter where it occurred.

CHECK IN

1 What would you identify as the most important reason for the existence of child-sex tourism? Explain your answer.

2 What evidence is there that government officials and police fail to enforce laws against child-sex tourism because it is good for the economy?

3 Design a poster or a computer graphic that could be used by the travel and tourism industry to help combat the child-sex trade.

Tourists and the Spread of Diseases

Hepatitis, AIDS, Ebola, and cholera are only a few of the deadly contagious diseases that exist in the world. These and other diseases have reached, or have the potential to reach, **pandemic** levels – that is, to infect a large population over a wide area. Because tourists travel to parts of the world where these diseases are more common than at home, they risk contracting these illnesses. Tourism could play a key role in spreading these diseases from one location to another at a rate far faster than would normally occur.

Tourists can also become victims of deadly diseases that are not contagious – that is, they are acquired by means other than direct person-to-person contact. Malaria and typhoid are two such diseases that can be contracted in tropical destinations. Tourists carry these diseases with them when they return to their home country. Some of these diseases can harm a person's health permanently.

Estimates of Illnesses Among Travellers to the Tropics	
Illness	**Rate per 100 000 Travellers**
Any health problem	45 000
Gastrointestinal infection	35 000
Malaria	2 100
Respiratory infection	1 400
Accident	500
Hepatitis (all types)	450
Gonorrhoea	300
Syphilis	40
Typhoid	3
Cholera	>1

Figure 11.10 Give reasons why gastrointestinal infections are so common among visitors to tropical areas.

Figure 11.11 Prior to visiting some countries, you must be inoculated for certain infectious diseases. Otherwise, you will be denied entry to Canada on your return. Even as a precaution, inoculation against some infectious diseases is a wise action.

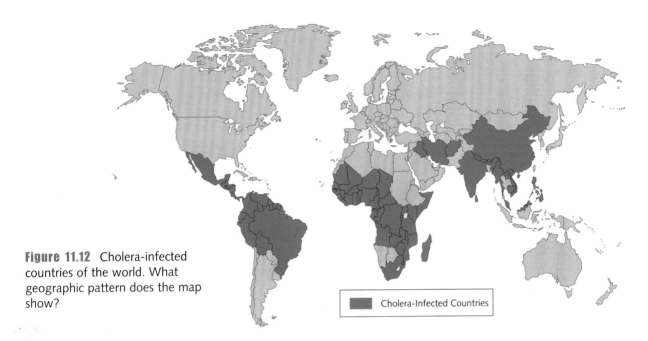

Figure 11.12 Cholera-infected countries of the world. What geographic pattern does the map show?

Cholera-Infected Countries

The Extent of the Problem

Studies show that up to 50% of travellers to developing countries contract some illness during their visits, although symptoms may not appear until they return home. The most common complaints are **gastrointestinal infections**, illnesses that tourists colourfully refer to as Montezuma's Revenge or travellers' diarrhoea. Most of these infections are cleared up with over-the-counter medicines and have no lasting harmful effects. Unfortunately, travellers may encounter more serious diseases, of which malaria, viral hepatitis, and typhoid are the most common. These diseases can cause long-term health problems and even death. Travellers who contract these diseases require immediate medical attention. Symptoms of most infections show up three weeks after exposure, although some infections may take up to six months to manifest themselves.

When trying to diagnose an illness, a doctor will want to know the patient's travel history up to a year earlier. Many diseases have

Canada Travels

In 2001, a very sick tourist from Africa was admitted to a hospital in Hamilton, Ontario. Doctors were puzzled by her condition and suspected that she might be suffering from the Ebola virus, a contagious disease from central Africa with a 90% death rate. The possibility of Ebola was eliminated through testing, and the patient eventually recovered. Nevertheless, the incident caused health officials to examine their responses to contagious diseases brought into Canada.

specific locations where they are most common. For example, yellow fever occurs in Africa, Latin America, and the Caribbean, but not in Asia. Typhoid is mainly confined to Africa, Asia, and Central America. The Ebola virus is limited to an area in northern Congo and Uganda. Knowing the recent destinations of a traveller is a clue to a diagnosis.

The patient's activities are also a clue to diagnosis. Doctors may ask about the level of hygiene in a place, types of food eaten, exposure to insects, sexual activities, and whether the patient's skin was broken by piercing or tattooing. These activities may point to higher risk for such illnesses as sexually transmitted diseases or insect-borne viruses.

Interact

Should incoming tourists and returning travellers be required to have health examinations to prevent the spread of diseases?

Figure 11.13 A woman arriving from Europe steps on an iodine footbath as she disembarks in Rio de Janeiro, Brazil, March 2001. During the European foot-and-mouth epidemic, many countries' ministries of agriculture inaugurated similar preventive footbaths at major airports.

Figure 11.14 A physician speaks to members of the media during a press conference at Henderson General Hospital in Hamilton, Ontario, to assure the public that the patient suspected of Ebola infection was tested and found to be free of all known viruses. The cause of her near-fatal illness was never determined.

Canada Travels

A huge outbreak of foot-and-mouth disease in Europe in 2000–2001 had implications for Canadian tourism. This highly contagious disease affects cattle, hogs, and sheep. A single instance of the disease in a herd means that the whole herd must be killed and the carcasses burned or buried. The disease spreads by animal-to-animal contact but also through the air and on the clothing of humans or their equipment. Outbreaks are very hard to contain. During the epidemic, many European locations were closed to tourists. Travellers returning from affected areas had to wipe their feet on disinfectant mats when they stepped off the aircraft. Tourists returning to Canada were warned not to visit farms for at least two weeks to protect the animals from disease.

Figure 11.15 The Anopheles mosquito, shown here under a scanning electron microscope, is a common carrier of the malaria parasite.

"Malaria represents the number one life-threatening infection that travellers to the developing world will face, and it is preventable. Even if you were to acquire it, it's curable, provided it's recognized early."

— Kevin Kain, MD, Centre for Travel and Tropical Medicine, Toronto General Hospital

Travel FACT

Some strains of malaria have developed resistance to anti-malarial medications, including the widely prescribed chloroquine.

Malaria

Malaria is the most common serious disease among tourists. It occurs in most of Africa, large areas of South and Southeast Asia, the Middle East, Oceania, Central and South America, and Haiti and the Dominican Republic in the Caribbean. This disease is transmitted to humans through the bite of an infected female mosquito. The severity of the disease varies depending on the species of the mosquito that transmitted the parasite that infected the person. Some types of malaria are fatal if untreated.

Symptoms of malaria include fever and a flu-like attack, including headache, nausea, vomiting, muscle pain, and general malaise. Chills and muscle spasms are also symptoms. Acute infections of the disease lead to enlargement of the spleen, seizures, kidney failure, coma, and a painful death.

Figure 11.16 (Left) This fourteen-year-old girl is suffering from a high fever due to malaria in a village near Delhi, India, in 1996. Over 50% of 140 000 residents in nearly 200 villages were infected. (Right) A baby sleeps under a mosquito net in Ho Chi Minh City, Vietnam.

Controlling Infections Tourists can reduce the risk of contracting malaria in two ways. The first is to reduce your exposure to mosquitoes. Since mosquitoes feed mainly during the evening and at night, staying in well-screened accommodations and sleeping under bed nets is good protection. At other times of the day, tourists should wear clothing that reduces the amount of exposed skin and apply insect repellent containing DEET (diethylmethyltoluamide).

Although not 100% effective, taking anti-malarial medication is another way to reduce the risk of contracting the disease. Several types of medication are available, and each has its own side effects. The medication must be taken before going into malarial regions and for a number of weeks after leaving because of the delayed onset of some strains of malaria.

Malaria in Canada Detection and cure of malaria cases brought into Canada is important. This country has three of the four factors necessary for an outbreak of malaria: standing water, warm weather at least three months of the year, and mosquitoes. The only missing factor is a large number of people carrying the parasite, an element that could occur if people with the disease go undetected.

Confirmed Malaria Cases in Canada	
Year	Confirmed Cases
1994	430
1995	637
1996	744
1997	1036
1998	552

Figure 11.17 What might be some reasons why the numbers of malaria cases vary so much from one year to the next?

CHECK IN

1 a) Explain the relationship between tourism and the spread of diseases.

   b) Suggest three actions by governments, groups, or individuals that could help reduce the risk of the spread of disease.

2 For what reasons should Canadians be concerned about malaria, a disease that is largely associated with tropical parts of the globe?

3 Create a cartoon or a list of sayings that could be used as part of a Canadian effort to educate tourists about the risks of contracting diseases in destinations.

Tourists as Targets of Criminal Activity

Crowds are ideal places for thieves who pick pockets, snatch handbags, or walk away with cameras. These criminals ply their trade around popular tourist attractions, main squares, train stations, and nightclubs.

Petty crimes are on the increase even in relatively safe destinations such as Belize, a small country in Central America. Officials there acknowledge that muggings, pickpocketing, and burglary are common, although these incidents are largely confined to Belize City, the largest urban area. In Belize as in most destinations, credit card fraud is growing, and moneychangers have been known to pass counterfeit bills. Violent armed robberies have occurred in more rural parts of the country, and tourists have occasionally reported assaults and rapes. Most tourist destinations are struggling with the same problems.

VIRTUAL TRAVEL

www.irwinpublishing.com

Personal safety is an important concern for vacationers in Mexico. Recent reports of crimes and violence directed toward tourists have Mexican officials worried. To help deal with this bad press, the Mexican Ministry of Tourism set up a Web site. If you would like to find out about safe travel in Mexico, visit the Student Page for *Canada Travels*.

Figure 11.18 A country's economic and social problems can negatively affect tourism. In Colon, near Panama City, Panama, once-beautiful houses crumble from neglect; more than 40% of the city's 100 000 residents are unemployed. Crime rates have risen to such frightening levels that some guidebooks advise potential tourists not to go.

Figure 11.19 Thieves who prey on travellers are common, and they often target those carrying new, brand-name cameras. Be aware that a thief may reach right into your backpack while you are walking around the city.

Police, particularly in developing countries, lack the resources and training to curtail crimes against tourists. There simply are not enough police officers to deal with the number of petty crimes reported. In some locations, criminal activity actually takes place with the consent or even cooperation of the police. This corruption means that there is little that can be done to recover stolen property while in a destination.

Why Target Tourists?

Tourists are easy targets for criminals. For one thing, their appearance makes them easy to spot. They often travel in large groups and are herded in and out of buses, usually wearing name tags or clutching carryall bags adorned with tour company logos. Their clothing, different from local manners of dress, identifies them as outsiders. The video camera or expensive SLR camera with a telephoto lens is another identifying characteristic of tourists.

Tourists are busy viewing attractions, reading travel guides, peering through camera lenses or talking excitedly with their companions. Often they are so preoccupied that they ignore their own security and that of their belongings. Many cameras, bags, and purses have disappeared when their owners "just turned away for a moment." Experienced thieves are opportunistic and will take advantage of tourists who are inattentive.

Some tourists are partly to blame themselves. Seeking new experiences, they can wander or be led into dangerous places where they become victims. Their lack of knowledge about a location makes them vulnerable to predators.

Figure 11.20 What strategies could tourists use to lessen the odds that they will be victimized by criminals?

Criminals also target business travellers, who may be carrying expensive electronic equipment, travellers' cheques, and cash. Canada's Department of Foreign Affairs and International Trade reports that 20% to 25% of the calls received on the 24-hour hot line are related to problems affecting businesspeople who are travelling. In fact, some Canadian companies routinely prepare risk assessments of locations for their employees travelling abroad.

TRAVELLERS' ALERT!

Petty thieves will watch you park and wait until you have entered a tourist attraction before stripping your car of valuables. They will be long gone when you return to find your vehicle ransacked. So, never leave documents, especially passports and visas, or valuable objects in a car unattended.

Figure 11.21 Victims in waiting: (Left) While some tourists enjoy experiencing the seamier aspects of their destination, they should recognize that criminal activity is more common in these locations. (Right) Tourists who are distracted by their surroundings are easy targets for petty criminals.

Violent Crimes

While petty theft is annoying and can disrupt your vacation, tourists must also face the reality that they could be targets of violent crimes. In remote parts of the world, it is not uncommon for robbers to kill their victims to ensure that they will not be identified. Women tourists have been sexually assaulted. And, in some countries suffering through political upheaval, tourists have been kidnapped and used as pawns to put international pressure on governments.

U.S. tourists, in particular business travellers, have been targeted by extremist groups in some tourist destinations, particularly in Central American, Middle Eastern, and Asian countries where anti-

> **"**Any tourist with an ounce of intelligence knows that in violent societies and crime-infested cities, it only comes down to being in the wrong place at the wrong time.**"**
>
> – *TTG Asia* (travel magazine)

American sentiment is strong. The U.S. State Department warns citizens travelling abroad to be on guard for their safety.

Victims of Criminal Activity

Many crimes against tourists are never reported. Tourists may feel that time spent in a police station filling out reports is wasted. Local authorities are unlikely to spend time tracking down petty criminals, and there is little chance that stolen property will be recovered. There may also be a language barrier. In the end, most tourists just move on to their next destination. They come to view their loss as a hidden cost of travel.

Impact of Crimes Against Tourists

Tourists have many options for travel. When a location begins to get a bad reputation for violence and crimes aimed at tourists, travellers see these as **barriers** and plan trips to other places. This has a substantial impact on the economic well-being of the industry. Japan and Singapore are popular tourist destinations because they are considered the safest in Asia. Macau, on the other hand, lost a large percentage of its tourist business between 1997 and 2000 because of feuds over control of casinos that put tourists in the middle of rival groups. When security is questionable, tourists will gravitate toward destinations that offer fun and excitement without fear of violence.

Figure 11.22 Travellers should be wary of entering poorly lit or deserted areas, such as parking lots, at night.

CHECK IN

1 Why do criminals target tourists?

2 With a partner, brainstorm a list of actions that tourists could take to help reduce the risk of being a victim of criminals. Share your ideas with the class and create a list of "Five Strategies for Personal Security" while on vacation.

CASE STUDY
Macau, China – Gang Violence and the Tourism Industry

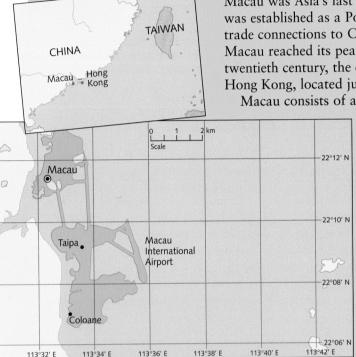

Figure 11.23 Location of Macau. Fill has been used to create causeways and the airport.

Macau was Asia's last colony. In the sixteenth century, Macau was established as a Portuguese colony to improve Portugal's trade connections to China and other parts of Asia. As a colony, Macau reached its peak in the early 1800s. Throughout the twentieth century, the colony was surpassed economically by Hong Kong, located just 60 km to the northeast.

Macau consists of a peninsula and two islands, Taipa and Coloane, that jut into the South China Sea just west of the Zhu Jiang (Pearl River) estuary. China's Guangdong province borders Macau on the north. Macau is tiny, just 17.4 km². It has hot, humid summers – annual precipitation totals about 2000 mm – and mild, dry winters.

In an agreement signed in 1987, control of Macau reverted to China on December 20, 1999. Under an arrangement that is scheduled to last until 2049, the former colony is allowed to keep its own political, social, and economic systems, which are very different from those of communist China. Cantonese and Portuguese will remain official languages for the 450 000 people who call the territory home.

Figure 11.24 (Left) Fireworks light up the sky over the statue of Kun Iam in Macau's harbour on December 20, 1999, when the territory celebrated its handover from Portugal to China. (Below) A Chinese opera performer stands out among the crowd. Chinese people make up 95% of Macau's population. The territory has one of the highest population densities in the world.

Tourism is the mainstay of the economy of Macau, contributing more than half of its Gross Domestic Product. Located only 45 minutes by hydrofoil from Hong Kong and the Chinese mainland and a short flight from Taiwan, Macau offers tourists from these areas services that are not available at home. In recent years, a good deal of investment has taken place in tourism infrastructure to capture a share of the expanding Asian tourism market.

Gambling and Tourism

Casinos have been part of Macau's economy since the mid-1800s, contributing to the territory's income and producing a life of prosperity. The organizations – gangs might be a better term – in charge of gambling operations kept a truce that allowed them to expand their businesses and earn high profits. However, this tranquillity was very much threatened in the late 1990s as the takeover by China approached. Rival gangsters began fighting for control of the multi-billion dollar gambling business. Each wanted to be in a position of great power when it came time to talk to the new Chinese administrators. The violence threatened to destroy Macau's tourism industry.

> "Macau has a bit of an image problem."
>
> – Maria Suzete Saraiva, deputy director, Macau Government Tourist Office

Figure 11.25 Casinos, massage parlours, and strip shows lead the list of tourist attractions in Macau. Casinos offer games from both the East and the West, appealing to a wide range of clients.

Gang Violence in Macau

Killings of rival gang members and public officials responsible for keeping the peace in Macau began in 1997 and escalated in the following years. In 1999, 37 murder cases were linked to organized criminal activity associated with the casinos. These incidents became front-page news, and tourists feared for their safety even though they were not the targets.

Tourist arrivals from Hong Kong in 1999 were down 15% over 1998. Arrivals from Japan fell close to 29%, and totals for the rest of Asia were down by 5%. Hotel occupancy rates for June 1999 showed that 62.9% of rooms were rented, well below the 72.5% rate for the same period the previous year. Tour companies reported cancellations and poor bookings as people reacted to the news from Macau.

The violence prompted countries to issue travel advisories. Australia encouraged its citizens to "maintain a high level of personal security" while travelling in the territory. Canada suggested that visitors should "remain vigilant." American citizens were instructed to "exercise prudence and caution in visiting Macau." These security concerns helped to undermine Macau's tourism even further, threatening the long-term success of the industry.

Interact

In what ways was the gang violence in Macau a barrier to tourism?

Figure 11.26 (Above) An open fish market and (left) a bicycle-driven rickshaw represent two of Macau's older traditions.

Figure 11.27 (Right) Macau's modern skyline and (above) a McDonald's restaurant point to the effects of globalization on the territory.

Struggling to Rebuild a Tourism Industry

In an effort to combat its negative image, Macau's tourism sector tried hard to emphasize safety and security on the island. Government officials worked hand-in-hand with authorities in China and Hong Kong to control the activities of the casino gangs. Their measures included drafting tough new laws against organized crime. Also, the Tourist Office turned to more aggressive marketing, promoting other assets of the territory, especially convention facilities, culture, food, and entertainment. Officials hoped to create an integrated industry in which gambling is just one aspect, not the main one.

The marketing especially targeted Chinese tourists. In addition, the government waived the departure tax for visitors staying less than 24 hours in a bid to encourage Hong Kong-bound travellers to land in Macau before continuing to their destination. Overall, tourist industry workers are hoping the territory's new status under China will bring about a stability that will allow them to reconstruct a positive public image and a vibrant tourism sector.

CHECK IN

1 a) What was the cause of the violence in Macau?

   b) How did the violence affect tourism?

   c) What actions were taken to deal with the problem?

2 Identify the motivators and barriers for Macau's tourist industry.

CASE STUDY
Florida, USA – Restoring a Reputation

Figure 11.28 Location of Florida

Florida's tourism industry was tarnished in 1992 and 1993. The murders of ten tourists and numerous robberies in the state made it seem that criminals were targeting tourists. Two incidents in 1994 strengthened this perception: a Canadian retiree was shot to death outside his winter home in Miami during a robbery, and a businesswoman from Panama was wounded by gunfire in a robbery attempt in Dade County. The criminals seemed to focus on people driving rental cars.

The economic impact of the violence against tourists was significant. Florida is a state dependent on tourism. Normally, over 40 million visitors a year contribute about US$38 billion to the economy. However, polls of potential tourists showed that many chose not to travel to Florida because of the perceived possibility of violence. Tourist arrivals dropped substantially, and the industry demanded that something be done to counteract the negative image that the state was acquiring.

Figure 11.29 Well-known tourist destinations in Florida: (Clockwise from top) Rocket Garden, Cape Canaveral; Busch Gardens, Tampa; Disney World, Orlando. Any slowdown in tourism results in job losses and reduced economic earnings.

Responding to the Criminal Threat

The tourism industry and the government responded to Florida's high crime rates. A new law that eliminated the identification of rental cars on licence plates was enacted. Routes were marked more clearly with new road signs that carry a distinctive sunburst logo encouraging tourists to "Follow the Sun" to their destinations. Tourist maps were distributed widely so that travellers would have less difficulty finding hotels and attractions. Crime Stoppers became involved, offering monetary rewards for information leading to the apprehension and conviction of persons who committed crimes against tourists.

Extra funding was allocated to programs such as the South Florida Violent Street Crime Task Force and the Tourist Robbery Abatement Program so that they could function more effectively. The Tourist Oriented Police (TOP) program was set up to help patrol the Miami International Airport. A special program was set up to provide round-the-clock prosecution for tourism-related crimes. The Greater Miami Convention and Visitors Bureau published a visitor safety brochure to help tourists avoid dangerous situations and neighbourhoods.

Figure 11.30 Route markings such as the "Follow the Sun" logo were one measure designed to improve the safety of tourists. How does this strategy work?

Figure 11.31 With public support, Florida police stepped up their campaign against crime, especially when directed against tourists.

Canada Travels

If you are planning to travel to the United States, consider purchasing a crime map of your destination from Safe T Maps. This company produces colour-coded crime maps based on FBI and police crime statistics. You can use these maps to identify areas of the city that have high crime rates, and those areas that are relatively safe. To find out more about Safe T Maps, visit the Student Page for *Canada Travels*.

Victory over Criminals

The actions by the tourism industry and the State of Florida substantially improved the situation. For example, in 1998, there were only 330 robberies compared with 2114 in 1992. Murders declined 17% and burglaries 15% from 1990. The non-resident victimization rate – the proportion of crimes committed against visitors as opposed to citizens – fell from 3.7% in 1990 to 2.5% by 1994, and even lower throughout the decade. The actions taken by the government, industry, and citizens helped reverse the perception that Florida was a violent state. Tourist arrivals began to rise, and the industry was again expanding. Since the mid-1990s, tourism to central Florida has grown at an annual rate of 6.2%, with Canadians making up the largest number of international tourists.

TRAVELLERS' ALERT!

The tourism industry in Florida recommends that you carry only a small amount of cash in your wallet, and the rest in another pocket or money belt. If somebody attempts to steal your wallet or purse, hand it over. Most injuries and deaths occur when victims refuse to surrender their money.

Figure 11.32 (Clockwise from top) Tampa, the commercial centre of Florida's west coast, boasts such visitor attractions as a waterfront convention centre, performing arts centre, fine arts museum, and cruise ship terminal; Old Hyde Park Village is a favourite neighbourhood for shopping and sidewalk cafés; fine dining in Tampa includes an eclectic mix of restaurants specializing in seafood and Spanish-inspired cuisine.

66 We [have] done a tremendous amount of work in making sure the traveller to Miami understands we are an urban environment, with some pluses and some minuses. 99

– Mayco Villafana, Greater Miami Convention and Visitors Bureau

Figure 11.33 Many Canadians spend a winter vacation in Florida. So popular is this destination that clubs and newspapers have been established so that Canadians can stay in touch with national views and events. (Above) Angus Kinnear, the founder and president of Canada 3000, stands by his airline's logo. The company, which quickly grew to become Canada's second largest airline, started out as a two-plane charter service taking vacationers to resorts in Florida and the Caribbean. In the fall of 2001, however, the company faced severe financial difficulties. (Left) A bicyclist in Hollywood, Florida, passes a restaurant sign aimed at French-speaking Canadian diners.

CHECK IN

1 a) List the different actions taken in Florida to deal with criminal activity targeted at tourists.

   b) Add two more actions that might be taken to improve conditions.

2 Do a plus–minus analysis to consider Florida as a vacation choice.

3 Create a flow chart to show how the government and the tourism industry worked to improve security in the state.

- identify selected factors that influence travellers' destination choices
- analyze tourist travel within selected regions and explain reasons for the observed patterns
- explain the effects of selected natural systems and phenomena on travel and tourism
- research and report on the impact of a natural or human-caused disaster on travel and tourism in a selected region
- demonstrate an understanding that cultural conflicts may result from the movement and interactions of people around the world
- analyze the effects of cultural, economic, and political motivators and barriers on travel and tourism patterns

Global Hot Spots: Tourist Destinations to Avoid

Purpose: To use ArcView and the Internet to create an interactive map of major events, social, economic, and political issues, and even extreme weather conditions that may affect the travel plans of international tourists.

Files: country.shp

Functions: View Properties, Legend Editor (Symbol Edit, Unique Value), Table Edit, Convert to Shapefile, label, Hot Link.

Hot Spots is a service provided by Air Security International. Via their Web site or fax, Air Security International provides a daily snapshot of pressing worldwide travel and security events that may affect the travel plans of international travellers. Hot Spots is a concise summary and analysis of current security, aviation, and international travel-related news from around the world. For the international traveller, this service has become an indispensable tool since many of these issues are not covered in the mainstream press, but are significant enough to affect travel plans.

Hot Spots is available by visiting the Student Page for *Canada Travels* at www.irwin publishing.com.

1. Your first step will be to follow the above link to access the Hot Spots page of Air Security International's Web site by visiting the Student Page for *Canada Travels*. Several hot spots will be listed and described under the following headings: Today's Focus, Snapshots, Situation Updates, and Government Warnings.

2. Next, start a word-processing program such as Notepad (Start – Programs – Accessories – Notepad). Use Alt-Tab (or the Task Bar at the bottom of your screen) to return to your browser (e.g., Netscape or Explorer). Copy and paste the first hot spot and its description into your word processor. Save it as a text (.txt) document, naming the file

with the name of the country. *It is crucial at this stage that you write down the directory path and file name, since you will be hot linking to it later in ArcView.* Repeat for the remaining countries listed and described in the Hot Spots page of the Air Security International Web site.

3. Now, start ArcView, create a blank View, and name it "Travel Hot Spots."

4. Next, add the c:\esri\esridata\world\country .shp theme to your View. Use the Colour Palette in the Legend Editor to change the theme's colour to white.

5. Now, open the theme table for the Country.shp theme. Select all of the countries that were listed as hot spots in the Air Security International Web site. Close the theme table to return to your View. Convert the selected countries to a shapefile, naming it "Hot Spots" and adding it to your View. Clear the selected countries.

6. Next, open the theme table for the Hot spots.shp theme. Under Table Properties, turn off the visibility of all of the fields except for "Cntry_name."

7. Now, place the table in Edit mode, then create two new string fields, naming one "Hot Link" and the other "Issue." (Note: make sure that the width of the Hot Link field is set to a number large enough to accommodate all the characters of the directory path that leads to the text files you created in Step 2.) In the Hot Link field, for each country enter the correct directory path and file name of the text file created in Step 2 (e.g., c:\windows\temp\colombia.txt). In the Issue field, for each country enter the type of travel and security event that is currently being experienced in that Hot Spot (i.e., political, social, economic, environmental). Stop editing the table, saving the edits that you have made. Close the theme table to return to your View.

8. Next, using the Legend Editor, apply a "Unique Value" legend type to the Hot spots.shp theme, using "Issue" in the values field. Apply a colour scheme of your preference.

9. Now, use the Callout Label tool to label all the countries belonging to the Hot spots.shp theme.

10. Lastly, open the Theme Properties window and complete setting up your hot links to the text files using the Hot Links field. Test your hot links!

TRAVELLERS' ALERT!

Air Security International publishes an annual list of Dangerous Places. Cities with important tourist industries included on the list are

- São Paulo, Brazil
- Rio de Janeiro, Brazil
- Lagos, Nigeria
- Johannesburg, South Africa
- Cape Town, South Africa
- Mexico City, Mexico

Extension:

Scan or download photos of the travel and security events currently being experienced in each of the countries designated as hot spots in this activity. Then, hot link these to the Hot spots.shp theme by creating new Views and adding the .jpeg photos as image data. (Hint: Don't forget to turn on the JPEG Support extension and name the Views appropriately!)

Extension:

Using the Cntry_95.shp file located on the ArcCanada 2.0 CD (and its "Tourists_k" field), create a graduated colour map illustrating the number of tourists received by the various countries of the world. Comment on the number of tourists received in 1995 by the countries designated as Hot Spots in this activity.

REVISIT THE chapter 11
Looking Back

Understanding the Concepts

1. Suppose you were asked to give a speech to a service club in your community about the causes and consequences of child prostitution and the exploitation of children. List five points that you would include in your speech.

2. List three criminal activities targeted at tourists. For each one, outline a preventative measure that might be taken.

Practising Your Skills

3. Read the newspaper article in Figure 11.34. Respond to this article by writing a letter to the editor suggesting steps that might protect children from future exploitation.

4. For Florida, identify conditions that encourage or motivate travel and tourism activities and those conditions that discourage or act as barriers to tourism. Organize your ideas in a chart with the headings "Motivators" and "Barriers."

Figure 11.34

THE GLOBE AND MAIL

Meet Rose, Age: 12; Price: $200

Nobody knows the Flower Man's name or exactly where he comes from.... His pockets stuffed with cash, he trolls the village, searching out the poorest of China's poor, peasants so destitute they will finally agree to sell their children into servitude.

The Flower Man prefers girls, since they are more profitable, the younger the better. The six-year-olds are put to work selling flowers in the bar districts of China's big cities.... As he does every trip, the Flower Man offered $200 to $300 a child.

You can find the sold children ... any night on Beijing's streets. They work ... under the chemical glow of the neon light shed by bars with names such as Orgasm and the Boys and Girls Club. They are part of the strip of mostly sleazy establishments on ... Beijing's Bar Street.

With the disarming smiles of children, they sell their bunches of withered red roses carefully wrapped in cellophane to strangers for $2 apiece.

To tourists such as Joe Balladaci, a pensioner from Florida, they seem like adorable hustlers trying to make a few bucks after school.... "She's a cutie pie," he says, patting the head of Chen Ying. Now 12, she is rake-thin in rumpled clothes with a heart-melting smile. "This kid is going places."

Chen, who has been working the street since the Flower Man bought her two years ago, ... holds the American's hand and says in broken English that her name is Rose, given to her by an American couple a few months ago.

"Xiexie, xiexie, thank you, thank you," she chirps in delight as the silver-haired American proffers a 50-renminbi note, about $10 Canadian, for a single rosebud.

But as soon as he disappears into a nearby bar, Rose's flower-girl smile disappears. Her eyes harden and she looks older as she scopes the street for her next customer. The Flower Man has set a stiff quota tonight: 50 roses need to be sold, and Rose doesn't want a beating.

Source: Adapted from Miro Cernetig, "Meet Rose, Age: 12; Price: $200." The Globe and Mail, April 28, 2001.

Applying Your Skills

5. Bangkok, Thailand, is a tourist destination city associated with child-sex prostitution. Use Internet and other sources to answer these research questions:
   - What has the tourism industry in Bangkok done to try to control child-sex tourism?
   - What actions have the governments of Thailand and Bangkok taken to deal with this problem?
   - Is it likely that child-sex tourism will be eliminated in this tourist destination in the future? Explain.

6. Countries in Africa see the growth in tourism as a way of stimulating their economies and creating jobs. Unfortunately, many of these countries have had incidents of criminal activity and violence that have discouraged tourists from travelling there. Choose one of Algeria, Nigeria, or South Africa and investigate its tourism future. Use Internet and other research sources and prepare a two-page written report to show your findings.

7. Identify the problem of crime faced by either Macau or Florida. Organize your points in a chart. Some topics that you might consider are:
   - sources of the problems
   - impacts on travel and tourism
   - government policies designed to solve the problems
   - the future

Figure 11.35 The Casbah district of Algiers, Algeria, has always been off-limits to tourists. Since the early 1990s, however, political unrest has closed the entire country to foreign travellers.

Thinking Like a Tourist

8. Research strategies for keeping yourself safe while enjoying your travel experiences in each of these situations:
   - while travelling
   - while in your place of accommodation
   - while at attractions or events

   Produce your findings as a booklet that could be distributed to tourists.

9. The World Tourism Organization has asked you to determine which destinations are the safest and which are the riskiest for tourists. Design a research study that you might undertake to satisfy this request.

J O B SKILLS

Workers in any industry have to take responsibility both for their own actions and for those of their industry and to contribute to their community. Workers in the travel and tourism industry can play a key role in dealing with problems such as tourists travelling for the purposes of having sex with children or to disrupt sports events. Work with others to draft a "Code of Conduct for Tourism Workers." Make sure your points deal with taking responsibility for your industry's actions and contributing in positive ways to the worldwide community.

CHAPTER twelve 12
Tourism Planning and Marketing

Successful Tourism

In recent decades, many developing countries of the world have turned to travel and tourism as a way to improve their economic and social conditions. For these countries, the travel and tourism industry offers some hope where few other opportunities exist. There have been some real success stories. You have read about some of these – South Africa (Chapter 1), Costa Rica (Chapter 3), St. Martin/St. Maarten (Chapter 9), and Mexico (Chapter 10). Even wealthy developed countries encourage tourism because it can stimulate or maintain economic vitality.

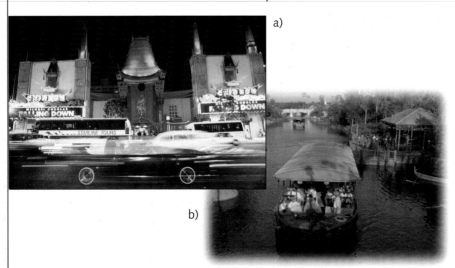

a)

b)

Figure 12.1 a) Mann's Chinese Theatre in Los Angeles, California, draws tourists who are fascinated by Hollywood's most famous and infamous people; b) visitors enjoy Animal Kingdom's Safari Village boat ride in Lake Buena Vista, Florida; c) Shakespeare's house and its Knot Garden are a focal point for tourists to Stratford-upon-Avon, England; d) workers construct a stage at Angkor Wat, a major cultural attraction in Siem Reap, Cambodia, as dancers practise their routines. Large tourist attractions like these do not happen by chance. Facilities exist as a result of the efforts of many individuals and organizations. Both governments and businesses are needed for a thriving and successful tourist industry.

Benefits of the Development of Tourism	Potential Problems Resulting from Tourism
Tourism can	**Tourism can**
• increase employment • attract money from other countries • raise incomes and improve the quality of life • develop the infrastructure • stimulate local businesses • increase government revenues • preserve cultural and natural resources • promote environmental protection • improve modernization by encouraging new technologies • develop costly recreational facilities	• lead to overcrowding of local facilities • divert development funds from other forms of economic activity • create social conflicts through differences in values and attitudes • increase crime rates • harm the natural environment • lead to commodification and a loss of cultural identity • inflate land values • increase prices of goods and services for local residents

Figure 12.2 When effectively developed, tourism can have many benefits for a society. But development of this industry can also result in overuse and overcrowding of resources.

c)

d)

There have also been many instances where investments in tourism did not produce the positive benefits that were expected. Hotels that remain underbooked, casinos that are little utilized, and theme parks on the verge of closing are just some examples of tourism that did not live up to expectations. Overall, we must conclude that tourism is not an automatic cure for every country's woes. To realize the many advantages of tourism, there must be careful planning and thoughtful consideration of the costs and benefits of the activity.

In this chapter, we will look at aspects of planning and developing tourism around the world.

EXPECTATIONS

In this chapter you will have the opportunity to

- identify criteria that planners must consider when planning for tourism development within a region
- analyze the impact of marketing and advertising on travel and tourism patterns
- produce a case study to investigate the future of tourism for a selected region or destination
- evaluate the impact of government policies on travel and tourism in a selected region
- identify selected factors that influence travellers' destination choices
- demonstrate an understanding that the travel and tourism industry consists of many interconnected components

Planning for Tourism

Combinations of natural, historic, archaeological, cultural, and climatic features can provide the impetus to develop a tourist industry. As you have learned, some places are better endowed with attractive features than others. These places have a comparative advantage. Each location must work with the features that it has to develop its own distinctive tourism industry. Tourism planning is about achieving maximum benefits from the resources that are available.

Features That Attract Tourism

Natural Factors

Natural beauty	General landscape; plants and animals; proximity to lakes, rivers, seas, and islands; caverns; waterfalls
Climate	Amount of sunshine; temperature; winds; precipitation patterns

Social Factors

Artistic and architectural features	Local architectural style; places of worship; monuments; art museums and galleries
Festivals and competitions	Music and dance festivals; sports events and competitions
Distinctive local features	Folk dress; folk music and dances; local food specialties; folk handicrafts
Fairs and exhibits	Fall fairs; annual events
Attitudes toward tourists	Local congeniality and friendly treatment of tourists

Historical Factors

Ancient ruins	Location, condition, and accessibility
Religious significance	Annual celebrations
Historical prominence	Links to important events and/or legends; monuments and plaques

Recreational Facilities

Sports facilities	Hunting; fishing; swimming; skiing; golfing; sailing; horseback riding
Educational facilities	Archaeological sites; museums; zoos; botanical gardens; aquariums

(continued)

Figure 12.3 Ontario's Stratford Festival, which began as a local initiative backed by business-people and residents, has grown into an internationally acclaimed annual dramatic event. (Top) Building the theatre for the festival's first performance, July 1953; (above) a scene from Shakespeare's play *A Midsummer Night's Dream*, as performed at the Festival Theatre.

Figure 12.4 Which combination of these features would you find most appealing? Why?

Relaxation facilities	Mineral-water and hot-water spas; hiking trails; picnic grounds; golf courses
Evening recreation	Casinos; clubs; theatres; cinemas
Shopping facilities	Souvenir and gift shops; handicrafts; duty-free shops
Infrastructure	
Basic services	Highways and roads; water, electricity, and gas; safety and health services; communications; public transportation facilities
Tourist facilities	Hotels and motels; restaurants; vacation villages; camping facilities

Figure 12.5 (From top) A maintenance crew checking the face of the gorge wall for hazardous loose rocks in Niagara Falls, Ontario; some of the attractions for tourists; a poker dealer at Casino Niagara. Which jobs should be done by the public sector? Why? Which jobs should be handled by the private sector? Why?

Developing the tourist potential of an area is typically a joint effort between the **public sector** (various levels of government) and the **private sector** (for-profit businesses and individuals). This partnership is quite apparent when you think about a well-known destination such as Niagara Falls. The public sector built and now maintains the parks and gardens that enhance our enjoyment of this natural wonder. The private sector constructed and operates the hotels and provides many other services that we enjoy while there. Each sector benefits from the efforts of the other.

The Public Sector's Role

One role of governments and their agencies in most of the developed countries of the world is to ensure that a favourable business environment exists for the private sector. This involves

- constructing a workable infrastructure (transportation facilities, water systems, and parks)
- providing services, including education to upgrade the skills of local workers
- promoting and marketing the region and special features of the destination

Governments should also consider the negative impacts of tourist developments and try to reduce them. Typically, the public sector is involved in

- developing policies to protect the environment
- ensuring that land-use planning has provided an organized use of space, so that conflict does not emerge between uses

- encouraging involvement of local people in protecting cultural and social qualities of the area

Revenues for government activities are raised through licensing, user fees, and taxation.

Government Incentives

In theory, government's support of tourism – by providing services and infrastructure – should encourage the tourist industry. However, this involvement is not always enough. Then, governments must consider using **incentives**, or rewards, to stimulate private sector developments. Incentives are designed to remove some of the risks of undertaking new projects. Governments argue that the costs of offering these incentives are more than recovered by the jobs and other income generated by the new developments. A variety of incentives have been used by different governments.

Financial Incentives One strategy is to make investment money more readily available to the private sector through such government agencies as investment banks, special credit facilities, or tourism development corporations. Interest rates on loans are usually lower than rates at most financial institutions. Businesses then face lower borrowing costs and potentially higher profits.

Reduction in Capital Costs By reducing the **capital costs** – the cost of building the facilities – government incentives improve profits for businesses. These incentives may involve offering land for free or below market value, removing taxes on construction materials, and building or expanding facilities like airports.

Reduction in Operating Costs **Operating costs** are the day-to-day costs of running of a business. These costs include such things as wages, energy, water supply, and materials and services used by the business. Governments can help businesses reduce operating costs by offering worker-training programs, tax breaks on materials, profit

> "Local government always has to balance the day-to-day needs of its residents and their economic future with the short-term exploitative needs of the tourism industry – determining the fine line between community good and industry good can be very difficult."
>
> – Ian Oelrichs,
> Australian Tourism Committee

Figure 12.6 Construction workers and photographers watch as the last section of the Tsing Ma Bridge, which links Hong Kong with its new Chek Lap Kok Airport, is lifted into place. Chek Lap Kok was an expensive endeavour because landfill was needed to expand the island's area.

Figure 12.7 Worker training strengthens the tourist industry by making workers more effective in their jobs.

tax "holidays," and low-interest loans. Offering reduced energy costs to large hotels in hot climates, where air conditioning costs are high, has proven to be an effective incentive.

Investment Security   The more business owners can be assured that their investments are safe, the more likely they are to invest in a project. Government incentives help to reduce the risk of loss. These incentives may include loan guarantees, work permits for key foreign employees, free technical advice, marketing of the region, and simplifying government regulations. Such incentives help the private sector be more comfortable with its development decisions.

The Private Sector's Role

The private sector has been, and remains, the driving force behind tourism developments. The private sector category is made up of for-profit companies that provide products and services for tourists. These companies base their decisions on what they think the market (tourists) wants and will buy. Private developers work within the infrastructure created by the government and use their financial, human, and physical resources to try to satisfy a consumer need. If they are correct in their judgements, they will make a profit and be successful. If they are wrong, they will lose their investment.

The range of facilities run by the private sector is enormous. Think about the accommodations industry: multinationals like Club Med or Holiday Inn compete for the same tourists as bed-and-breakfast facilities. This diversity means that a variety of needs are being met. The diversity also encourages small-scale development that can have positive impacts for local communities, especially through creating jobs.

Small-scale Tourism   Offering tourism services on a small scale has helped many communities around the world. Some services offered include bed-and-breakfast accommodations, transportation in the owner's vehicle, meals served from the family kitchen, and handicraft sales. Local people modify what they already own to provide goods and services to tourists. Their increased revenue is often reinvested in the business, and tourism services expand. Family members are employed in the businesses, and the owners gain status in the community if they are successful.

Other Voices

Besides governments and businesses, a wide range of other voices may be involved in the development of tourism resources. Residents close to a potential destination site will likely want to express their views, either for or against a proposal. Consumer, environmental, and cultural groups often choose to express their views. In an ideal

Interact

If a government supports the development of a tourist industry, should that government be obligated to support all other types of industries as well? Discuss.

VIRTUAL TRAVEL

www.irwinpublishing.com

Helping workers develop appropriate skills to build careers in the travel and tourism industry can start as early as high school. Check out the Ontario Tourism Education Corporation on the Student Page for *Canada Travels* to find out how this organization helps young people prepare for entry into this growing industry.

Travel FACT

In spite of the growing popularity of the Internet, in 2000, 95% of business and leisure travel transactions were still booked directly through travel agents.

world, the different levels of governments and the businesses involved listen to these voices and consider their messages in the development of tourism activities.

Public and Private Sector Planning

Both the public and private sectors can stimulate development of the travel industry. Figure 12.9 outlines a typical process that would occur as the two sectors work through the planning of a tourist facility.

Figure 12.8 Some tourist "developments," like this bed-and-breakfast lodging, are modest in size. Who benefits from this type of activity?

Figure 12.9 The difficulties of putting all the pieces in place mean that many potential developments never reach completion. Profitable developments successfully combine the resources of both the public and private sectors.

The Planning Process for Travel and Tourism Developments

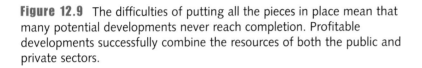

Stage	Activities
Conceptualizing the Project	Developers carefully consider their available resources including capital, the intended market, suitable activities, possible sites, competition, and the potential for a profit. If a project seems possible, the developers begin to prepare a preliminary project plan.
Preparing a Preliminary Plan	This plan outlines the project being considered. A site is chosen, land-use plans prepared, artists' conceptual drawings are sketched, investors recruited, and cash flow projected.
Approving the Plan	Approval of a plan involves a variety of stakeholders. Investors and stockholders will want to know that their capital is secure. Local governments check that the proposed project fits the goals and values of residents. Other groups and individuals, including Aboriginal peoples, environmentalists, and current users of the land, will study the plans. Any or all of these groups may want changes to the plan. Approval may take a long time and may require substantial changes to the preliminary plans.
Developing a Final Plan	Details for the development are finalized. This stage often includes making sure that the local infrastructure can support the project, taking steps to protect the natural environment, ensuring that construction standards will be met, setting up administrative structures, getting necessary permits and approvals, and putting financing in place.
Completing the Project	Time and money will have been spent on a project before construction actually begins. At this stage the facilities are constructed, staff hired and trained, and marketing conducted. The project becomes a reality.

1 Find a tourist activity in your area that has not been as successful as was expected. Suggest a reason for its lack of success.

2 Which benefit of tourism is most important to an impoverished developing country? Explain your answer.

3 In a two-column chart, compare the roles of the public and private sectors in the development of tourism.

4 a) Think about a tourist service in your local area. Identify three ways that governments might help that business.

   b) In what ways might governments hinder a tourist business?

5 a) Which of the incentives for encouraging tourism do you think small-scale tourism would find most useful? Explain why.

   b) Which of the incentives identified do you think large-scale tourism would find most attractive? Explain why.

The Market and the Product

The majority of international tourists are people from countries in the developed world. These people have the finances and freedom to travel. They represent the **market** for the travel and tourism industry, which tailors its **products**, or destinations, to suit the wants and needs of this market.

Tourism provides a unique trade export situation. Other export commodities or products are moved to the market. For example, tropical fruit (the product) grown in South America is shipped to consumers in Canada (the market). Tourism works exactly the opposite. Tourists (the market) are shipped to the destination (the product).

Figure 12.10 The tourist trade export market expands during peak vacation periods, when people are eager to visit destinations for sun and fun.

Marketing

One of the key roles of the public sector in tourism is marketing and promoting travel destinations. **Marketing** involves a system of planning, pricing, promoting, and placing (distributing), known as the **four Ps**.

In marketing tourism, *planning* involves identifying the needs and interest of consumers (the market). *Pricing* involves developing products (destinations) at a price that the market will find attractive. *Promoting* involves informing the market about those products, and *placing* is making sure the product is available for sales.

In most industries, marketing is handled by the private sector, usually by the manufacturers or suppliers of services. If a firm develops a new computer product, for example, that firm will also manage the marketing and promotion of the product. Travel and tourism is different in that the industry is a collection of complementary services tied to specific destinations. Transportation, accommodations, entertainment, and sales of souvenirs, among other activities, contribute to the total tourist experience and economic value of a destination. Each of these services on its own would find it difficult to do a good job executing the four Ps of tourism marketing. For this reason, the public sector has usually been responsible for marketing travel destinations.

Knowing Your Target Market

Not everyone looks for the same thing in a destination, and one destination cannot meet everyone's needs. Because of this, marketing specialists focus on certain groups or **target markets**. These people are segments of the entire market that are considered most likely to travel to a particular destination. Target groups can be chosen based on a wide range of attributes, including their

- location
- income level
- demographics (age, education, or family status)
- socio-cultural characteristics
- interests and lifestyle characteristics

Consider two destinations – Algonquin Park and Las Vegas. The target market for one destination might be young people, with limited funds, who love the outdoors. For the other location, it might be people in their early fifties, with disposable income, who love to be entertained.

Economic Factors People are most likely to travel if they are experiencing good economic conditions. The usual indicators are high levels of disposable income, low and stable unemployment rates, and strong consumer confidence. Advertising to markets in countries or regions where these conditions exist will yield greater returns than marketing to places with weaker economies.

Demographic Factors Retirees and double-income households are two good demographic indicators of potential tourists. These indicators signal people who may have the time and the money to travel. Figure 12.12 demonstrates one demographic factor.

BEAUTIFUL BRITISH COLUMBIA
EXPLORE STRATHCONA PROVINCIAL PARK

Relax among the towering pines that surround Campbell Lake. Enjoy your own log cabin by the water – paddling a canoe on clear water – backpacking and hiking along pristine trails – fine country inns. Visit our Web site for complete tourist information www.bc-tourism.com

Figure 12.11 Marketing typically sells the destination, rather than specific businesses in the destination.

Interact

Prepare your own tourist profile by listing your attributes. For which type of destination might a marketing specialist target you?

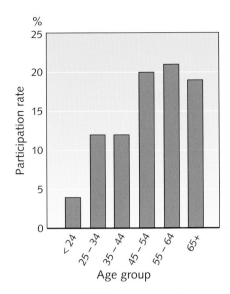

Figure 12.12 Travel participation rates for Canadians who travel outside North America, by age groups, (1990s)

Figure 12.13 A young family enjoys ice fishing in Northern Ontario. Participation in tourism is often related to age and stage in life.

Socio-cultural Backgrounds Because Canada has a large multiethnic population, many people travel to Canada from other countries to visit their families and friends. These visits are a contributing factor to Canada's travel and tourism success.

Figure 12.14 A Japanese Canadian family visits ancestral gravesites in Nagoya, Japan. Millions of Japanese travel to family gravesites each summer for the Festival of the Dead, one of the country's oldest and most important holidays.

Canada Travels

Since 1980, Europe's share of Canada's outbound travel has declined, from 60% of overseas trips at the end of the 1970s to only 41% in 1999. Destinations in Asia took most of the difference. This shift largely reflects the changing immigration sources for Canada.

Shaping Tourists' Wants

Successful marketing is about making people want to travel to your destination. Tourists have to choose *your* destination over all other options. Sometimes this is just a matter of informing them of your destination's attractions. The Grand Canyon, for example, is an attraction that cannot be rivalled, and it draws tourists to Arizona. Not every destination has a feature as spectacular as the Grand Canyon, however. Many destinations may have attractions comparable to those of your own region. Consider how many large cities have professional sports teams, shopping, nightlife, and zoos. It usually takes hard work to make your destination stand out from the rest.

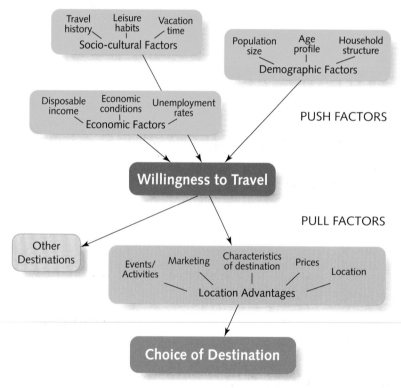

Figure 12.15 Factors affecting arrivals in a destination. Some of the factors are "push" factors, encouraging people to travel, while other factors are "pull" factors, drawing tourists to specific destinations.

Packaging Tourism

Travel packages have become very popular, and they are a good way to get attention in the marketplace. Packages are combinations that usually include transportation, accommodation, meals, and activities. Working together, the sectors of the tourist industry in a particular destination design packages that fit specific target markets. The industry benefits through the wider exposure and more customers. Consumers appreciate the convenience, better prices because of volume sales, and activities that cater to their specific interests.

The Importance of Distance

Costs, time, and convenience make geographic proximity important. Distant destinations increase the costs and time required for travel. Destinations that are farther away increase the likelihood that there will be **intervening opportunities** – other destination options closer to potential customers. Marketing strategies may have greater return for those places closest to your destination, all other factors being equal.

Figure 12.16 Diamond Rock, Martinique. Geographic proximity is one advantage that the Caribbean, Mexico, and Florida have for attracting sun-seeking Canadian tourists.

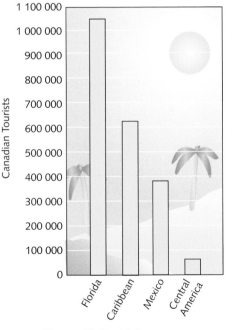

Figure 12.17 Major sun destinations of Canadians, 1999

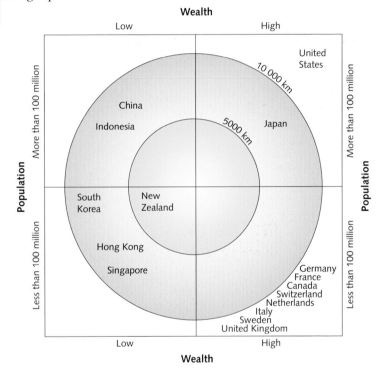

Figure 12.18 Australia's major markets, organized by wealth, population, and distance

CHECK IN

1 Explain how each of the four Ps – planning, price, promotion, and place – affects the success of marketing of a destination.

2 Figure 12.18 shows a marketing target for Australia. The grid is constructed using population and wealth data, with concentric circles for distance from the destination. The countries are the top 15 sources for tourists to Australia. Using this target, on which countries would you suggest Australia concentrate its marketing efforts? Explain your answer.

CASE STUDY
Tourism Planning and Marketing in India

Figure 12.19 Location of India

In 2000, India's share of world tourism amounted to only 0.2%, ranking 43rd in the world. The country hosted 2.4 million international visitors, one-third of whom travelled to the Taj Mahal. The travel and tourism industry contributed a modest 5.9% of total employment and 6% of the country's Gross Domestic Product.

Despite these statistics, India is a country with a great tourism potential. Its ancient civilizations, rich culture, and spectacular physical environment are just now starting to attract more visitors. Between 1999 and 2010, revenues are forecast to grow by 8.3% annually, more than double the annual global rate of 4.1%. India's share of world tourism is predicted to grow to over 1% by 2005. India needs the economic vitality that tourism will bring. However, to accomplish this goal requires effective marketing efforts shared by the country's public and private sectors.

Figure 12.20 What do these photographs tell you about the potential for tourism in India? (Clockwise from top) A musician and traditional dancer in Jaisalmer; the majestic Ajanta caves, carved out of the mountainside, in Maharashtra state; rafting on the Zanskar River in the Ladakh region

"India is a tourist destination for all reasons, all seasons, and for tourists of all means and tastes."

— Department of Tourism, State of West Bengal

Figure 12.22 Commuters travel on the rooftop of a bus in New Delhi, India, an example of the overcrowded conditions for much of the country's transportation infrastructure.

Investment in Tourism

The key to success is investment in travel and tourism infrastructure and facilities. India needs at least US$10 billion in domestic and international investment if it is to see maximum growth. To spur growth, the national government has declared tourism a high-priority industry, a designation that removes some obstacles to investment. For example, foreign investors can control up to 51% of tourism developments, a level much higher than allowed for most other industries. Approval for international investors under 51% is virtually automatic. Allowing an increase in investments has stimulated growth in such areas as travel agencies, tourist accommodations, transportation facilities, and entertainment and convention facilities.

The national government has offered other incentives to the private sector. An interest rate subsidy of 3% is available to hotel projects in areas outside the largest cities. A capital subsidy for up to 10% of the cost of renovating heritage hotels has helped to preserve historic properties.

State governments have developed their own strategies to complement national actions. For example, the government of the state of Maharashtra offers tax exemptions and reduced water and electricity charges for new tourism projects with at least ten rooms.

Challenges for Tourism

Even though governments at both the state and national levels have programs to stimulate private sector investment in travel and tourism, the industry faces some severe challenges.

Inadequate Infrastructure Government incentives to attract private sector investments are undermined by the country's weak infrastructure. Transportation facilities are woefully overcrowded, water supplies and sewage treatment are inadequate, and education and training

systems are underfunded. Of greatest concern are the air transportation facilities, which are incapable of handling the growth in tourism.

Restrictions on Foreign Ownership   Some of the key obstacles, according to many critics, are detrimental government policies, such as those on foreign ownership. Even though the percentage of foreign ownership allowed has now been increased to 51%, having a ceiling discourages large multinationals from expanding into India when other countries willingly accept higher levels of foreign ownership. Multinationals refuse to be involved in projects in which they are forced to be a partner with local firms or where their control of financial resources is weakened. On the other hand, citizens who support restrictions on foreign ownership argue that controls are necessary to give Indian entrepreneurs time to establish themselves and to develop the expertise to take advantage of the anticipated growth in the industry.

Weak Government Policies   The World Travel and Tourism Council has criticized the Indian government's education and training efforts. Governments have not been expanding training facilities at a rate that will support the predicted expansion of the industry.

Conflict and Violence   Ongoing violence has also limited the growth of tourism in some parts of the country. The population of India is largely Hindu. India has experienced periodic violence concerning such issues as the treatment of minorities, including adherents of the Sikh religion and India's control of Kashmir, a state in the northern part of the country with a Muslim majority. Continuing disputes with neighbouring Pakistan, a mainly Muslim country, have prompted both countries to develop nuclear weapons.

Such conflicts discourage private investment in tourism. At the same time, these conflicts divert limited government funds that could be spent on infrastructure improvements to military spending. Military funding totals 15.8% of government expenditures, much higher than Canada's 1.2%.

Poverty   Millions of people in India live in poverty, a condition that limits the growth of both domestic and foreign tourism. The annual Gross Domestic Product (GDP) per capita is barely above $1700. Poverty contributes to other conditions that make expansion of tourism more difficult, including high population growth rates (1.7% per year, compared with Canada's 1.0%), low literacy rates (53.5% of adults), and high unemployment (around 11%).

Interact

What are the benefits of controlling the amount of foreign ownership in the travel and tourism industry? Should the government of India remove restrictions on foreign investment in order to stimulate development of the travel and tourism industry?

Travel FACT

In India, education accounts for only 3.0% of government spending. Find out what percentage of government spending goes toward education in your province.

Figure 12.23 Students cram into a makeshift school on a loading platform next to the train tracks in Calcutta's flower market.

Figure 12.24 Women and children leave the desert village of Pushkar, India, on foot after a week-long camel bazaar, a centuries-old gathering in the Rajasthan desert.

The Future for Travel and Tourism in India

Until some of these problems are solved, even the best marketing efforts will not build a strong tourism industry for India. The industry needs investment, but domestic sources are limited by the widespread poverty, and foreign sources are hesitant because of risks. While a bright future is possible, in reality, the future for tourism is uncertain in India.

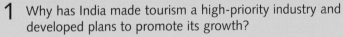

CHECK IN

1 Why has India made tourism a high-priority industry and developed plans to promote its growth?

2 In a chart, compare the motivators and barriers for tourists in India and Canada.

3 What attitudes toward expanding foreign investment in tourism in India do you suppose the following groups of people might have:
  ● Canadian tourists thinking of travelling to India
  ● large multinational hotel chains
  ● Indian hotel owners
  ● workers in the Indian tourism industry

4 As a manager of a Canadian tour company considering expanding routes to include destinations in India, list five questions you would ask Indian officials to help you decide whether to expand.

Travel FACT

The average length of stay for international tourists in India is 30 days, substantially longer than for competing destinations.

- identify selected factors that influence travellers' destination choices
- analyze tourist travel within selected regions and explain reasons for the observed patterns
- explain the importance of geographic knowledge and skills in the travel and tourism industry
- use statistics effectively to analyze travel and tourism patterns
- produce and interpret different types of maps, graphic organizers, and diagrams
- produce a plan of action and conduct an independent inquiry that synthesizes concepts, skills, and applications relating to a geographic issue involving travel and tourism either within a region or on a global scale

Canada's Tourist Market: Where Should Efforts Be Emphasized?

Purpose: To use ArcView to identify and produce a map layout of the countries in which Canada should focus its tourism marketing strategies. Three variables will be used: proximity, population, and income.

Files: cntry_95.shp, cities.shp, country.shp

Functions: View Properties, Convert to Shapefile, Select by Theme, Query Builder, Legend Editor (Symbol Edit, Unique Value), Table Edit, Zoom, Layout.

1. Your first step will be to create a blank View, name it "Canada's Marketing Target," and change the Distance Units to kilometres.

2. Next, add the x:\world\cntry_95.shp theme to your View.

3. Now, convert the Cntry_95.shp theme to a shapefile, naming it "Countries" and adding it the View. Delete the original Cntry_95.shp theme.

4. Next, add the c:\esri\esridata\canada\cities.shp theme to your View. Use the Identify tool to locate Toronto, then the Select Feature to highlight it. Convert the selected record to a shapefile, naming it "Toronto" and adding it to your View. Delete the Cities.shp theme.

5. Now, with the Countries.shp theme active, use the Select by Theme function to select all countries that are within a distance of 10 000 km of Toronto. Convert the selected countries to a shapefile, naming it "Potential Market" and adding it to your View. Delete the Countries.shp theme.

6. Next, with the Potential market.shp theme active, use the Query Builder tool to select all of the potential market countries that have populations of greater than 10 000 000 and per capita incomes greater than $10 000: ([Pop_cntry] > 10000000) and ([Inc_pcap] > 10000). Convert the selected records to a shapefile, naming it "Market" and adding it to your View. Delete the Potential Market.shp theme.

7. Now, using the Legend Editor, apply a "Unique Value" legend type to the Market.shp theme using "Cnrty_name" for the Values Field and "Pastels" for the Colour Scheme.

8. Next, open the theme table of the Market.shp theme. Using the Table Properties function, turn off the visibility of all attributes except for "Cntry_name," "Pop_cntry," and "Inc_pcap." Return to your View by selecting Canada's Marketing Target from the Window menu.

9. Now, since it is obvious that Canada should continue to market its tourist industry both within its own borders as well as the United

States, let's focus on the overseas market. Zoom in closely on the European countries in the View. To provide a spatial perspective, add the c:\esri\esridata\europe\country.shp theme. Using the Legend Editor, apply a "Single Symbol" legend type and make the theme transparent. Drag the theme to the bottom of the legend.

10. Finally, create a Layout of your View, selecting "Portrait" in the Template Manager. Change the Units of the scale bar to "Kilometres" and the Style to one of your choice. Move and resize items in the layout to make room in the bottom right section for a table. Add the Attributes of Market.shp table to the view. Right click on the table and select Simply. Using the Pointer tool, select and delete the outside border of the table header and the outside border of the table body. Select all rows in the table by clicking and dragging to draw a box around the entire table. Select Group from the Graphics menu. Move and resize all layout items until you are satisfied.

Figure 12.25 Montreal's Biodome is among a new breed of ecological tourist attractions that simulate conditions in the wild. Other examples are the Pacific Canada Pavilion in Vancouver, which replicates life in the Strait of Georgia, and the Toronto Zoo, with seven tropical pavilions.

Extension:

Redo the activity, introducing different criteria that may be used in determining the countries in which Canada should focus its tourism marketing strategies.

Extension:

Repeat the activity, except this time use Vancouver instead of Toronto as the point from which proximity is determined. How different are the results?

Extension:

Use ArcView to create a series of scatter charts to illustrate the correlations between the number of visitors arriving in Canada from various countries and

- the distance of these countries from Canada
- the population of these countries
- the per capita income of these countries
- any other related variables that come to mind

Extension:

Use ArcView to determine the geographical target market of a local, regional, or provincial tourist attraction. In addition to using proximity, population, and income criteria, you may also wish to introduce demographic data such as age. If identifying local target areas, the enumeration district data for Kingston that is included with ArcCanada 2.0 Disk #2 will be helpful. If you are identifying regional or provincial target areas, the census divisions data included with ArcCanada 2.0 Disk #1 will be more appropriate.

Understanding the Concepts

1. Brainstorm a list of at least ten criteria that must be considered when planning for tourism developments. When your brainstorming is complete, rank your items. Record an explanation for your top three choices.

2. a) Choose one tourist facility or service in your local area. Identify the target market for this facility/service, listing three important characteristics of the market.
   b) Identify a marketing strategy that this facility/service should use to attract tourism, giving an explanation for your choice.

3. a) Prepare a PMI (Pluses, Minuses, Interesting) chart for the travel and tourism industry in India. Compare your chart with those of your classmates. Discuss differences in your charts.
   b) Using the top three criteria developed in question 1, rate the potential for development of the tourist industry in India on a scale of one to seven, with seven representing "very good." In a paragraph, explain your rating.

Practising Your Skills

4. Select a destination within Canada (province, territory, city, or region). Write a two-page case study about the future of tourism for the location you selected. Use Internet and other resources to gather data about the potential and problems in the tourist industry in the destination.

5. Find an example of tourism marketing, perhaps a television commercial, a brochure, or a magazine advertisement. Analyze the item by noting
   • its intended market
   • the images or symbols used to create its message
   • its apparent message
   Discuss its effectiveness in attracting tourists to the destination.

Figure 12.26 A young woman carries firewood home in rural India.

Applying Your Skills

6. Identify a small-scale tourist service that you plan to open and operate in your community. It might be a bike rental concession, a pitch'n putt, a souvenir kiosk, an ice cream stand, or another business of your choosing. Following the tasks outlined under activities in Figure 12.9, prepare a preliminary plan for your business operation.

7. What are some impacts of marketing and advertising on travel and tourism patterns? Investigate by designing a short questionnaire that asks respondents how they make their travel decisions and where they get their information about where they want to travel. Ask ten people to fill in your questionnaire. Work in groups to organize your data and prepare a report to answer the question.

8. Working with a partner, list as many forms of media as you can think of that can be used to market travel destinations. For each medium, identify a target market that would receive this message.

9. Study the photographs in Figure 12.27. These pictures show scenes from a place that wants to increase its tourism earnings. Script a 15-second television advertisement that could be used to attract more travellers to the area. For each element of your ad, explain its purpose.

Figure 12.27 Nunavut, Canada's youngest territory, celebrated its creation on April 1, 1999. (Clockwise from top) Fireworks light up the night sky over Iqaluit, the new capital; Inuit drum dancers perform during the celebration; a 72-year-old carver of soapstone sculptures in his Iqaluit workshop. In a community such as this, how might tourism be increased?

Thinking Like a Tourist

10. Think about the images in tourism marketing that you find most attractive.
    a) Describe two images that you find very appealing.
    b) For each image, explain why you are attracted to it.
    c) Based on your analysis, describe yourself as a target market.

11. How can you make sure that you are well informed about tourist destinations? Prepare a database of ten Internet sites that you might go to for marketing information about travel destinations. Your database may include e-zines, travel agencies, newsgroups, or more general-purpose sites like About.com. For each of your sites, write a brief description of its contents.

J O B   SKILLS

Successful planning and marketing efforts are built on effective teamwork, with team members sharing creative ideas and setting common goals. Use the Internet and other sources to identify five to seven personal characteristics that are essential for teams to function well. Rate yourself on these characteristics.

APPENDIX

Geographic Information Systems (GIS) Tutorial

Welcome to the ArcView tutorial! If you are a new ArcView user, it is strongly recommended that you do this tutorial before attempting the many ArcView activities in this text. This tutorial uses a "recipe-style" format to teach you the various functions of ArcView. The tutorial is based on the concepts of regions, issues, and world travel, themes that are central to this text. Each part of the activity contains a *header* that tells you the function you are about to perform. This way, if you forget how to do something you can simply refer back to this tutorial for a refresher. Sound easy? Well, it actually is, so sit back, follow the instructions carefully, and enjoy the wonderful world of Geographic Information Systems!

Note: Much of the data for this tutorial can be found on ArcCanada Disk 2 (a data disk that comes with the ArcView 3.2 K–12 package). The tutorial instructions refer to "d:\" as the drive on which the data from this CD is located (assuming "d:\" is your CD ROM drive). If, however, you are not accessing this data from the CD, your teacher will inform you of the drive onto which the data has been loaded.

Creating and Naming Views

1. Start ArcView and click New to create a new View. Select Properties from the View pull-down menu. In the Name field, key "Continents of the World," then click OK.

Adding Themes

2. Click the Add Theme button and locate x:\af\cont_bnd.shp. Click OK. Turn on the Cont_bnd.shp theme by checking the box next to its name.

Adding Tables

3. Select "1" from the Window pull-down menu to return to the project window.

4. Click on the Tables ![Tables icon] icon, then click Add. Locate x:\af\tables\wri_3m.dbf then click Add.

Joining Tables

5. Select Continents of the World from the Window pull-down menu.

6. Click the Open Theme Table ![Tables icon] button to open the Cont_bnd.shp attribute table. Select Tile from the Window pull-down menu. Click to depress the "Cntry_name" field header in the wri_3m.dbf table, then do the same in the Attributes of Cont_bnd.shp table. Click the Join ![Join button] button. Close the Attributes of Cont_bnd.shp window and maximize the Continents of the World window.

Converting to a Shapefile

7. Select Convert to Shapefile from the Theme pull-down menu. Key "Africa" in the File Name field. *Remember the directory and folder into which the shapefile is saved* (usually c:\windows\temp unless the default has been changed or you have set the working directory or specified a different folder). Click OK, then click Yes to add the shapefile to the view. Select Delete Themes from the Edit pull-down menu, then click Yes. Turn on the Africa.shp theme by checking the box next to its name.

   Repeat Steps 2 to 7 for the remaining six continents as shown in Columns A and B in the table below. Each time you finish, click the Zoom to Full Extent ![Zoom button] button so that all continents are in view.

A	B
x:\an\cont_bnd.shp	Antarctica
x:\as\cont_bnd.shp	Asia
x:\eu\cont_bnd.shp	Europe
x:\na\cont_bnd.shp	North America
x:\oc\cont_bnd.shp	Oceania
x:\sa\cont_bnd.shp	South America

Table Edit

8. Click on the Africa.shp theme to make it active, then click on the Open Theme Table ⊞ button. Select Start Editing from the Table pull-down menu, then select New Field from the Edit pull-down menu. Key "Continent" into the Name field and select "String" in the Type field. Click OK. Click the Edit 🖎 button, then click inside the first cell in the Continent field. Key "Africa" into each of the cells of this new field. (Hint: Using Ctrl-C to copy the continent name after you type it once, then Ctrl-V to paste it into the remaining cells, will save a lot of time.) *Remember to hit Enter after inserting the continent name in the last cell.*

9. If you study the table closely, you will notice that in some of the fields there are several occurrences of the value "–99." The producers of the data set use this value when data is n/a (not available). Since in the next step of this activity you will be performing some mathematical functions on the data set, it is important that we do something with these values. At best, we can change the values to "0" since we are not equipped to make more accurate estimates. To do so, for each of the following fields, click to depress the field header, then click the Sort Ascending 📊 button. Click the Edit 🖎 button, then change all of the values of "–99" to "0."

   Select Stop Editing from the Table menu and save your edits. Close the Attributes of Africa.shp window.

   Repeat Steps 8 and 9 for all remaining continents. Remember to enter the names of the continents, exactly as they appear in Column B above, into the new fields you create.

Field	Definition	Field/Operation
Cons_tot89	total energy consumption	Cons_tot89 by Sum
Co2_sol89	industrial carbon dioxide emissions in solid fuels	Co2_sol89 by Sum
Co2_liq89	industrial carbon dioxide emissions in liquid fuels	Co2_liq89 by Sum
Co2_gas89	industrial carbon dioxide emissions in gas	Co2_gas89 by Sum
Co2_cap89	average carbon dioxide emissions in metric tons/capita	Co2_cap89 by Average

Geoprocessing (Dissolving)

10. Select Continents of the World from the Window pull-down menu. Select Extensions from the File pull-down menu. Locate and check the box next to "Geoprocessing." Click OK.

11. Click on the Africa.shp theme to make it active (i.e., raised). Start the Geoprocessing Wizard by selecting it from the View pull-down menu. Select "Dissolve features based on an attribute," then click Next. Select "Africa.shp" as the theme to dissolve and "Continent" as the attribute to dissolve. Click on the Open Folder 📂 button, then key in "Continent of Africa" in the Name field. Click OK, then click Next. Select additional operations by holding down the Shift key and clicking on each of the fields/operations shown in the table opposite. Click Finish. Open the Edit pull-down menu and select Delete Themes to delete the original Africa.shp theme.
    Repeat Step 11 for the remaining six continents.

Geoprocessing (Merging)

12. Start the Geoprocessing Wizard again by selecting it from the View pull-down menu. Select "Merge themes together," then click Next. Select all seven of the continental themes by holding down the Shift key and clicking on each one. Click on the Open Folder 📂 button, then key in "Continents of the World" in the Name field. Click OK, then click Finish. Make all seven of the continent themes active by holding down the Shift key and clicking on each. Select Delete Themes from the Edit pull-down menu. Click Yes to all when asked to confirm. Turn on the Continents of the World.shp theme by checking the box next to its name.

Table Editing/Creating and Calculating a Field

13. With the Continents of the World.shp theme active, click the Open Theme Table button. Select Start Editing from the Table menu, then select Add Field from the Edit menu. In the Name field, key in "Co2_tot89," in the Type field, select "Number," and in the Decimal Places field, key in "4." Click OK. Click the Calculate 🔢 button. By double-clicking on the appropriate Fields and Requests, enter the following equation: [Sum_Co2_sol89] + [Sum_Co2_liq89] + [Sum_Co2_gas89]. Click OK. Select Stop Editing from the Table menu. Click "Yes" when asked "Save Edits?"

14. Close the Attributes of Continents of the World.shp window and return to the Continents of the World View.

Legend Editing (Unique Value)

15. Double-click on the Continents of the World.shp theme to open the Legend Editor. In the Legend Type field, select "Unique Value" and in the Values Field, select "Continent." Select a Colour Scheme of your preference, then click Apply. Close the Legend Editor.

Copy and Pasting Themes

16. Select Copy Themes from the Edit pull-down menu. Then, select "1" from the Window pull-down menu to return to the project window. Ensure the Views [icon] icon is selected, then click New. Select Paste from the Edit menu.

Legend Editing (Graduated Colour)

17. Double-click on the Continents of the World.shp theme to open the Legend Editor. In the Legend Type field, select "Graduated Colour," and in the Classification Field, select "Ave_co2_cap." Select a Colour Ramp of your preference, then click Apply. (Experiment with different classification types by clicking the Classify button). Close the Legend Editor.

Renaming Themes

18. Select Properties from the Theme pull-down menu, key "CO2 per capita (metric tons)" in the Theme Name field, then click OK.

Renaming Views

19. Select Properties from the View pull-down menu, key "CO2 Production Per Capita by Continent" in the Name field, then click OK.

Legend Editing (Chart)

20. Repeat Step 16.

21. Double-click on the CO2 per capita (metric tons).shp theme to open the Legend Editor. In the Legend Type field, select "Chart." Under Fields, hold down the Shift key, select

Sum_co2_sol, Sum_co2_liq, and Sum_co2_gas, then click Add. Double-click on the Background Symbol to open the Fill Palette. Click on the transparent square in the top left corner of the palette then close it. Click the Properties button. In the Size Field, select "Co2_tot89," then OK. Click Apply, then close the Legend Editor.

Renaming Themes

22. Select Properties from the Theme pull-down menu, key in "CO2 Sources" in the Theme Name field, then click OK.

Renaming Views

23. Select Properties from the View pull-down menu, key in "CO2 Production and Sources by Continent" in the Name field, then click OK.

Creating Charts

24. Click on Open Theme Table [icon] button to open the attribute table. Click on the Create Chart [icon] button. In the Name field, key in "Total Energy Consumption by Continent." Under Fields, select "Sum_cons_tot89," then click Add. In the Label series using field, select "Continent," then click OK. Click on the Chart Element Properties [icon] button, then click on the "Title." Key in "Total Energy Consumption by Continent," then click OK. Click on the vertical y-axis. Check the box next to Axis Label, then key in "Energy Consumption" in the Axis Label field. Click OK. Click on the horizontal x-axis. Check the box next to Axis Label, then key in "Continent" in the Axis Label field. Click OK. Close the Total Energy Consumption by Continent window.

Hot Linking Images (Part 1)

25. Select "1" from the Window pull-down menu to return to the project window. Ensure the Views [icon] icon is selected, then click New. Select Properties from the View pull-down menu. In the Name field, key in "Africa," then click OK. Click the Add Theme [icon] button and locate the Africa.shp theme created in Step 7. Click OK. Turn on the Africa.shp theme by checking the box next to its name.

Geoprocessing (Dissolving)

26. Select Geoprocessing Wizard from the View pull-down menu. Select "Dissolve features bases on an attribute," then click Next. Select "Africa.shp" as the theme to dissolve and "Region" as the attribute to dissolve. Click on the Open Folder button, then key in "Regions of Africa" in the Name field. Click OK, then click Next. Do not select any additional operations. Click Finish. Open the Edit pull-down menu and select Delete Themes to delete the original Africa.shp theme. Turn on the Regions of Africa.shp theme by checking the box next to its name. Important: Since many of the continents consist of different parts (e.g., Islands) that are distributed over large expanses, it is important to click the Zoom In tool and zoom in on the main land masses of the continent.

Legend Editing (Unique Value)

27. Double-click on Regions of Africa.shp theme to open the Legend Editor. In the Classification Type field, select "Unique Value," and in the Values Field, select Region. Select a Colour Scheme of your choice, click Apply, then close the Legend Editor.

Labelling (Auto-label) and Changing Fonts

28. Select Auto-label from the Theme pull-down menu. In the Label Field, select "Region." Check the box next to Allow Overlapping Labels, then click Apply.

29. Select Select all Graphics from the Edit pull-down menu. Then, select Show Symbol Menu from the Window pull-down menu. Select a Font, Size, and Style of your choice, then click on the paintbrush. In the Colour field, select "Text," then click on a colour of your choice. Close the Colour Palette. (If one or more of your labels appears in a different colour than the others then it means it is, or was, overlapping. If so, select Convert Overlapping Labels from the Theme pull-down menu.) Click on the Pointer tool, then click on any blank space in the View to deselect the labels.

30. Close the Africa View, then repeat Steps 25 to 29 for the remaining six continents.

Hot Linking Images (Part 2)

31. Select "1" from the Window pull-down menu to return to the project window. Ensure the Views icon is highlighted. Select Continents of the World, then click Open. With the Continents of the World.shp theme active, select Properties from the Theme pull-down menu. Click on the Hot Link icon. Change the Field to "Continent" and the Predefined Action to "Link to Document." Click OK. Click the Hot Link button, then test your links by clicking on each of the continents and closing the Views after each appears.

Hot Linking Text Files

32. Start any word-processor (such as Word Pad, Word, or WordPerfect) that allows you to save files as "ASCII DOS Text." Create seven files, each with a description of one of the continents. (You may wish to research and write about unique features of each continent that attract tourists.) Save each file as an ASCII DOS text file, naming it with the name of the continent. Write down the directory path and the name of the files you create (e.g., c:\windows\temp\Africa.txt).

33. Select Continents of the World from the Window pull-down menu (or return to the project window and open Continents of the World under Views). With the Continents of the World.shp theme active, click on the Open Theme Table button.

    Select Start Editing from the Table pull-down menu. Select Add Field from the Edit menu. Key in "Hot Link" in the Name field, select "String" in the Type field, and change the Width field to "48." (You can choose a number greater than "48" if there will be more than this number of characters in the directory paths that you will be typing in for your text files.) Click OK. Click the Edit button, then click inside the first cell in the Hot Link field. Key in the directory path and file name of the text file you have created for this record, i.e., the continent. (You may have to scroll back to see the name of the continent, e.g., c:\windows\temp\Africa.txt.) *Remember to hit Enter after you have keyed in the last entry.* Select Stop Editing from the Table pull-down menu. Click Yes when asked "Save Edits?" Close the Attributes of Continents of the World.shp window to return to the view.

34. With the Continents of the World.shp theme active, select Properties from the Theme pull-down menu. Click on the Hot Link ⊞ icon. Change the Field to "Hot Link" and the Predefined Action to "Link to Text File." Click OK. Click the Hot Link ⚡ button, then test your links by clicking on each of the continents and closing the text files after each appears.

Adding Event Themes

35. Select "1" from the Window pull-down menu. Click on the Tables ▦ icon, then click New. Key in "Busiest Airports" in the File Name field, then click OK. Select Add Field from the Edit pull-down menu. Key in "Airport" in the Name Field, select "String" in the Type field, and change the Width to "32." Click OK. Select Add Field from the Edit pull-down menu again. Key in "Tot_Passengers" in the Name Field and click OK. (Click Continue if informed that ArcView will truncate the field name.) Select Add Field from the Edit pull-down menu again. Key in "Latitude" in the Name Field and change the Decimal Places to "2." Click OK. Repeat for "Longitude." Hold down the "Ctrl" key and click the "A" key 30 times to add 30 records. Click the Edit ↕ button, then click inside the first cell in the "Airport" field. Key in the data as shown in the following table. *Remember not to put any spaces in the numbers and to hit Enter after keying in the last number.*

Top 30 Airports by Passenger Traffic (January – May 2000)			
Airport	Latitude	Longitude	Total Passengers
Atlanta	33.60	−84.36	33117711
Chicago	41.83	−87.64	28840310
Los Angeles	34.00	−118.25	27094312
London	51.49	−0.18	25126039

Dallas/ Ft. Worth	32.76	−96.66	24789407
Tokyo	35.68	139.81	21999016
Frankfurt	50.13	8.67	18877180
Paris	44.88	2.43	18502329
San Francisco	37.73	−122.31	15901663
Denver	39.75	−105.07	15594436
Phoenix	33.51	−112.11	15100705
Amsterdam	52.37	4.89	15020112
Las Vegas	36.21	−115.22	14968094
Seoul	37.54	126.94	14746076
Detroit	42.39	−83.08	14555656
Miami	25.83	−80.27	14526317
Minneapolis/ St. Paul	44.92	−93.31	14336971
Houston	29.77	−95.41	14129183
Newark	40.72	−74.20	13500000
Hong Kong	22.43	114.15	13134000
Orlando	28.51	−81.37	13085967
Madrid	40.44	−3.89	12674964
Bangkok	13.75	100.55	12499727
New York	40.75	−74.10	12300000
St. Louis	38.64	−90.34	12094616
Singapore	1.23	104.18	11426451
London	51.49	−0.18	11426279
Toronto	43.72	−79.41	11220724
Boston	42.38	−71.10	10769427
Seattle/ Tacoma	47.59	−122.32	10733726

Source: ACI – Airports Council International www.airports.org/traffic/busiest.html (09/21/2000)

Select Stop Editing from the table menu and save your edits. Close the Busiest Airports.dbf window, then select Continents of the World from the Window pull-down menu. Select Add

Event Theme from the View pull-down menu. Select "Busiest Airports.dbf" in the Table field, "Longitude" in the X field, and "Latitude" in the Y field. Click OK.

36. Turn on the Busiest Airports.dbf theme by checking the box next to its name.

Setting View Properties (Distance)

37. Select Properties from the View pull-down menu. Change the Distance Units to "kilometres," then click OK.

Drawing and Measuring

38. Click and hold on the Draw Point button to reveal the pull-down drawing tools bar. Click on the Draw Line tool. Click on the airport farthest east, then begin moving west, clicking on each airport along the way until you have reached the last one. Double-click on the last airport to complete the "route." Look in the bottom left corner of the screen and make note of the total distance travelled, as well as the distance travelled during the last leg of the journey.

39. Select Select all Graphics from the Edit pull-down menu. Select Show Symbol Window from the Window pull-down menu. Select a Line Type of your choice and a Size of your choice. Click on the paintbrush, then select a Colour of your choice. Close the Colour Palette. Click on the Pointer tool, then click on any blank space in the View to deselect the line you have created.

40. Click on the Measure tool. Click on the airport farthest to the east, then double-click on the airport farthest to the west. Note the distance shown on the bottom left corner of the screen.

Legend Editing (Graduated Colour)

41. Double-click on the Busiest Airports.dbf theme to open the Legend Editor. In the Legend Type field, select "Graduated Colour" and in the Classification Field, select "Tot_Passengers." Select a Colour Ramp of your preference, then click Apply. (Experiment with different classification types by clicking the Classify button.) Close the Legend Editor.

Symbol Editing and Loading Palettes

42. Double-click on the Busiest Airports.dbf theme again to open the Legend Editor. Double-click on the first symbol to open the Marker Palette. Click on the ⊙ Palette button, then click Load. Locate c:\esri\av_gis30\arcview\symbols\municipl.avp and double-click on it. Click the Marker ⊘ button, then select one of the airport symbols. Select a size of your choice, then close the Marker Palette. Change the remaining symbols to the same type and size of marker. Click Apply, then close the Legend Editor.

Renaming Themes

43. Select Properties from the Theme pull-down menu. Key in "Passengers 01/00–05/00" in the Theme Name field, then click OK.

Creating Layouts

44. Select Layout from the View pull-down menu and click OK to accept the "Landscape" default. Double-click on the scale bar, select a Style of your choice, then change the Units to "kilometres." Click OK. Click on various objects in the layout to select, resize, and move them. Double-click on the title and change it to "A Trip Through the World's Busiest Airports." Resize and centre the title.

Congratulations! You should now have a general understanding of the concepts of regions, issues, and world travel, and possess all the basic skills you will need to complete the GIS activities in this text. Bon voyage – and do not hesitate to return if you experience some turbulence!

GLOSSARY

adventure travel vacations that usually take place in an outdoor setting and offer experiences that are both mentally and physically challenging

alternative tourism individually planned tourist activity that explores destinations or events that are considered out-of-the-ordinary

area of influence the area around a place that is influenced by the place, usually economically

barriers negative aspects of a location that discourage travellers from visiting a location

biodiversity variety of animal and plant life

boundaries edges of a region; can be clearly defined or can be amorphous

capital costs amount of money spent to construct, furnish, and equip a facility

centrally controlled state a nation where the government controls every aspect of development

child-sex tourism travel to other countries for the purpose of seeking sex with children

city-centred region the area that encompasses a city and its hinterland

commercialism exchange of merchandise with emphasis on money and profits

commodification exploitation that treats a culture as a commodity

cultural motivators reasons for travelling based on interests in various cultural pursuits

cultural tourism travel that focusses on learning about characteristics of life of the people in different destinations

cultural transmission the transfer of traits when different cultures meet

culture various characteristics of life shared by a group of people in a particular community or nation

democratization open to all, e.g., travel opportunities

demonstration effect the phenomenon of valuing another culture more than one's own

destinations places that tourists visit

direct impacts tourist dollars spent on easily identified transactions, with positive economic benefits

direct tourist spending money spent by travellers on necessary items, such as accommodation and food, and things they desire

discretionary money income available after living expenses are covered

domestic tourism travel within one's own country

ecological footprint the impact of people's way of life on natural systems

economic functions activities in and around a city that influence the city's welfare

ecotourism environmentally responsible travel to natural areas that conserves the environment and sustains the well-being of the local people

empowerment control of decision making

endangered space an area threatened by destructive human activity

ethical travel choice of destination based on sustainable tourism practices

ethnic cleansing when one group forces other groups to leave an area

ethnocentrism valuing one's own culture above others

external market people who live outside the area of the destination

extraterritorial laws laws in the traveller's home country for acts committed in another country

fertility rate the number of live births per 1000 women of child-bearing age per year

foreign investment money invested in a country by an investor from another country

four Ps marketing system of planning, pricing, promoting, and placing or distributing

fully independent tourist (FIT) traveller who makes all his or her own travel arrangements

functional region an area defined by its ongoing activities or functions

gastrointestinal infections the presence of micro-organisms in the stomach or the intestines that cause cramps and diarrhoea; sometimes called Montezuma's Revenge

green space natural areas or parks in a city

hard adventure travel that involves a level of risk and requires a person to have experience and be physically and mentally fit

hedonism the pursuit of pleasure

heritage conservancy preservation of important cultural and physical environments

high culture aspects of culture that include such activities as opera, ballet, and theatre

hinterland a city's surrounding zone of influence

homogeneous the presence of uniform factors within a geographic region

incentives rewards to stimulate activity

independent travellers people who make their own travel arrangements and plan their own activities as they travel

indirect impacts secondary transactions generated by the direct spending of tourists

indirect tourist spending money generated from supplies and support services required for tourists' activities

infant mortality rate the number of deaths of young children per thousand in the population

informed opinion a viewpoint based on reliable information and sound reasoning

infrastructure human systems that deliver important services within a city

internal market people who live in the same area as the destination

interpersonal motivators reasons for travelling based on interests in meeting people while doing things

intervening opportunities destination options between a distant destination and the potential customer

intrinsic value a place or a thing that has value on its own

issue a significant concern that involves different viewpoints

issues approach dealing with a significant problem by examining the arguments of the people involved

invisible export income generated by tourism

leakages money that leaves the local economy and reduces economic impact

life cycle six stages that a tourist destination experiences as it grows and changes

life expectancy the average number of years one can expect to live at birth

literacy rate the percentage of people in a country over age 15 who can read and write

location characteristics the natural or physical attributes of a place

market people who have the finances and freedom to travel

marketing a system of planning, pricing, promoting, and placing or distribution to sell a destination

mass tourism organized movements of large groups of travellers to specialized tourist areas

multifactor region an area identified using many characteristics

multinational corporations companies that have their head offices in one country and branch locations in many other countries

multiplier effects rounds of respending that increase total economic activity

non-governmental organizations (NGOs) organizations that are administrated privately and supported by private donations

operating costs amount of money required for the day-to-day operation of a business

pandemic spread of a disease to large populations over a wide area

physical motivators reasons for travelling based on interests in physical activities

pilgrimage devotional journey to a place that has special significance

planned travellers people who purchase packaged vacations and rely on travel agents to make all arrangements

poaching illegal hunting

popular culture current cultural practices and activities of a society's general public

prestige motivators reasons for travelling based on interests in personal benefits

private sector activities that include for-profit businesses and individuals

product travel services and destinations

proximity nearness or closeness of a destination

public sector activities that include various levels of government and government organizations

region an area of the Earth's surface that has characteristics that make it unique or different from other places

reluctant travellers people who do not care much for travelling and prefer to return to the same location and remain in one spot once they reach their destination

reunification the process of bringing back together or unifying

safari expeditions that take tourists into wilderness parts of a country

satellite accounting system an international accounting system for the tourist industry that links national accounting systems to give up-to-date information about travel and tourism

savanna a tropical or subtropical grassland area with tall grasses during the wet seasons and low sparse grasses in the dry seasons

single-factor region an area identified using only one characteristic

site factors the natural or physical attributes of a place

soccer hooligans soccer fans who commit acts of vandalism or violence

societal guidance state involvement in an advisory capacity

socio-cultural characteristics history, culture, and social organization of a location

soft adventure travel that is less physically demanding than hard adventure and involves less risk

sports tourism travel that focusses on attending sporting events

stakeholders people involved in or concerned about an issue

subterranean systems systems that are underground

superstructure a destination's tourism complex of hotels, places of entertainment, shopping centres, and restaurants

sustainable meeting needs and protecting the environment at the same time for the needs of future generations

sustainable tourism responding to the needs and expectations of tourists, while considering the interests of local residents

system something made up of different parts and joined to form a unified whole

target markets certain segments of the market that are considered most likely to travel to a particular destination

tourist arrivals the number of tourists who enter a country

transculturation the integration of different traits from one culture to another

transition zone an area with fewer visible characteristics of the region

travel and tourism economy the direct and indirect spending associated with travel and tourism

travel and tourism industry the provision of goods and services for travellers and tourists

travel motivators reasons people have for travelling

travel packages combinations that usually include transportation, accommodations, meals, and activities

trickle down flow of benefits from one group to another

variables conditions, such as age, education, health, responsibilities, free time, and income level, that influence how people respond to travel motivators

wildlife corridors strands of protected areas that link national parks and reserves, through which animals can migrate

CREDITS

Literary Credits

The authors and publisher would like to acknowledge the following people or organizations who gave permission to reproduce the excerpts listed below.

Chapter 1

1.22 Courtesy of Terrestrial Ecology Research Unit; 1.24 Reprinted with permission by *The Sunday Times*; 1.25 Reprinted with permission by the *Eastern Province Herald*; 1.26 Terrestrial Ecology Research Unit; 1.28 Reprinted with permission by Southern Africa Environment Project; 1.29 Reprinted with permission by the *Eastern Province Herald*; 1.32 Copyright Environment News Service (ENS) 2000. Republished with permission from ENS online at <http://ens-news.com>.

Chapter 2

Page 49 Reprinted courtesy of *The Hamilton Spectator*.

Chapter 5

5.27 Toronto Film & Television Office; 5.29 Green Tourism Association.

Chapter 6

6.9(a) From *Frommer's® Alaska 5th Edition* by Charles P. Wohlforth with Peter Oliver. Copyright © 1998 by Hungry Minds, Inc. All rights reserved. Reproduced here by permission of the publisher. Frommer's is a registered trademark of Arthur Frommer used under exclusive license by Hungry Minds, Inc.; 6.9(b) Copyright © 1999 by Douglas Rand. From LET'S GO:

ALASKA AND THE PACIFIC NORTHWEST, ed. 1999 by Douglas Rand. Reprinted by permission of St. Martin's Press, LCC; 6.15 Adaptation from "Blockbuster Summer" by Martin Knelman, *The Toronto Star*, June 3, 2001. Reprinted with permission–The Toronto Star Syndicate; 6.23 Copyright © <www.worldmusicnight.com>.

Chapter 7

7.4 Reprinted with permission. Copyright Reuters 2000; 7.12 *The World Factbook, 2000*, Central Intelligence Agency; 7.23 Courtesy of WTO.

Chapter 9

9.6 From TRAVEL & TOURISM: WORLD REGIONAL GEOGRAPY, A TEXT, 1st edition, © 1992. Reprinted with permission of Nelson Thomson Learning, a division of Thomson Learning; 9.7 From TRAVEL & TOURISM: WORLD REGIONAL GEOGRAPHY, A TEXT, 1st edition, © 1992. Reprinted with permission of Nelson Thomson Learning, a division of Thomson Learning.

Chapter 11

11.21 Reprinted with permission from *The Globe and Mail*.

Photo Credits

The authors and publisher would like to acknowledge the following individuals or organizations that supplied the photographs listed below.

AP = Associated Press
CP = CP Picture Archive
GVA = Geographical Visual Aids
Stone = Stone Images

Chapter 1

1.1 SA National Parks, Praetoria, RSA; Ministere du Tourisme du Quebec; 1.3, 1.4 V. Last/GVA; 1.5, 1.7 Ontario Ministry of Tourism & Recreation; 1.9 Leesa Price; 1.10 London Pictures Service; 1.13 Ontario Ministry of Tourism & Recreation; 1.15 Francine Geraci; 1.16 CP /Chuck Stoody; 1.17 Daniel Bosler/Stone; 1.18 Image courtesy <www.adbusters.org>; 1.19 Vince Streano/Stone; 1.22, 1.30, 1.32 SA National Parks, Praetoria, RSA; 1.33 J.P. Williams/Stone.

Chapter 2

2.1, 2.2, 2.3 Dr. B. Lynne Milgram; 2.6 Jake Rajs/Stone; 2.7 Yann Arthus-Bertrand/CIDA; 2.8, 2.13 V. Last/GVA; 2.14 Dr. B. Lynne Milgram; 2.16, 2.19 Ontario Ministry of Natural Resources; 2.20 V. Last/GVA; 2.21 (left) Ontario Ministry of Tourism & Recreation; (left centre) Joe McBride/Stone; (right centre and right) Niagara Escarpment Commission; 2.22 Metropolitan Toronto Zoo; 2.23, 2.24, 2.25, 2.26, 2.27 Niagara Escarpment Commission; 2.28 Coalition on the Niagara Escarpment; 2.29, 2.30 Niagara Escarpment Commission; 2.31 Bob Handelman/Stone; 2.32 Jan Kopec/Stone; 2.33 Institute for Space & Terrestrial Science.

Chapter 3

3.1 Ministere du Tourism du Quebec; Ontario Ministry of Tourism & Recreation; 3.4 Trudy Rising; Lori Adamski Peek/Stone; Ken Fisher/Stone; V. Last/GVA; 3.7 (winter, summer, spring) Parks Canada; (fall) Michael Cullen/Trent Photographics; 3.9 Robert Frerk/Stone; Phil Schermeister/Stone; 3.12 V. Last/GVA; 3.13 CP; 3.16 Earthwatch/Luke Dollar; 3.18 Daniel J. Cox/Stone; V. Last/GVA;

3.19 Alfred Wolf/Stone; 3.20 V. Last/GVA; 3.23 Larry Crackower.

Chapter 4

4.1 UNESCO/Dominique Roger; 4.3 Public Affairs Alberta; Ontario Ministry of Tourism & Recreation; 4.4 Leesa Price; 4.5 CP/*Edmonton Journal*/Ian Scott; 4.7 Patricia Healy; Mike Timo/Stone; 4.8 Chris Harvey/Stone; 4.9 Glen Allison/Stone; 4.10 Tom Bean/Stone; 4.12 CP/AP/John McConnico; Grand Canyon National Park/Public Affairs Office; 4.14 Corbus/Magma; 4.15 Dr. B. Lynne Milgram; 4.16 Nova Scotia Tourism; 4.17 Robert Weight/CORBIS; 4.19 Amanda Bramall; 4.20 Nicholas Parfitt/Stone; 4.21 Amanda Bramall; 4.23 CP/AP/Sara-Jane Poole); CP/AP/Sayyid Azim; 4.25 CP/*Halifax Daily News*/Paul Darrow; 4.27, 4.29 CP/AP/Robert Sorbo; 4.30 CP/AP/Vincent DeWitt; 4.32 CP/AP/Robert Sorbo; 4.33, 4.37 Nick Didlik/*Vancouver Sun*; 4.38 CP/Bayne Stanley; 4.39 Nick Didlik/*Vancouver Sun*; 4.40 UNESCO/F. Charafi; 4.41 Andreas Pollok/Stone.

Chapter 5

5.1 V. Last/GVA; 5.2 Jeffry W. Myers/Firstlight.ca; 5.4 (a) Will & Deni McIntyre/Stone; (b) Harvey Lloyd/Firstlight.ca; (c) V. Last/GVA; 5.6 Sam Sargent/Stone; 5.7 Greg Pease/Stone; 5.8 CP/AP/Bob Macy; CP/AP/Lennox McLendon; 5.9 CP/AP/Christine Nesbitt; 5.11 Grace Groetzsch; 5.15 Harbourfront Centre; 5.16 Leesa Price; 5.18 CP/AP/Lauren McFalls; 5.21 TVOntario; 5.23 London Pictures Service; 5.25 David Stoecklein/Firstlight.ca; 5.27Shaun Egan/Stone; 5.29 CP/Frank Gunn; 5.30 Ontario Ministry of Tourism & Recreation; 5.31 CP/Fred Lum; CP/Chantal Poirier; 5.33 CP/Kevin Frayer; 5.34 Jan Kopec/Stone; 5.37 CP/Tom Hanson; 5.38 CP/AP/Ian Mainsbridge; 5.40 Restaurant aux Anciens Canadiens; 5.41 Ed Bohon/Firstlight.ca; 5.42 Brendan Beirne/Stone; 5.43 Photo by Chris Collins/Corbis Stock Market/Magma; 5.45 CP/AP/Vincent Yu; 5.47 CP/*Toronto Star*/Mitchell Smyth; 5.49 V. Last/GVA; 5.50 Harvey Lloyd/Firstlight.ca; 5.51 V. Last/GVA.

Chapter 6

6.1 Dilip Mehta; The Japan Foundation, Toronto; 6.3 Ethel Johnston; 6.4 Doug Armand/Stone; 6.5 CP/AP/Victoria Arocho; 6.11 Doug Mazell/Stock Market/Firstlight.ca; 6.12 Ethel Johnston; 6.13 CP/AP/Thaksina Khaikaew; Francine Geraci; 6.14 V. Last/GVA; 6.16 Canadian Art Gallery; The Montreal Museum of Fine Arts; Michal and Renata Hornstein Pavilion/Photo; Brian Merrett, MMFA; 6.17 (left, right) Ethel Johnston; (centre) Nova Scotia Information Service; 6.18 Photo ITAR-TASS; 6.20 UNESCO; 6.21 (top, left, and centre) Toronto Reference Library; (top, right) Jean-Dominique Dallet/Firstlight.ca; (centre, left) Jim Zuckerman/CORBIS/Firstlight.ca; (centre, centre) Alvaro de Leiva/Firstlight.ca; (centre, right) Tibor Bognar/Firstlight.ca; (bottom, left and left centre) Toronto Reference Library; (bottom, right centre) Angela Brown/Firstlight.ca; (bottom, right) G. Rowell/Firstlight.ca; 6.22 CP/Ryan Remiorz; Kennan Ward/Firstlight.ca; 6.25 (top) CP/AP/Diether Endlicher; (centre) CP/AP/Michel/Lipchitz; (bottom) CP/Fred Greenslade; 6.26 CP/AP/Dennis Doyle; CP/Ryan Remiorz; 6.27 Nordic Combined Training Centre; 6.29 CP/AP/Frank Prevel; 6.31 CP/John Lehmann; CP/AP/Saurabh Das; 6.32 CP/AP/Paris Saris; 6.34 CP/AP/Mark Lennihan; 6.35 CP/AP/Yonhap; 6.37 Ethel Johnston; 6.38 John Henley/The Stock Market/Firstlight.ca.

Chapter 7

7.1 (top left) CP/AP/Andrew Medichini; (bottom left) CP/AP/Ivan Sekretarev; (centre) CP/Rod Currie; (right) CP/AP/Martyn Hayhow; 7.4 CP/AP/Michel Lipchitz; 7.6 CP; 7.7 CP/Nelle Oosterom; 7.8 CP/AP/Saurabh Das; 7.9 CP/AP/Elizabeth Dalziel; CP/AP/Yaron Kaminsky; 7.11 CP/AP/Amr Nabil; 7.12 CP/AP/Kamran Jebreili; CP/AP/Amr Nabil; 7.13 CP/AP/Kamran Jebreili; 7.14 CP/AP/John Riley; Cosmo Condina/Stone; 7.16 CP/AP/Enric Marti; 7.17 Wm. J. Hebert/Stone; 7.19 (left, centre) Herb Schmitz/Stone; (right) David Hanson/Stone; 7.21 Ethel Johnston; 7.22 National Information Centre of India; 7.23, 7.24 Ethel Johnston; 7.25 World Tourism Organization; 7.27 David Hiser/Stone; 7.28 Stone/Will & Deni McIntyre; 7.29 CP/AP/Pier Paolo Cito; 7.30 (left) CP/AP/Denis Gray; (right) CP/AP; 7.28 CP/AP/Remy de la Mauvinière; 7.29 UNESCO.

Chapter 8

8.1 (a) CP/AP/David Longstreath; (b) CP/AP/Victor R. Caivano; (c) Paul Chesley/Stone; (d) Bernard Grilly/Stone; (e) Connie Coleman/Stone; 8.3 CP/AP/Shirley Salemy Meyer; 8.6 The Highlands of Scotland Tourist Board; 8.11 Canadian Broadcasting Company; 8.13 CP/AP/Richard Vogel; 8.17 Ethel Johnston; Owen Franken/Stone; 8.20a CP/AP/Richard Vogel; 8.20b Glen Allison/Stone; 8.23 CP/Fred Chartrand; 8.24 (top) CP/AP/Richard Vogel; (bottom, left) CP/Ray Rudowski; (bottom, right) Ethel Johnston; 8.26 CP/AP/Richard Vogel; 8.27 CP/*Globe & Mail*/Taras Kovaliv; 8.29 Hudson Bay Polar Bear Park Expeditions; 8.30 CP/Tom Hanson; 8.31 CP/AP/Rusty Kennedy; 8.33 CP/*Winnipeg Free Press*/Marc Gallant; 8.34 Ethel Johnston; 8.35 Hugh Sitton/Stone.

Chapter 9

9.1 (page 230, left) David Hanover/Stone; (centre) Cameron Davidson/Stone; (right) Lori Adamski Peek/Stone; (page 231, left) David Hanover/Stone; (centre) Jon Riley/Stone; (right) David Hanover/Stone; 9.3 CP/AP/Koji Sasahara; 9.5 Bob Thomas/Stone; 9.11 CP/AP John Moore; 9.12 CP/AP; 9.14 CP/AP/Dimitri Messinis; CP/AP/Joe McDonald; 9.16 Bruce Ayres/Stone; 9.17 V. Last/GVA; 9.18 (left) Laurence Monneret/Stone; (top) Martin Barraud/Stone; (right) David Hanover/Stone; (bottom) Harold Pfeiffer/Stone; 9.19 Wm. S. Helsel/Stone; 9.21, 9.22, 9.23, 9.24, St. Maarten Tourist Office; 9.25 George Armitage; 9.26 CP/AP/Ricardo Figueroa; 9.27 St. Maarten Tourist Office; 9.28 Office du Tourisme de la Martinique; 9.29 St. Maarten Tourist Office; 9.30 Office du Tourisme de la Martinique.

Chapter 10

10.1 (a) Sylvain Grandadam/Stone; (b) Office du Tourisme de la Martinique; (c) Nick Dolding/Stone; 10.3 Paul Steel/Firstlight.ca; 10.6 CP/Jose Goita; 10.8 CP/*Calgary Sun*/Jim Wells; 10.11 CP/Kevin Frayer; 10.13 CP/Michelle MacAfee; 10.14 CP/*Maclean's*/Phill Snel; 10.16 Chris Saunders/Stone; 10.17 New Internationalist/Polyp; 10.18 Stock Image/Firstlight.ca; 10.19 CP/Mike Ridewood; 10.21 Didier Hubert/Stone; 10.22 CP/*The Standard*/Denis Cahill; 10.25 Atlantide SNC/Firstlight.ca; 10.26 (left)

CP/AP; (right) CP/AP/Rikard Larma; 10.27 (left) CP/AP/Michael Stravato; (centre) CP/AP/Hidajet Delic; (right) CP/AP/Dragan Fiipovic; 10.28 CP/AP/Hidajet Delic; CP/AP/Enric Marti; 10.30 Robert Landau/Firstlight.ca; 10.32 Bob Krist/Stone; 10.33 John Scheiber/The Stock Market/Firstlight.ca; 10.35 (left) Jose Enrique Molina/Firstlight.ca; (right) Bruce Herman/Stone; 10.36 (top) Demetrio Carrasco/Stone; (bottom) Mark Segal/Stone; 10.37 Office du Tourisme de la Martinique; 10.38 Francine Geraci; 10.39 (left) Joseph Gladstone; (right) Minden Images/Firstlight.ca; 10.40 Robert Van Der Hilst/Stone.

Chapter 11

11.1 (left) Louis Datlas/Firstlight.ca; (right) Daniel Bosler/Stone; 11.2 (left, top) CP/AP/Giulio Broglio; (left, bottom) CP/AP/Saurabh Das; (right) CP/AP/Sayyid Azim; 11.4 CP/AP/Shizuo Kambayashi; CP/AP/Sakchai Lalit; 11.5 Dilip Mehta/CIDA; 11.6 CP/AP/Eraldo Peres; 11.8 CP/AP/Sakchai Lalit; 11.9 CP/AP/Ulf Isacson; 11.11 CP/*Winnipeg Sun*/John Woods; 11.13 CP/*Hamilton Spectator*/Gary Yokoyama; 11.14 CP/AP/Silvia Constanti - Agencia Fotosite; 11.15 Tim Flach/Stone; 11.16 CP/AP/Saurabh Das; Robert Van Der Hilst/Stone; 11.18 CP/AP/Tomas van Houtryve; 11.19 Enrique Algarra/Firstlight.ca; 11.20 John Chard/Stone; 11.21 CP/AP/Mark Lennihan; Andrea Booher/Stone; 11.22 Matthias Clamer/Stone; 11.24 CP/AP/ David Guttenfelder; Michel Setboun/Stone; 11.25 (top) CP/AP/Bullit Marquez; (bottom) *Seattle Post-Intelligencer*; 11.26 Baiba Morrow/Firstlight.ca; CP/AP/David Guttenfelder; 11.27 Patrick Morrow/Firstlight.ca; Photographic Society of Macau/Lam Sao Wa; 11.29 (top) Richard Elliott/Stone; (left) Leesa Price; (right) Doug Armand/Stone; 11.31 Baron Wolman/Stone; 11.32 Tampa Bay Visitors & Convention Bureau; 11.33 (left) CP/AP/Wilfredo Lee; (right) CP/*Toronto Star*/Dick Loek; 11.35 Francine Geraci.

Chapter 12

12.1 (a) Robert Yager/Stone; (b) CP/AP/Peter Cosgrove; (c) Tony Craddock/Stone; (d) CP/AP/David Longstreath; 12.3 (top) National Archives of Canada; (bottom) Courtesy Stratford Festival; 12.5 (top) CP/*Niagara Falls Review*/Mike DiBattista; (centre) CP/Bill Sikes; (bottom) CP/AP/John Hickey; 12.6 CP/AP/Anat Givon; 12.7 Chuck Savage/The Stock Market/Firstlight.ca; 12.8 Alan Marsh/Firstlight.ca; 12.9 David Hanover/Stone; 12.10 CP/*Toronto Star*/Tony Bock; 12.11 Tourism BC; 12.13 Ontario Ministry of Natural Resources; 12.14 CP/AP/Chiaki Tsukumo; 12.16 Office du Tourisme de la Martinique/Pierre Courtinard; 12.20 (top left) Ben Edward/Stone; (bottom left) CP/AP/Arthur Max; (right) CP/Kristy Phillips; 12.22 CP/AP/Manish Swarup; 12.23, 12.24 CP/AP/John McConnico; 12.25 CP/Sean O'Neil; 12.26 John Flanders/CIDA; 12.27 (top) CP/Kevin Frayer; (bottom left) CP/Jonathan Hayward; (bottom right) CP/Shaun Best.

INDEX

E

Ebola virus, 291
ecological footprint, 122
economic benefits of tourism, 206–207, 258–59
economic conditions, in St. Martin/St. Maarten, 245
economic development, in Mexico, 272–77
economic functions, of cities, 115–17
economic issues, 15, 206–207, 258–59
economic patterns, 235–43
economics, and tourism, 232–34, 256–67
economy
    and tourism, 90–91, 92
    trickle down effect, 190
ecotourism, 64–65
education, as travel variable, 8
endangered spaces, 64–65
endangered species, 97–98
environment, effect of tourism on, 93
environmental issues, 15
    in Madagascar, 74
ethical travel, 205
ethnic cleansing, 269
ethnocentrism, 287
Eurail pass, 155
exploration stage, 265
external market, 210
extraterritorial laws, 288

F

facts, 17
fertility rate
    in Canada, 73
    in Madagascar, 73
finances
    and discretionary money, 7
    as travel variable, 7
Florida, and crime, 302–305
foot-and-mouth disease, 292
foreign investment, 261
fully independent tourist, 154
functional regions, 39

G

Gaelic Council of Nova Scotia, 208
gambling, 116
    in Macau, 299
gangs, in Macau, 300
gastrointestinal infections, 291–92
Golden Gate Biosphere Reserve, 83
government, and tourism, 316–17
Grand Tour, 151
Great Lakes, 87
Greater Addo National Park, 22–27
green space, 131
Green Tourist Association, 131
guidebooks, 152

H

Haida, 106
hard adventure, 61
health, as travel variable, 8
hedonism, 245
heritage conservancy, 158, 159
Herzegovina, and tourism, 268–71
high culture, 154
hiking trails, 84
hinterland, 114
historical influences, preserving, 214
Hockey Hall of Fame, 128
homogeneous, defined, 36
Hong Kong, 136–38
hostels, 154, 155, 156
Hudson Bay Polar Bear Park Expeditions, 221
Hunter, Sam, 221
hunting, 95
hurricanes, 62
    effect on tourism, 248, 273

I

illness, and travel, 291–94
incentives, to tourism, 316
independent travellers, 238
India
    Goa, 192–95
    and tourism marketing, 324–27
indirect impacts, 257
infant mortality rate
    in Canada, 73
    in Madagascar, 73
informed opinion, 20
infrastructure
    of city, 119–20
    improving, 122
    in India, 325
integration, and culture, 150
interactions, as geographic concept, 37, 38
internal market, 209
International Council on Monuments and Sites (ICOMOS), 158
International Cultural Tourism Charter, 158
International Hotel Association, 289
International Olympic Committee, 132
International Union for the Conservation of Natural Resources (IUCN), 82
International Year of Tourism, 64
International Youth Hostelling Federation, 155
intervening opportunities, 323
Intracoastal Waterway, 85
involvement stage, 265
Islam, 186–88
isolation, and culture, 150
issues approach, 11–14
issues
    cultural, 15
    economic, 15
    environmental, 15
    political, 15
    social, 15
    stating, 15–16
Ivey, Grace, 155

J

Japan, 168–73
jobs, and tourism, 234

K

Kawartha Lakes Tourism, 63
Kawartha Lakes, 87
Knappen House Youth Hostel, 155